The MAILBOX

The Education Center

SUPERBOOK

Grade 1

Everything You Need for a Successful Year!

- Literacy
- Math
- Science and Health
- Social Studies
- Graphic Organizers

- Centers
- Games
- Differentiation Tips
- Bulletin Boards
- Arts and Crafts

And Much More!

Revised and Updated!

Managing Editor: Gerri Primak

Editorial Team: Becky S. Andrews, Kimberley Bruck, Karen P. Shelton, Diane Badden, Thad H. McLaurin, Sharon Murphy, Lynn Drolet, Amy Erickson, Kelly Robertson, Karen A. Brudnak, Juli Docimo Blair, Hope Rodgers, Dorothy C. McKinney

Production Team: Lori Z. Henry, Pam Crane, Rebecca Saunders, Jennifer Tipton Cappoen, Chris Curry, Sarah Foreman, Theresa Lewis Goode, Greg D. Rieves, Eliseo De Jesus Santos II, Barry Slate, Donna K. Teal, Zane Williard, Tazmen Carlisle, Marsha Heim, Lynette Dickerson, Mark Rainey, Amy Kirtley-Hill, Ben Wooster

www.themailbox.com

D1452260

Manufactured in the United States
10 9 8 7 6 5 4 3 2 1

TABLE OF CONTENTS

TABLE OF CONTENTS

Holidays and Seasonal Activities

Back-to-School!

Welcome Back!

On the first day of school, ask your students what they hope to learn during the year. Write their individual responses on chart paper and have each child sign his name on the paper. Then store the paper in a secure spot. On the last day of school, display the chart paper. Students will see just how much they've learned during the year!

First-Day Friends

Try this welcome warm-up on the first day of school! Cut pictures from magazines, glue them onto construction paper, and then cut each picture into two irregular shapes. As you greet each child, ask him to choose a shape. After everyone has arrived, have each child find the person with the shape that completes his picture. Then let the new friends get acquainted for a few minutes. If desired, have each student exchange shapes with someone other than his partner and repeat the activity.

How We Get Home

Get your first day on the road by inviting youngsters to share how they plan to travel from school each afternoon. To prepare for each child, copy the pattern from page 8 that best depicts his mode of transportation. Make extra patterns for those students who travel from school using several different means. Then program a sheet of chart paper labeled to correspond to each mode of transportation used.

Have each child tell how he plans to travel from school each afternoon. Ask him to select a pattern that corresponds with his mode of transportation. Have him color it, cut it out, and write his name on it. If the student rides a bus home, write the bus number on the front of the bus. Then have him tape his pattern in the appropriate row on the graph. Discuss what the completed graph reveals.

At the end of the day, refer to the graph to group students based on their modes of transportation. What a great way to ease those first-day dismissal problems for youngsters with apprehensions!

How We Get Home

car Anna · Scott · Mary · Carly · Sam

bus Julie #10 · Alexa #203 · Cathy #11 · Pam #73

walk Tia · Sue · Allen · Bud

bike Pete · Joe · Becky

Personality Bags

Getting to know each other is in the bag with this clever activity! Use the parent note on page 9 to have each student bring a grocery bag containing five personal items. Each day choose a few bags and unpack them in front of the class. Students try to guess the identity of the bag's owner. It's a fun way for students to share information about themselves with their classmates!

Kids Say the Cutest Things!

The comments kids make can be both humorous and inspirational. Throughout the year, record funny, insightful, or interesting comments made by your students. At the end of the year, bind all the comment pages into a class book to share with students and parents during your year-end activities. You're guaranteed to see lots of smiles!

Memory Book

Preserve special days as a treasured keepsake with a memory book. At the beginning of the school year, make a memory book for each student. To make a memory book, staple several pieces of blank paper between two construction paper covers. Have each student personalize and add decorations to his front cover; then collect the books and store them until your class takes part in a special event, such as a field trip. At that time, have each student write about his favorite part of the event; then have him illustrate the page accordingly. What a treasure each student will have at the end of the year!

A New Look

Each school year brings new students and new experiences. So why not try a new look for your classroom? Scan the list below and choose a theme. Then put your imagination in gear to design nametags, a helpers' chart, a bulletin board, and a door decoration around this theme.

"Toad-ally" Cool in First Grade—Students will jump at the chance to be in a colorful classroom decorated with toad cutouts, lily pads, and other pond decorations.

Tracking Down a Good Year—Get your supersleuths off to a great start in a classroom decorated with detectives and magnifying glasses.

Making a Splash in First Grade—Students are sure to dive into learning when they enter a classroom decorated with fish, seashells, and other beach decorations. For even more fun, set up a small plastic wading pool in the corner of the room to serve as a reading center.

The First-Grade Express—All aboard! Your youngsters will be sure to hop aboard when you choose a train theme for your classroom. Be sure to display a railroad track cutout labeled with all the stops for learning they'll be making this year.

Bushels of Help

Here's a unique way of asking for supplies at open house that will "a-peel" to parents! In advance, draw a large tree shape on the board. Copy and cut out several construction paper apples using the patterns on page 9. Label each apple cutout with the name of a needed supply, such as resealable bags or cotton balls. If needed, label more than one apple with the same supply. Place a piece of magnetic tape on the back of each cutout, and then place the apples on the tree. Write a note on the board explaining that any parent who is willing to donate an indicated item should take the corresponding apple cutout. Each parent can place the magnetic apple on her refrigerator as a reminder to send in the supply at her convenience.

Tree with apples labeled: yarn, felt, lunch bags, craft sticks, glitter, resealable bags

Parents: If you are able to donate any of these items, please take one of the apple cutouts and send the item to school at your earliest convenience.

Thank you!
Ms. Beckwith

Find the Footprints

This open house activity will have parents in step with their children. Several days before open house, ask each student what his favorite classroom area or learning center is. Have each child trace and cut out a set of his footprints. Encourage him to decorate and personalize his footprints as desired. Then, right before open house, tape each child's footprints in his favorite classroom area. Also, in each area, display manipulatives that would be used and lessons and activities that would take place there. During open house, have each child's parents search the room to find their child's pair of footprints. When the parents find the footprints, encourage them to look around the area to try to discover why it is their child's favorite. What a unique way for parents to learn about their child's favorite activities!

Classroom Mascot

It's Nice to Meet You

Choose a colorful stuffed animal to be your class's very special friend, and the learning possibilities will go on and on! To create a sense of ownership, have your students cooperatively name the class mascot. Once a name has been chosen, have your new friend introduce himself to the class. The students will be thrilled to learn all his favorites!

Across the Curriculum

Students will be ready to jump into science to learn what kind of habitat the real version of their animal mascot lives in. After sharing information about the real animal, have each child draw a picture of himself visiting the animal in its habitat. Compile the completed pictures into a class book titled "A Visit to [class mascot's name]'s World."

We could visit Puddles at the pond. We would watch him swim around and we would feed him.

Weekend Adventures

Help foster positive home-school relationships by giving each child the opportunity to take the mascot home for a weekend. In advance, place a supply of story paper in a three-ring binder and label the cover "[Class mascot's name]'s Travelog." Instruct the child to write and illustrate an entry in the travelog about an event that took place with the mascot during the weekend. On Monday morning, have the child share her entry about her weekend adventures with the mascot. At the end of the year, compile all the accounts into a book and send a copy home with each child.

Puddles' Travelog

Puddles and I went on a picnic.

Molly

Extra Adventures

Imagine the students' excitement when they hear that the class mascot will be going home with the principal! In advance ask your principal to participate in the activity. On the Friday of the event, have your principal visit the classroom to meet the mascot. Ask student volunteers to tell the principal what to do with the travelog. Then have students wave goodbye as your principal leaves with their special friend. Students will be more than eager on Monday to read the mascot's travelog! For added fun, invite other school workers, such as your librarian or physical education teacher, to take the mascot home too!

Check out the reproducibles on pages 10 and 11.

Patterns

Use with "How We Get Home" on page 4.

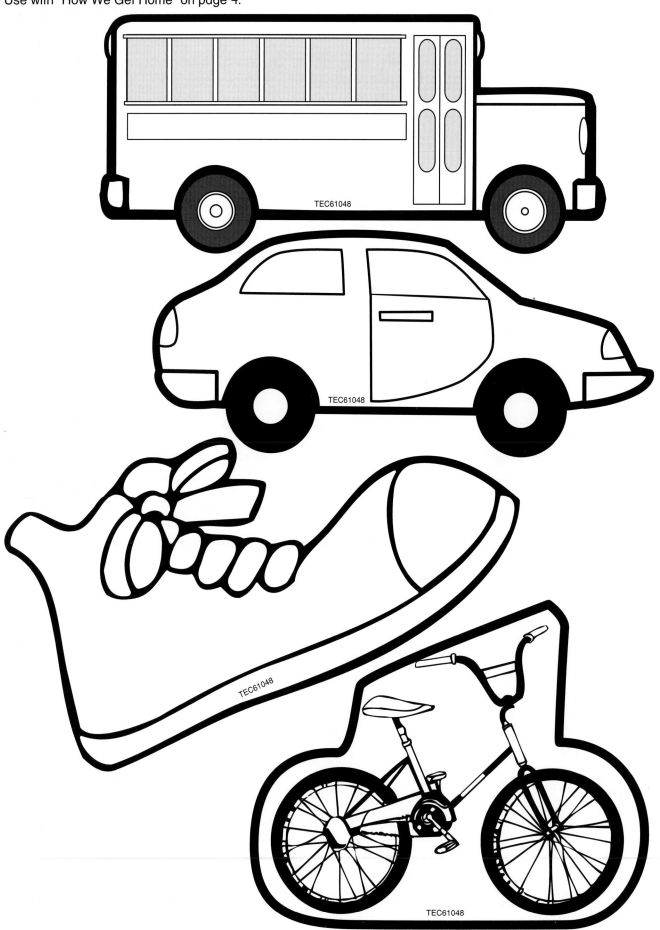

TEC61048

TEC61048

TEC61048

TEC61048

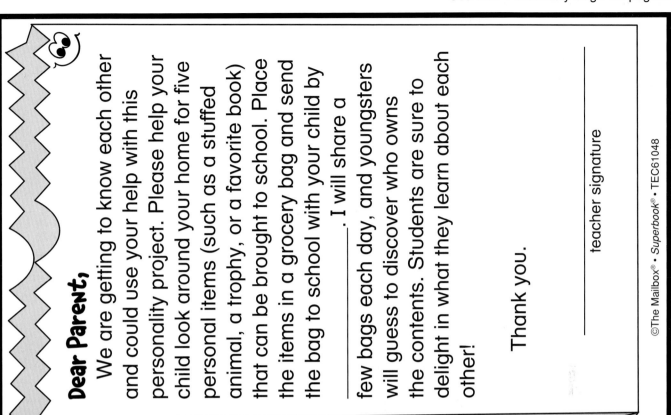

Dear Parent,

We are getting to know each other and could use your help with this personality project. Please help your child look around your home for five personal items (such as a stuffed animal, a trophy, or a favorite book) that can be brought to school. Place the items in a grocery bag and send the bag to school with your child by _____.

I will share a few bags each day, and youngsters will guess to discover who owns the contents. Students are sure to delight in what they learn about each other!

Thank you.

_____
teacher signature

©The Mailbox® • *Superbook*® • TEC61048

Apple Patterns
Use with "Bushels of Help" on page 6.

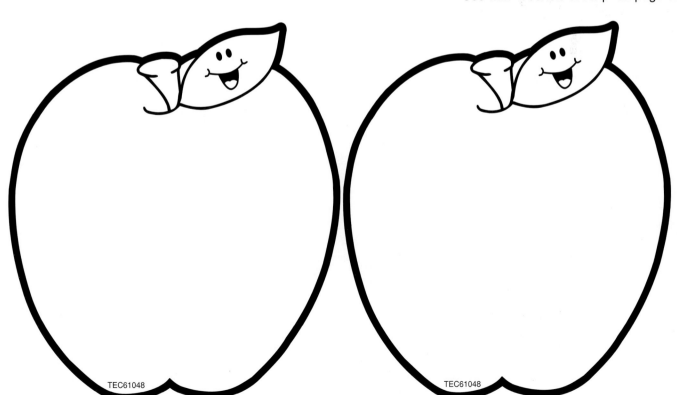

TEC61048

TEC61048

WELCOME

_____
student

_____
year

_____
teacher

TO FIRST GRADE!

©The Mailbox® • Superbook® • TEC61048

Student Information Card

Student no.

First name _____ Last name _____

Address _____

Student's birthdate _____

City _____

State _____ Zip _____

Mother's name _____

Mother's phone _____

Mother's email _____

Father's name _____

Father's phone _____

Father's email _____

Comments: _____
_____

Medical concerns: _____
_____

Emergency contact _____

Emergency phone _____

Transportation to and from school: _____ walks _____ rides bus (#_____) _____ other

©The Mailbox® • Superbook® • TEC61048

Note to the teacher: Make one copy of the "Welcome to First Grade!" certificate and program it with the year and your name; then make a class supply and write each child's name on a certificate to welcome him to your class. Make a class supply of the "Student Information Card" and send one home with each student.

Parent Roundup

We would like to have you be a part of our classroom and help make our school year a big success. If you have a little extra time and the desire, your help would be greatly appreciated. If possible, please participate in our roundup by completing this form and returning it to school with your child. I look forward to hearing from you.

_____
teacher

I would like to be involved in the following classroom activities:

_____ small-group work with students
_____ grading papers
_____ filing papers
_____ making copies
_____ constructing bulletin boards
_____ other _____

I would like to assist in the following special activities:

_____ chaperoning field trips
_____ reading program
_____ organizing class parties
_____ assisting in plays
_____ telephoning from home
_____ raising funds
_____ helping at parties or on special days
_____ other _____
_____ other _____

_____   _____
parent's name   child's name

_____
phone number

©The Mailbox® • Superbook® • TEC61048

Note to the teacher: Make one copy of the "Parent Roundup" letter and sign your name. Then make a class supply and send a copy home with each student.

11

Phonological Awareness and PHONICS

Rhyme Time

In advance, collect old game pieces and small toys that are rhyming pairs. Place the items on a table. Next, gather students in a circle. Invite a student volunteer to choose an item. Then ask another to try to find an item that rhymes with the first one. Have students continue in this manner until all the rhyming pairs have been discovered. Rhyming

Chant and Rhyme

Use this interactive chant to help students generate rhyming words! Lead students in the verse shown, inserting a word that has several words that rhyme with it. Then invite each of several students to repeat the featured word and name a corresponding rhyming word. Repeat the chant several times, choosing a different rhyming word each time. **Rhyming**

LOOK! A Book!

Students will be full of giggles after making this hilarious rhyming book. To begin, have your students name sets of three rhyming words—one set of words per student. Write their responses on the board. Next, have each student select one set of words. On a sheet of paper, have the student write and illustrate a sentence that includes his three words. Encourage each student to share his completed project; then bind the papers into a class book and place it in the library for all to enjoy! **Rhyming**

We can rhyme
Any old time!
Our ears are in gear,
And we're ready to hear.
Name a word that rhymes with
   [cake].

The frog and the dog sat on a log.

A to Z
Treasure Chest

Practice initial-consonant sounds with this idea for a class book. Program a craft stick for each letter of the alphabet; then place the sticks in a container. Have each student draw a stick and then think of five objects beginning with the letter that he would like to find in a treasure chest. Next, the student draws and labels the objects on a sheet of drawing paper. As students are completing their projects, create a story introduction similar to the one shown. Place the introduction atop students' completed work; then bind the compiled pages between two construction paper covers. This treasure of a story is sure to be a popular addition to your classroom library. **Initial consonants**

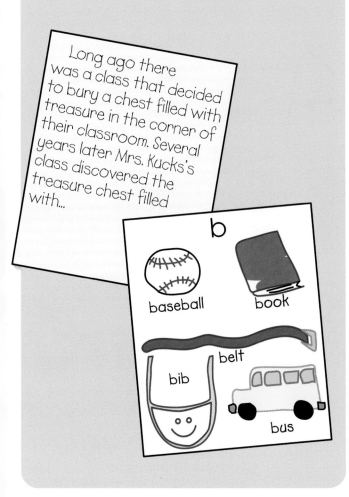

Long ago there was a class that decided to bury a chest filled with treasure in the corner of their classroom. Several years later Mrs. Kucks's class discovered the treasure chest filled with...

b

baseball   book

belt

bib

bus

Say and Sort

Youngsters practice matching pictured words to their beginning letters with this adaptable center! Cut out a copy of the picture cards on page 26. Glue each card to a slightly larger piece of construction paper for durability. Choose cards for several beginning sounds that you would like youngsters to practice; set the other cards aside. For each chosen sound, label the front of an envelope with a corresponding letter. Place the envelopes and the selected picture cards at a center. When a youngster visits the center, he names a picture, listens for the beginning sound, and places it in the appropriate envelope. He continues in the same manner for each remaining card. Periodically replace the cards and envelopes for practice with different letters and sounds. **Initial consonants**

Consonant Call

What better way to review initial sounds than with a lively group game! To begin play, gather students in a circle and announce a consonant. Then quickly toss a soft ball or beanbag to a child. That youngster repeats the letter, names the sound associated with the letter, and says a word that begins with the sound. Then she tosses the ball to another child while she names a different consonant. Play continues in the same manner until each child has had a turn. **Initial consonants**

Singing for Sounds

In advance, place several small objects with different beginning consonants in a container (or use the picture cards on page 26). Invite a child to remove an object, name it, and say its beginning letter and sound. Then lead youngsters in the song shown, inserting the beginning letter, letter sound, and word in the appropriate lines. Repeat the song several times with different objects. If desired, repeat the activity to reinforce ending consonants. **Initial consonants**

(sung to the tune of "Three Blind Mice")

Starts with *p*.
Starts with /p/.
What can it be?
What can it be?
We see a pig that starts with *p*,
We see a pig that starts with /p/,
p and /p/ go together, you see.
Starts with *p*!

Star Power

Looking for a quick way to assess students' knowledge of beginning or ending consonant sounds? Try this! On a copy of page 27, program the lines on the circle with different letters you would like youngsters to practice. Then make a construction paper copy of the page for each child. Have each child cut out the patterns and tape a craft stick handle to the back of the star. Next, help her cut out the window on the dotted lines and use a brad to attach the circle behind the star.

To begin, announce a word and have students identify the beginning or ending letter. Direct students to manipulate their circles so that the corresponding letter shows through the window. Scan for accuracy and verify youngsters' answers. Then continue in the same manner with several other words. **Initial or final consonants**

Make a Match

Gather a class supply of blank cards. Program half of the cards each with a different consonant and the other half to match. (If you have an odd number of students, include yourself in the count.) Give each child a card and ask her to keep her letter hidden from her classmates' view. Invite one child to stand up and give clues about her letter. The student who has the matching letter stands up and announces his letter. After verifying his response, invite another student to give clues for the next round! **Letter knowledge**

Noteworthy Reference

For each blend you would like to introduce, cut out a black construction paper music note like the one shown. Explain to youngsters that just like letters, music notes have their own sounds. When two notes are blended together they make a new sound. Then tell students that a blend is two letters that when blended together make a new sound. Use a white crayon to write each letter of a blend on a separate note and the blend on the connecting bar. Next, lead students in saying the sounds of the letters and the blend. Continue in this manner for each remaining blend. Display the music notes in a prominent location for students' reference. **Initial blends**

A Full Load

Here's a center idea that gets phonics skills on the move! Gather a supply of smooth rocks and label each rock with a different blend. Place the rocks in a toy dump truck. Label several blank cards each with a different rime. (See the suggestions for blends and rimes.) Place the cards and truck at a center. A student takes a card, places a rock in front of the rime, and reads the resulting word. If it is a real word, he chooses a new card and rock. If it is not a real word, he continues placing a rock on the card until he forms a word. He continues in the same manner as time allows. Initial blends

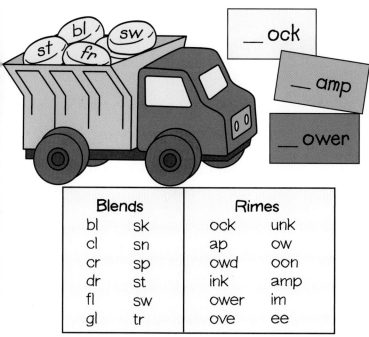

Blends		Rimes	
bl	sk	ock	unk
cl	sn	ap	ow
cr	sp	owd	oon
dr	st	ink	amp
fl	sw	ower	im
gl	tr	ove	ee

A Scoop of Blends

Give your youngsters the scoop on blends with this cooperative-group activity. Before beginning the lesson, copy four or five ice-cream cones onto light brown construction paper and a large supply of ice-cream scoops onto various colors of construction paper (patterns on page 28). Cut out the patterns. Next, write a blend on each cone and mount them in a location that is accessible to your students. Divide students into groups; then assign a cone to each group. Challenge each group to list on scrap paper as many words as it can that begin with the blend on its cone. When time is up, check each group's list. Have students rewrite the correct words on separate ice-cream scoops. Then, in turn, have the members of each group read their words for the class before they attach the scoops to their cones. **Initial blends**

Blast Off With Blends

This stellar activity doubles as a classroom display! Trim three sheets of bulletin board paper to resemble three rocket ships. Label each rocket with a different blend; then display them in a prominent location. Assign each youngster a blend and direct her to write a word that begins with her blend on a yellow construction paper star. After each youngster has written her word, invite a volunteer to read her word aloud. Ask her classmates to name the beginning blend. Then have her tape her star near the corresponding rocket ship. Continue in this manner for each remaining child. **Initial blends**

Digraph Shutters

This visual reminder will help youngsters remember the sound of the digraph *sh*. Help each child fold in the sides of a horizontally positioned sheet of construction paper so that they meet in the middle. Have her write "s" on one flap and "h" on the other. Then invite her to add details so the flaps resemble a pair of shutters. Next, direct her to open the shutters and visually divide the center section into fourths to represent a windowpane. Ask her to draw and label in each section an object whose name begins with *sh*, like shutters. Encourage youngsters to share their finished projects before displaying them for all to see! **Digraph *sh***

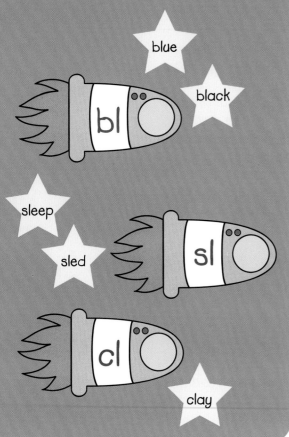

The Search Is On!

Get youngsters on the lookout for digraphs! Divide a sheet of paper into four sections and label each section with a different digraph *(ch, sh, th, and wh).* Then copy the paper to make a class supply. Give each child a copy of the prepared paper and have him name the sound associated with each digraph. Next, ask each child to visually search the room for objects or pictures of objects whose names begin with the digraphs. Direct him to write the name of each item on the corresponding section of his paper. After a predetermined amount of time, signal students to stop writing and invite them to share their lists. If desired, write their responses on a sheet of chart paper to create a class digraph reference. **Initial digraphs**

See the Ready Reference on page 23 for a list of blends and digraphs.

Vowel Verse

Youngsters are sure to remember the names of the vowels with this catchy tune! **Vowels**

(sung to the tune of "Bingo")

There are five letters that we know,
And vowels are what we call them.
A, e, i, o, u.
A, e, i, o, u.
A, e, i, o, u.
And vowels are what we call them!

Thumbs-Up!

Good vowel-sound discrimination will *pop* up everywhere with this quiet activity. Specify a vowel sound for students to listen for; then announce a word. If a student hears the sound, he puts his thumb up. If not, he puts his thumb down. After announcing several words, invite student volunteers to take turns announcing words. **Vowels**

Helping Hand

This handy reference will help youngsters remember the different sounds associated with vowels. Cut a large sheet of bulletin board paper into a hand shape. Label the palm with a title to designate the display for short or long vowels. Then label each finger with a different vowel and add a picture to represent each vowel sound. Display the hand within students' reach. To use the display, announce a word; then invite a student to point to the finger with the corresponding vowel sound. Continue in this manner as time allows. **Vowels**

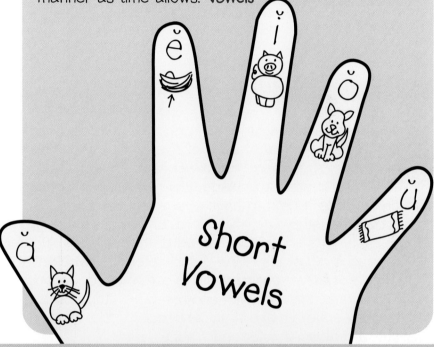

Vowel Munchers

These gobbling guys provide an engaging way to reinforce vowel sounds. Copy, color, and cut out ten monsters using the pattern on page 28. Label each monster with a different long or short vowel. Post the monsters at the top of a chart. To begin, announce a word that contains an appropriate vowel sound and ask a student volunteer to name the vowel. If the student is correct, he writes the word on a construction paper card. Then he "feeds" the card to the corresponding monster by taping the card under it. Continue in the same manner for several rounds. **Vowels**

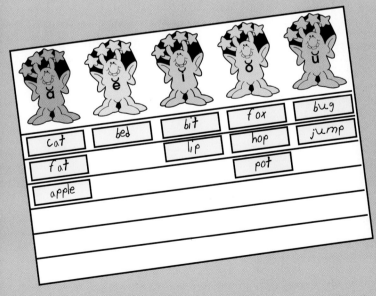

Vowel Jars

Review short- or long-vowel sounds with this sweet idea! Trim bulletin board paper into five candy jar shapes. Label each jar with a different vowel and then display them on a wall or bulletin board. Give each child five construction paper candy cutouts. Have her draw and label on each candy a picture for a different vowel sound. Then invite each youngster to attach her candies to the corresponding jars. **Vowels**

Real or Nonsense?

To prepare for this small-group activity, write on separate sentence strips different CVC words, omitting the vowels. Also label each of five blank cards with a different vowel. Place the vowel cards facedown in your small-group area and place a word strip in a pocket chart. Invite a child to choose a vowel card and place it over the strip to form a word. Encourage each group member to silently read the word; then ask a volunteer to read it aloud. Have the group determine whether the word is real or nonsense. If it is a real word, continue in the same manner with another word strip. If it is a nonsense word, have a student replace the vowel card until a real word is formed. **Short vowels**

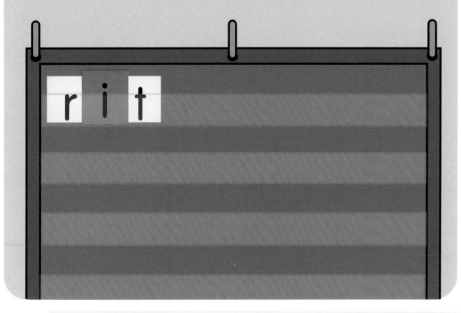

Amazing E!

With the help of your students, short-vowel words transform into long-vowel words! Program large cards each with a different letter to spell several of the CVC words shown. Also program one card with the letter e. Give each of three youngsters a letter to spell a chosen word and have them stand in order to display the word. After the remaining students read the word aloud, have a child hold the e card and position himself at the end of the word. Then invite a volunteer to read the new word. Repeat the activity several times, inviting different students to hold the letters each time. **Silent e**

Word List

bit	hop	pal
can	kit	pin
cap	man	rob
cub	not	tap
fin	mad	

See the Ready Reference on page 24 for 100 short-vowel and 100 long-vowel words.

Names
Brad
Chad
Dan
Jan
Kit
May
Kay
Jill
Bill
Kate
Nat
Pat

Word Family Photos

This unique photo album features members of different word families! Program a sheet of paper with a picture frame similar to the one shown. Copy the programmed paper to make a class supply. Label each paper with one of the names from the list shown, repeating names as necessary. Give each child a prepared paper and have her draw a picture of the fictional named person. Then ask her to write words in the same word family as the featured name. Bind students' completed papers to resemble a photo album and invite youngsters to refer to the book as a writing reference. **Word families**

Word Family Houses

Introduce youngsters to word families with construction paper houses. For each word family being introduced, trim a sheet of construction paper into a house shape. Label the roof of each house with a different word family. Then, as you introduce a word family, write a student-generated list of words that "live" in the house. Post the houses in a prominent location for students to refer to in their independent writing. Before long, students will know each family very well! **Word families**

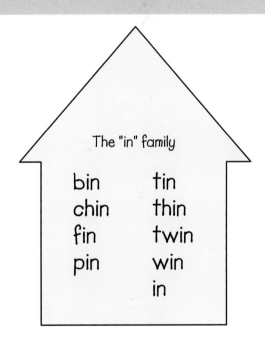

The "in" family

bin   tin
chin   thin
fin   twin
pin   win
        in

Flip Books

These unique books will have students flipping over word families! To make a book, staple a desired number of two-inch paper squares to the left edge of a 2" x 5" construction paper rectangle. Give each child a prepared book and have her write a word family on the construction paper as shown. Then, on each white paper square, direct the student to write a letter that makes a word when joined with the rime. To read the flip book, the student flips each paper square and reads the word. No doubt students will be eager to flip through their classmates' books too! **Word families**

Mail Sort

For this center activity, label each of three shoeboxes with a different rime; then cut a four-inch slit in the top of each lid to represent a mailbox. Program several cards with different words from the chosen word families. Add details to the cards to resemble envelopes; then place the cards in a paper bag labeled "Mail." Place the mailbag and mailboxes at a center. A center visitor removes a card, reads the word, identifies the word family, and places it in the appropriate mailbox. After she sorts all of the cards in this manner, she empties the boxes one at a time and reads each group of words. **Word families**

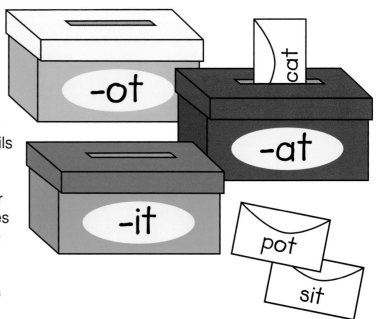

Feed the Elephants

When youngsters pretend to feed hungry elephants peanuts, they are also practicing their word family skills! Label a supply of peanut cutouts with different words from three different word families. Write the chosen rimes on separate paper bags. Invite three students to act as elephants and give each one a paper bag. If desired, have each volunteer wear paper elephant ears attached to a tagboard headband. Then give each remaining student a peanut. In turn, have each child read the word on his peanut and then feed it to the corresponding elephant. For an added challenge, give each student three blank peanut cutouts and have him write on each cutout a word to correspond with each word family. **Word families**

What a Home!

The result of this center is an extra large word family house! Trim a large sheet of bulletin board paper into a house shape. Draw lines to divide the house into rooms. (Make as many rooms as word families that you want to practice.) Label each room with a different rime. Display the house within students' reach at a center stocked with markers. When a child visits the center, she labels each room with a word from its word family. Then she quietly reads the words in each room. **Word families**

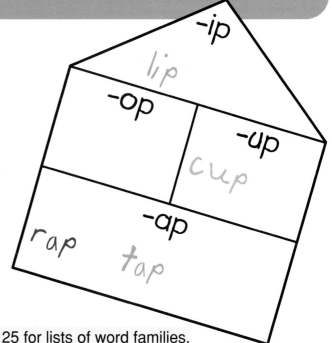

See the Ready Reference on page 25 for lists of word families.

Dig In!

Plant the seeds of learning with a garden-themed center that helps young-sters practice syllabication! Cut from magazines pictures of objects whose names have one, two, and three syllables. Glue each picture to a construction paper seed cutout. Label the back of each seed with the number of syllables for self-checking. Bury the seeds in a large container filled with brown paper shreds to resemble dirt. Place the container, a pair of child-size gardening gloves, and a small plastic shovel at a center. A youngster dons the gloves and uses the shovel to remove a seed. Then she names the picture, claps the number of syllables, and checks her response. After she sets the seed aside, she continues in the same manner for each remaining seed. **Syllables**

Fill 'er Up!

Students sharpen their syllable skills when they fill up these pails with raindrops! Label each of three plastic pails with a different number from 1 to 3. Program a supply of construction paper raindrop cutouts with different one-, two-, and three-syllable words. Store the raindrops in a white paper bag (cloud) and place the pails in your large-group area. Invite a child to remove a raindrop and read the word (provide assistance as needed). Next, have the class clap the word parts (syllables); then direct the volunteer to place the raindrop in the appropriate pail. Continue the activity until each raindrop has been sorted. **Syllables**

Word Links

This class activity provides a tactile way for students to practice identifying the number of syllables in words. Give each child four Unifix cubes. Announce a one-, two-, three-, or four-syllable word. After each student repeats the word, direct her to link together a cube for each syllable. To check for accuracy, ask students to hold up their connected cubes. Then have students disconnect their cubes and repeat the process with a different word. **Syllables**

Phonics Pockets

Students can show off their phonics skills using these individual display pockets. To make a pocket, position a 4½" x 9" piece of construction paper horizontally. Create a pocket along the lower edge by folding approximately 1½ inches of the paper upward. Staple the folded edges in place. Next, program the top third of a 1½" x 3½" construction paper rectangle for each letter of the alphabet. Place the letter cards and the pocket in a resealable plastic bag. To practice phonics skills, have each child remove the letter cards and the pocket from her bag. Announce a word that reflects your students' spelling abilities (without duplicating letters). Each child forms the word by placing the correct letter cards in her pocket. Have each student display her pocket before she clears it and you announce another word. At the end of the activity, have students store their letter cards and pockets in the bags. **Making words**

Wordplay

This cheerful chant is a fun way to build students' phonetic skills! As you lead youngsters in the verse shown, have students say the resulting word part for the last line. Repeat the chant several times, inserting a different one-syllable word each time. **Deleting sounds**

Teacher and students: Wordplay, wordplay, what do you say?
Teacher: Take [/m/] from [mat]…
Teacher and students: And then you will have…
Students: [at]!

Where's the Sound?

Invite youngsters to step right up for a class activity that provides practice with segmenting words. To begin, write a grade-appropriate word on the board. Lead youngsters in reading the word, emphasizing each sound. Then announce one phoneme (sound) and ask students to silently identify whether the sound is at the beginning, middle, or end of the word. Invite a volunteer to stand up, name the location of the sound, and point to the corresponding part of the word. Repeat the activity in this manner for several other words. **Isolating sounds**

Check out the skill-building reproducibles on pages 29-31.

Consonant Blends and Digraphs

Ready Reference

bl
black
blame
blank
blast
bleed
blend
blind
blink
block
blow
blue
blush

br
brag
brain
brake
brand
brave
breeze
brick
bring
broke
broom
brother
brown
brush

ch
chain
chair
chalk
chance
change
chase
chat
check
cheek
chest
chick
chin
choose
chop

cl
clam
clap

class
claw
clay
clean
climb
clock
close
clown

cr
crab
crack
crash
creep
crib
crime
crop
cross
crow

dr
drag
draw
dream
dress
drip
drum
dry

fl
flag
flake
flame
flap
flash
flat
flip
float
flow
fly

fr
frame
free
freeze
fresh
friend
frog

from
front
fry

gl
glad
glass
glove
glow
glue

gr
grab
grape
grass
green
grin
grip
grow

pl
place
plan
plane
plate
play
please
plot
plug
plus

pr
press
price
pride
prince
prize

sh
shade
share
shark
she
sheep
sheet
shell
shine
ship

shirt
shop
shot
should
show
shut

sl
slam
sled
sleep
slid
slip
slow

sm
small
smart
smell
smile
smoke

st
stand
stare
step
sting
stop
store

th
that
the
then
these
they
thin
think
this
thumb

wh
whale
what
when
where
white
why

100 Short-Vowel Words

Short *A* Words	Short *E* Words	Short *I* Words	Short *O* Words	Short *U* Words
add	bed	big	box	bug
bad	beg	bill	cot	bus
bag	desk	crib	dog	cub
bat	egg	dish	drop	cup
cab	fed	fib	fog	drum
cap	fence	grin	fox	fun
dad	get	hill	hop	gum
fan	help	in	hot	hut
fat	jet	king	jot	jug
ham	leg	lid	knob	luck
hat	met	milk	lock	mud
jam	nest	pig	mom	mug
man	pet	rip	mop	nut
map	red	ship	not	pup
nap	sent	six	on	rug
pan	ten	this	pot	run
rag	test	tin	rock	sun
ran	vet	whip	song	tub
sad	web	win	top	umbrella
tag	yes	zip	toss	up

100 Long-Vowel Words

Long *A* Words	Long *E* Words	Long *I* Words	Long *O* Words	Long *U* Words
ape	bee	bite	bone	amuse
bake	cheese	bride	close	cube
cape	deep	fire	cone	cute
cave	feet	five	dose	fume
date	free	hive	froze	fuse
face	he	ice	globe	huge
flame	heat	kite	hole	human
gate	key	life	home	humor
grape	knee	line	joke	mule
hate	lead	mice	lobe	music
lake	meet	mine	mole	mute
make	pea	nice	nose	pupil
name	please	nine	note	unicorn
page	read	pine	pole	unicycle
plane	see	ripe	robe	uniform
rake	she	size	rope	unit
same	three	smile	stove	universe
skate	tree	time	tote	use
take	we	vine	vote	useful
tape	week	wide	woke	yule

Short-Vowel Word Families

-ack	-an	-at	-ed	-est	-in	-ip	-op	-uck
back	can	bat	bed	best	bin	chip	chop	buck
black	clan	cat	bled	chest	chin	clip	cop	cluck
crack	fan	chat	fed	nest	fin	dip	drop	duck
jack	man	fat	fled	pest	grin	drip	flop	luck
pack	pan	flat	led	rest	pin	flip	hop	stuck
quack	plan	hat	red	test	shin	hip	mop	truck
rack	ran	mat	shed	vest	skin	lip	pop	
sack	tan	pat	sled	west	spin	nip	shop	-ug
shack	than	rat	wed		thin	rip	stop	bug
snack	van	sat		-ill	tin	ship	top	dug
stack		that	-ell	bill	twin	sip		hug
track	-ap		bell	chill	win	skip	-ot	jug
	cap		cell	dill		slip	blot	mug
	chap		fell	drill		tip	cot	rug
	clap		jell	fill		whip	dot	slug
	flap		sell	grill		zip	got	snug
	lap		shell	mill			hot	tug
	map		smell	pill			knot	
	nap		spell	skill			lot	
	rap		tell	spill			not	
	slap		well	still			plot	
	snap		yell	will			pot	
	tap						spot	
	trap							
	wrap							

Long-Vowel Word Families

-ail	-ain	-ake	-eed	-ight	-ine	-oat
fail	brain	bake	bleed	bright	fine	boat
jail	chain	brake	feed	flight	line	coat
mail	drain	cake	greed	fright	mine	float
nail	grain	fake	need	knight	nine	goat
pail	main	flake	seed	light	pine	oat
rail	pain	lake	speed	might	shine	throat
sail	plain	make	weed	night	spine	
snail	rain	rake		right	vine	
tail	train	shake		sight		
trail		snake		tight		
		take				
		wake				

Picture Cards

Use with "Say and Sort" on page 13.

TEC61048

TEC61048

TEC61048

TEC61048

TEC61048

TEC61048

TEC61048

TEC61048

TEC61048

TEC61048

TEC61048

TEC61048

TEC61048

TEC61048

TEC61048

TEC61048

TEC61048

TEC61048

TEC61048

TEC61048

TEC61048

TEC61048

TEC61048

TEC61048

TEC61048

TEC61048

TEC61048

TEC61048

TEC61048

TEC61048

TEC61048

Ice-Cream Patterns
Use with "A Scoop of Blends" on page 15.

Monster Pattern
Use with "Vowel Munchers" on page 17.

TEC61048

Name _____

Team Cheer

✂ Cut.

🫙 Glue to match the pictures and the beginning letters.

r

m

b

t

Name _____

30

Doggie Bowls

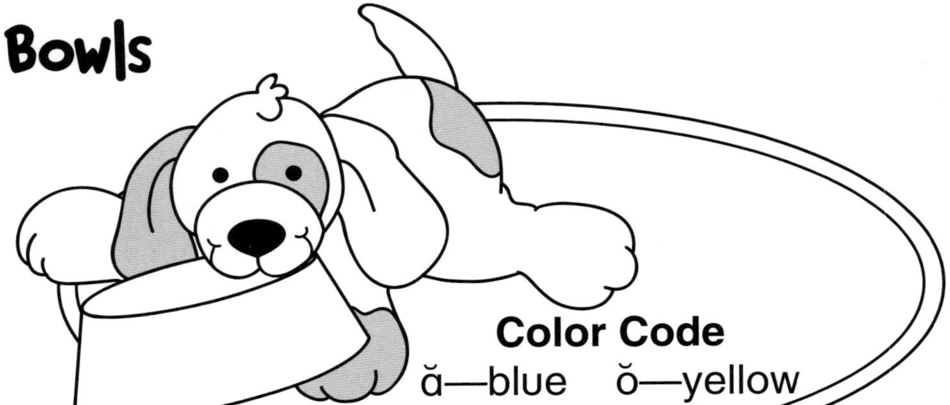

Color Code
ă—blue   ŏ—yellow

✏️ Write each vowel.

🖍️ Color the bowls by the code.

s __ ck

c __ t

h __ t

fl __ g

p __ n

b __ x

m __ p

d __ g

Showtime!

 Cut.

 Glue under the correct word family.

Write the word.

-ug   **-un**

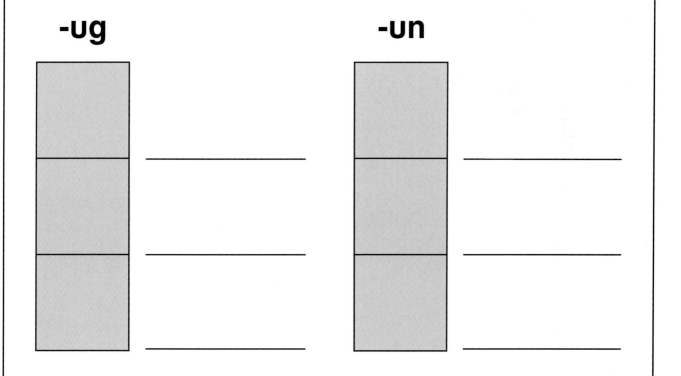

Word Skills

What's the Password?

Give students reading practice on the go! To prepare, write several familiar words on separate blank cards. Display the cards within student reach on the doorframe of your classroom. Whenever a student leaves the room, remind him to give the password a high five. To do this, he touches or high-fives a chosen word and reads it softly. Rearrange or replace the words periodically to help students gain sight words by leaps and bounds! **Word recognition**

Winning Pairs

This partner game is a literacy-boosting version of Go Fish. Program each of 12 index cards with a different familiar word, and then make a duplicate set. Place the cards in a resealable plastic bag at a center. To begin, one student deals seven cards each to himself and another player; then he stacks the remaining cards facedown to form a draw pile. Each player sets aside all his matching pairs of words. Player 1 begins by asking Player 2 for a word to match one that he is holding. If he receives the match from Player 2, he places the pair on the table and takes another turn. If Player 2 does not have the requested card, he says, "Go fish," and Player 1 draws a card from the pile. If Player 1 draws the card he requested or makes another match, he may lay down the pair and take another turn. If he does not draw a match, he keeps the card and Player 2 takes a turn. Any time a player lays down his last card, he takes one card from the draw pile. When the draw pile is gone, the game ends. The player with more pairs wins! **Word recognition**

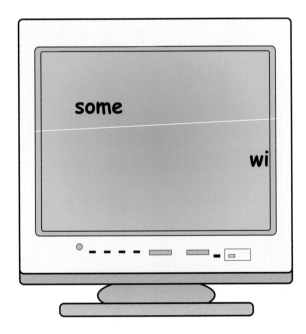

Look and Read!

This technology tip is a surefire approach to increasing students' sight-word vocabularies. Position a computer monitor in a prominent classroom location. Then set the monitor's screensaver to continuously scroll several familiar words. Whenever students read the screen, they'll get valuable skill reinforcement! **Word recognition**

It's a Match!

This activity is a memorable approach to high-frequency words. Choose ten or more words and write each word on two identical blank cards. Then display the cards in random order in a pocket chart with the blank sides facing outward. To begin, one player turns over a card and reads it aloud. Then she turns over another card and reads it. If the words are the same, she takes the two cards. If they are not the same, she turns the cards back over. Each remaining player takes a turn in the same manner. Alternate play continues until the pocket chart is empty. **Word recognition**

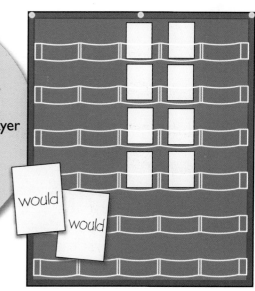

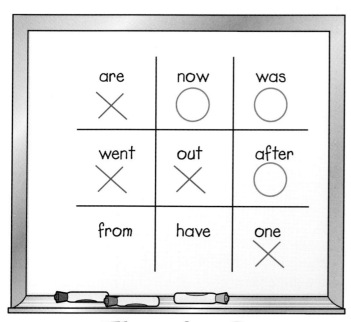

Three in a Row

Looking for a kid-pleasing warm-up for a reading group? Try this! Draw a tic-tac-toe grid on the board and then program each grid space with a different familiar word. Divide students into two teams and assign each team a symbol (X or O). To begin, a player from Team 1 points to a word and reads it aloud with his teammates' help as needed. If he reads the word correctly, he draws his team's symbol in the corresponding space. If he does not read the word correctly, help him identify it but do not have him mark the space. Team 2 takes a turn in a similar manner. The teams alternate turns until one team claims three spaces in a horizontal, vertical, or diagonal row and is declared the winner or until every space has been claimed and the game is declared a tie. Word recognition

Tower Power

Here's a fun way for students to build their reading vocabularies! To prepare, collect a supply of blocks. Label one side of each block with a different high-frequency word. Set the blocks in a paper bag at a center. Arrange for two or three students to visit the center at a time.

One youngster takes a block at random. She reads the word with the help of another center visitor as needed and then places the block on the floor to establish the base of a tower. The next student takes a block, reads the word, and then adds it to the tower. The students continue taking turns as described until the bag is empty or the tower falls. If the tower falls, the students read and build again! **Word recognition**

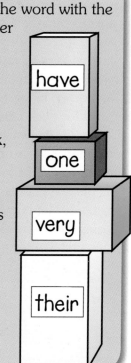

Pleasing Practice

Use the contract on page 42 to help your first graders improve their study habits. Give each youngster a copy. Have each student write his spelling words on the lines. Each day of the week that he studies his words, have him color the corresponding illustration. For additional reinforcement, encourage him to display the contract on his family's refrigerator. His family is sure to see the list and help him practice spelling the words. Spelling

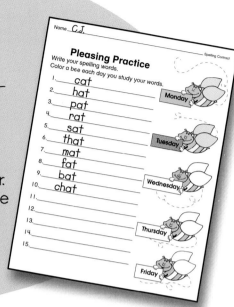

Word Aerobics

This spelling review is sure to receive rave reviews! In an open area, display a list of spelling words. Have students spread out; then encourage students to copy your aerobic movements as you spell each word. For example, hop up and down or perform jumping jacks for each letter of a word. After spelling each word in this manner, invite student volunteers to decide movements as the class spells the words again. Students will love exercising their way to spelling success! **Spelling**

Ways With Words

Invite students to try these creative alternatives to paper and pencil spelling practice. Count on the variety to keep student interest high! **Spelling**

- Arrange for students to use clean paintbrushes and water to "paint" spelling words on individual chalkboards.
- Place a spelling list and a shallow container of play sand at a center. When a student visits the center, have him use his fingertip to "write" a word in the sand. After he checks his work against the list, instruct him to smooth the sand and form a different word.
- Place a length of white paper on a table. Invite students to write their spelling words with various colors of markers.
- Have students roll modeling clay into snake shapes and then manipulate the shapes to form their spelling words.

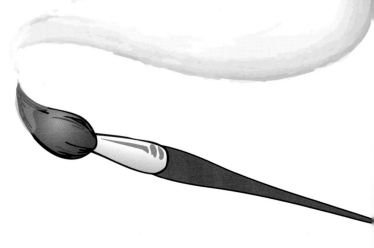

Magnetic Spelling

Attract student interest in spelling practice with this nifty idea! For an individual or a partner activity, place two small magnetic boards (or cookie sheets), a supply of magnetic alphabet letters, and a spelling word list at a center. Each student uses the magnetic letters to spell the words from the list. If two students are working together, they can trade magnetic boards and check each other's spelling. **Spelling**

Letter-Perfect Bottle Caps

Forming words is loads of fun with these durable manipulatives. Collect at least 26 light-colored, blank bottle caps from water bottles or two-liter soda bottles. Use a permanent marker to write the lowercase form of each alphabet letter on the bottle caps, writing one letter per cap. Program any remaining caps with frequently used letters. Place the letters in a shallow box. Dictate words for small groups of students to form with the caps, or have individual students use the caps to form words from a provided list. **Spelling**

How Colorful!

Here's a bright way to give students practice writing words. Give each student a large sheet of paper. Dictate a spelling word and have him use a pencil to write it with large letters. Confirm the correct spelling and then instruct each youngster to trace the word with a highlighter. After he completes his tracing, invite him to trace the word again with different-colored highlighters. **Spelling**

Scrambled Eggs

For this center activity, number 12 plastic eggs from 1 to 12. Inside each egg, place letter manipulatives that can be used to form a different spelling word. Set the eggs in an empty, sanitized egg carton. Set the carton and a spelling list at a center stocked with paper. To complete the activity, a student numbers his paper from 1 to 12. Next, he opens an egg and arranges the letters to form a spelling word. After he writes the word on his paper beside the appropriate number, he returns the letters to the egg. Then he continues in the same manner with the remaining eggs. Spelling

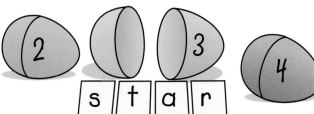

Topic Tools

New vocabulary words take shape with this ongoing idea. When you begin a new topic of study, use bulletin board paper to make a poster-size shape that represents the subject. For example, you might make a large flower for the topic of plants. Title the poster "[Topic] Words" and then display it on a classroom wall. Whenever you introduce a topic-related word to students, write it on the poster. Periodically review the displayed words with students as desired. The poster will be a handy reference during group discussions as well as when students write about what they have learned! Vocabulary

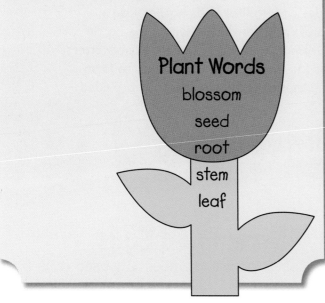

Plant Words

blossom

seed

root

stem

leaf

Word Keepers

This storage idea makes it fun for students to learn vocabulary words. Collect a class supply of clean, empty margarine containers with lids. Have each student use provided arts-and-crafts materials to personalize her container as desired. Next, give each youngster a copy of a vocabulary word list formatted like the one shown. Ask each youngster to cut apart her words and then place them in her container. Familiarize students with the words as desired. For example, have each youngster sort her words into categories. Or announce the meaning of each word, in turn, and instruct each student to hold up the corresponding word.

After students are familiar with the words, give each youngster a blank booklet. Ask her to glue her words in the booklet and title the corresponding page(s). Throughout the year, present new words for her to store in her container and then add to her booklet as described. **Vocabulary**

More Than One

Words with multiple meanings are the topic of this picture-perfect display. Program each of several blank cards with a different multiple-meaning word (see the suggestions on this page). Place the cards in a container. To begin, invite a student to take a card at random and read it aloud. Next, guide students to dictate at least two sentences that convey different meanings of the word. Write each sentence along the bottom of a separate sheet of paper. Then have volunteers illustrate the sentences. After the illustrations are complete, display the word card on a hallway wall and post the papers below it. Repeat the sentence-writing and illustrating process each day until all of the words are added to the display.

Multiple-meaning words

bark
bat
fly
play
roll
show
sign
sink
trip
watch

Building Compound Words

Use plastic or wooden building blocks to help students build compound words! Attach a piece of masking tape to one side of several blocks. Program each block with a word that could be used to make a compound word. Place the blocks and a supply of writing paper at a center. A student arranges the blocks to create compound words and records them on a sheet of paper. (Be sure to inform students that not all word combinations will make compound words.) If desired, include an answer key with all the correct combinations. **Compound words**

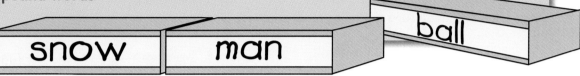

Picture These Compound Words!

To begin this picture-perfect activity, write a student-generated list of compound words on the board. Next, have each student select a compound word. Then have him fold each end of a 4½" x 12" piece of white construction paper to the center. On the outside of the folded ends, the student illustrates and labels the two words that make up his compound. On the inside middle section of the paper, he illustrates and labels the compound word. Invite each student to share his completed work before mounting the pictures on a bulletin board titled "Picture These Compound Words!" Compound words

Butterfly Buddies

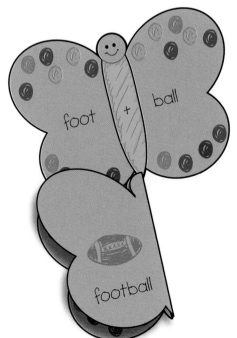

Students' compound word skills are sure to soar with this three-dimensional display. Give each student a colorful copy of the butterfly pattern on page 43 and assign her a compound word. Have her write on her butterfly the two words that form the compound word, writing the first word on the left wing and the second word on the right wing. Invite her to color the body of the butterfly and decorate the wings as desired. After she cuts out the butterfly, have her fold it in half and position it so that the fold is on the right. Instruct her to write and illustrate her compound word on the butterfly and then unfold it.

To display students' completed work, title a bulletin board "Soar With Compound Words!" Then staple the body of each youngster's butterfly to the board, leaving the wings free. For reinforcement, have a student read the words on the front of a butterfly, say the corresponding compound word, and then look on the back of the butterfly to check the word. **Compound words**

See the Ready Reference on page 44 for a list of compound words.

Move Together!

Here's a simple way to demonstrate how contractions are formed. On individual blank cards, write the letters that spell the two words that form a chosen contraction. Write an apostrophe on a separate card. Give each letter card to a different student. Then have the students with the letters stand at the front of the classroom and form the two words. After the seated students read the words, give a volunteer the apostrophe card. Then help the youngsters form the contraction. Repeat the activity with different words to give each student a turn modeling a contraction. **Contractions**

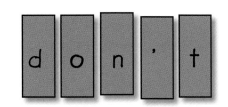

Clever Cover-Up

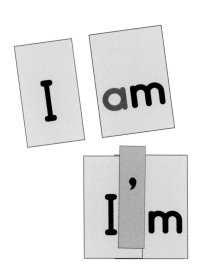

Slide into contractions with this pocket-chart activity. Write the words *I* and *am* on separate cards, as shown, using a red marker to write the *a*. Write an apostrophe on a different-colored card. In a similar manner, write the words that form chosen contractions with *is* and *are,* using a red marker to write each letter that is omitted in the contractions. Prepare an apostrophe card for each contraction.

Display each pair of words in a pocket chart. Next, demonstrate how to slide the first card over the second card in each pair and set an apostrophe in place to create a contraction. Then have students form contractions with the remaining cards in the same manner. **Contractions**

Search and Sort!

To prepare this contraction review, divide a large piece of paper into nine sections and title them as shown. Display the paper within student reach. Then set out a supply of sticky notes and children's books. To begin, pair students and have each twosome look through books for contractions. When partners find a contraction, they write the word on a sticky note and flag the page with it.

After each twosome finds at least one contraction, invite each student pair, in turn, to read aloud a contraction it found. If the word is not already displayed, have the partners place their sticky note in the correct section of the paper. Then write the two corresponding words beside the sticky note. If the contraction is already displayed, ask the partners to place their sticky note atop the matching sticky note. Have students share all of their finds in this manner. Encourage them to look for different contractions to add to the poster whenever they read. Contractions

Contractions		
am	are	has
I'm I am	we're we are	
	you're you are	
have	is	not
	he's he is	
us	will	would

See the Ready Reference on page 45 for a list of contractions.

Busy Bears

With this group activity, students learn the "bear" facts about adding -s to verbs. Draw a line down the center of a sheet of chart paper. Title the two columns as shown. Then ask a volunteer to name an action that three bears (real or imaginary) might do. Write the verb in the first column. Then say, "Three bears [verb] but one bear...," prompting students to say the appropriate verb form. After they say the correct word, write it in the second column. Continue adding pairs of verbs to the chart in this manner. Then ask students what they notice about the verbs. They're sure to conclude that most verbs that tell about only one bear end with -s! **Verbs that end with -s**

Three Bears	One Bear
eat	eats
sleep	sleeps
walk	walks
sit	sits

Yesterday

Take a look at the past with this class book project. Assign each student the -ed form of a different verb and give him a 12" x 18" sheet of white paper. Have him write a sentence that includes the verb and begins with the word *Yesterday*. Then ask him to illustrate his work. On another sheet of paper, write in large letters, "It was a busy day!" Stack students' completed papers on your paper. Bind the entire stack between two construction paper covers and then title the resulting book "Yesterday." **Verbs that end with -ed**

Yesterday my dog jumped into the water.

Roll Into Action!

This group activity is a quick and easy way to give students practice adding –ed to words. Label each side of a small, empty tissue box with a different regular verb, such as *jump, look, paint, skip, smile,* and *walk.* To begin, sit with students in a circle. Pass the box to one youngster and have her toss it. Ask her to read the word on the top of the box. Then invite a volunteer to use the –ed form of the verb in a sentence. After the volunteer says an appropriate sentence, have the student who rolled the box pass it to the youngster on her right. Continue the activity as described until each student has had a turn rolling the box. For another round, have students use the –ing form of the verbs. **Verbs that end with –ed and –ing**

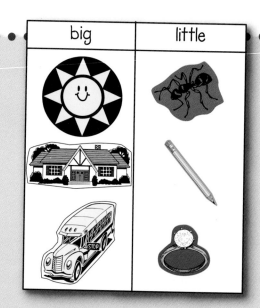

"Send-sational" Synonyms

This center delivers first-class practice with word meanings. To prepare, gather a lidded shoebox and several different picture postcards. Cut a slit in the box lid that is large enough for a postcard. Label the box "Synonym Mailbox" and decorate it as desired. On the back of each postcard, write a word and a synonym for the word side by side. Then cut between the words to divide each card into two pieces. Drop all of the prepared postcards in the box and then place the box at a center stocked with paper.

To complete the activity, a student removes the postcards from the box and replaces the lid. Then he spreads out the cards word side up. He reads a word and finds the synonym. He flips the two cards over and reassembles the postcard to check his work. If the two parts of the postcard match, he writes the word pair on his paper and then deposits the cards in the mailbox. If they do not go together, he tries a different pairing.
Synonyms

Opposite Posters

For each of several pairs of opposites, divide and label a large sheet of paper as shown. (Consider using pairs such as *big* and *little, hot* and *cold, living* and *nonliving.*) Then divide students into as many groups as there are posters. Give one poster to each group and have students cut pictures from old magazines to illustrate the words. Then instruct the students to glue their pictures in the appropriate columns of their posters. Ask a student from each group to share his group's completed poster. Then display the posters on a classroom wall. *Antonyms*

Mix and Match!

Secretly assign each student a different word so that each youngster has an antonym for a classmate's word. (If you have an odd number of students, assign one word to two students.) Have each youngster illustrate her assigned word on a provided blank card. Then ask each child, in turn, to stand, show the class her illustration, and use her assigned word to tell about it. If a seated student illustrated an antonym for the word, he stands and shares his work next. After he tells the class about his illustration, have the two students sit together. Continue the activity as described until all of the cards are paired in this manner. **Antonyms**

See the Ready Reference on page 44 for a list of antonyms.

Easy as ABC!

What better way to teach alphabetical order than by using your youngsters' first names? Have each student write her first name on a construction paper strip and then use a highlighter to highlight the first letter. To begin, slowly recite the alphabet, stopping after each letter to ask students to stand if their names begin with the announced letter. When more than one student has a name that begins with the same letter, have those students highlight one or more additional letters in their names. Display the strips in alphabetical order on a wall. The final result will be an eye-catching and alphabetized list of important words—students' own names!
Alphabetical order

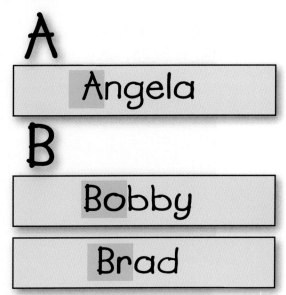

Quick and Easy Alphabetizing

Have each student select five crayons from her crayon box or a classroom supply. (If desired, tell students not to select more than one crayon that begins with the same letter.) Have her arrange the crayons in alphabetical order. Then have a classmate check her work before the student returns the crayons to the box.

Instruct each student to think of five toys whose names begin with different letters. Next, have him draw a picture of each toy on a separate index card and label it. Then have each student arrange his cards alphabetically on his desk. Check each student's work; then have each student scramble his cards and paper-clip them together. Collect the card sets and redistribute them for different students to alphabetize. **Alphabetical order**

Check out the skill-building reproducibles on pages 46–49.

Personal Dictionaries

This ongoing project is not only a simple way to practice alphabetical order, it is also a handy spelling reference. Early in the school year, staple 13 half sheets of paper between two construction paper covers to create a blank dictionary for each student. Have each youngster personalize his front cover as desired. Then instruct him to label his pages from *A* to *Z*, writing on the front and back of each page. Throughout the year, have each student write words—such as number words, classmates' names, color words, and vocabulary words—on the appropriate pages of his dictionary. Encourage him to refer to his dictionary whenever he writes. Each time he enters or looks up a word, he'll sharpen his alphabetizing skills! **Alphabetical order**

Pleasing Practice

Write your spelling words.
Color a bee each day you study the words.

1. _____

2. _____

3. _____

4. _____

5. _____

6. _____

7. _____

8. _____

9. _____

10. _____

11. _____

12. _____

13. _____

14. _____

15. _____

Monday

Tuesday

Wednesday

Thursday

Friday

Compound Words

airplane	downstairs	mailbox	seahorse
barnyard	fingernail	newspaper	sidewalk
baseball	firecracker	nobody	skateboard
bathtub	flashlight	notebook	snowflake
bedroom	football	outside	snowman
beehive	goldfish	paintbrush	somebody
birdbath	grandparents	pancake	something
birdhouse	grasshopper	patchwork	strawberry
butterfly	groundhog	peanut	suitcase
chalkboard	hairbrush	playground	sunlight
cowboy	haircut	policeman	sunshine
cupcake	handshake	popcorn	teamwork
daydream	homework	railroad	teapot
daylight	indoor	rainbow	toothbrush
doghouse	keyboard	sailboat	underline
dollhouse	ladybug	sandpaper	watermelon
doorbell	lighthouse	scarecrow	weekend

Antonyms

above—below	come—go	give—take	old—young
alike—different	crooked—straight	happy—sad	on—off
always—never	dark—light	hard—soft	polite—rude
asleep—awake	day—night	healthy—sick	pull—push
back—front	deep—shallow	heavy—light	rich—poor
beautiful—ugly	difficult—easy	high—low	rough—smooth
before—after	down—up	kind—mean	save—spend
begin—end	dry—wet	large—small	short—tall
best—worst	early—late	leave—stay	start—stop
big—little	easy—hard	left—right	strong—weak
bottom—top	empty—full	long—short	tame—wild
bright—dull	far—near	loose—tight	thick—thin
clean—dirty	fast—slow	lose—win	true—false
close—open	first—last	many—few	wide—narrow
cold—hot	forget—remember	noisy—quiet	yes—no

Contractions

A contraction is a shortened form of a single word or word pair. An apostrophe is used to show where a letter or letters have been omitted to create the shortened form.

word with "am"
I am   I'm

words with "are"
they are   they're
we are   we're
you are   you're

words with "has"
he has   he's
it has   it's
she has   she's
what has   what's
where has   where's
who has   who's

words with "have"
I have   I've
they have   they've
we have   we've
you have   you've

words with "is"
he is   he's
it is   it's
she is   she's
that is   that's
there is   there's
what is   what's
where is   where's
who is   who's

words with "not"
are not   aren't
cannot   can't

could not   couldn't
did not   didn't
do not   don't
does not   doesn't
had not   hadn't
has not   hasn't
have not   haven't
is not   isn't
must not   mustn't
should not   shouldn't
was not   wasn't
were not   weren't
will not   won't
would not   wouldn't

word with "us"
let us   let's

words with "will"
he will   he'll
I will   I'll
she will   she'll
they will   they'll
we will   we'll
you will   you'll

words with "would"
he would   he'd
I would   I'd
she would   she'd
they would   they'd
we would   we'd
who would   who'd
you would   you'd

Fitting Together

Write to complete each compound word.
Use the word bank.

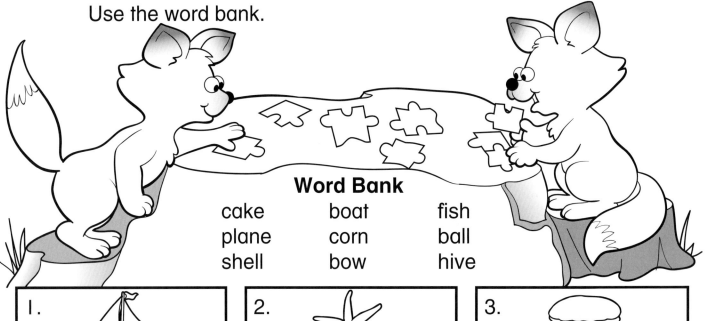

Word Bank

cake	boat	fish
plane	corn	ball
shell	bow	hive

1.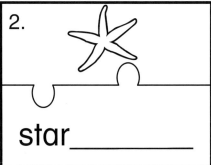

sail_____

2.

star_____

3.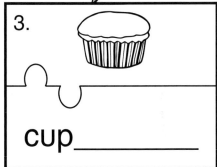

cup_____

4.

pop_____

5.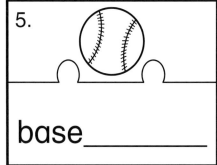

base_____

6.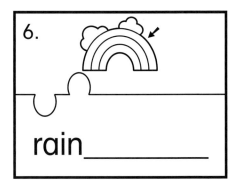

rain_____

7.

bee_____

8.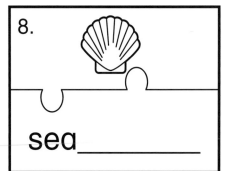

sea_____

9.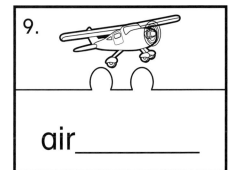

air_____

Name _____

Amazing Changes

✂ Cut.

Glue to match the words.

1 do not	2 you are	3 that is	4 we are

5 was not	6 it is	7 I am	8 is not

that's	I'm	don't	we're
you're	it's	wasn't	isn't

47

Piggy Pictures

✏️ Write. Use the word bank.

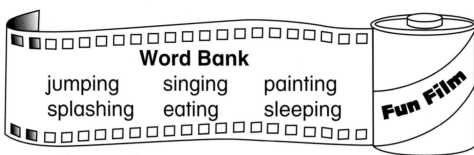

Word Bank

jumping	singing	painting
splashing	eating	sleeping

Fun Film

_____   _____   _____

_____   _____   _____

Complete each sentence with the best word from above.

1. I like the song that he is _____.

2. I saw him _____ up and down.

3. He is _____ the old barn red.

4. Is he _____ all the corn I picked?

5. He always has fun _____ in the mud.

6. Now he is _____ in the hay.

    ©The Mailbox® • Superbook® • TEC61048

Name _____

Just Sniffles!

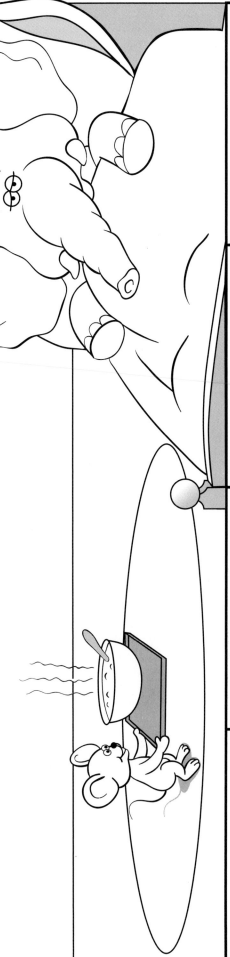

Write each group of words in ABC order.

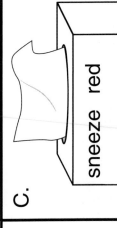

A.

bed	sick
rest	cold

1. _____
2. _____
3. _____
4. _____

B.

soup	hot
cracker	juice

1. _____
2. _____
3. _____
4. _____

C.

sneeze	red
nose	better

1. _____
2. _____
3. _____
4. _____

D.

rest	drink
well	flowers

1. _____
2. _____
3. _____
4. _____

Purposeful Blunders

Reinforce reading strategies by having students correct your deliberate oral-reading mistakes. Before beginning the activity, tell students that you are going to make some mistakes in the sentences you will be reading. Then have students follow along as you read several sentences, deliberately making mistakes as you read. Ask students to name the words you mispronounced. Then have students describe reading strategies you could have used to determine each unfamiliar word. Strategies might include using picture clues, chunking the word into parts, sounding out each letter, or listening to yourself read. After students have explained several reading strategies, reread the sentence correctly. Continue in this same manner in various parts of the story. **Reading strategies**

Sam sees a snack.

Sam sees a snake.

Hoop Help

The result of this small-group activity is a human graphic organizer. In advance, tie one end of a long length of yarn to a plastic toy hoop. Continue to add yarn lengths around the hoop until there is one for each student. Select a volunteer to wear a headband programmed "Reading Strategies," and have her stand in the middle of the hoop. Then ask students to share ways to improve reading. Each time a child shares, encourage her to pick up a piece of yarn, gently lifting that portion of the hoop. Students are sure to be engaged as each idea contributes to lifting the hoop off the floor! **Reading strategies**

Pencils With a Purpose

Add meaning to your storybook collection with these nifty bookmarks. Write the title and author of a selected book on a construction paper copy of the pencil pattern on page 62. Read the story aloud and then ask your students why they think the author wrote the book. Summarize your youngsters' responses and write them on the back of the pencil. Then place the pencil in the book for students' future reference when reading the book. Repeat the activity with other stories to make additional bookmarks. **Author's purpose**

Book Title _____Corduroy_____

Author _____Don Freeman_____

Even though someone or something is not perfect, it is no less special.

What Next?

This unique idea gives youngsters the opportunity to make predictions throughout a story. Preread a selected book, adding sticky notes to ideal pages to stop and ask, "What do you think will happen next?" Then gather your youngsters and introduce the book. Encourage students to make predictions based on the book's front cover. Then read the story aloud, pausing at each sticky note to recognize actual story events and for youngsters to make new predictions. Children are sure to be engaged and curious to find out how close they are to the author's direction in the book. **Making predictions**

The Very Hungry Caterpillar

I think the catrpilr is hngree. He wil et los uv levs and get fat!

He ate los uv food and seeps. He is a buterfi.

A New View

Youngsters compare their predictions to an author's written message with this trifold project. Have students fold down the top 1½ inches of a sheet of paper and tuck the bottom of the paper under the top fold. Instruct each child to write the title of a chosen book on the top fold. Then ask him to look at the front cover, consider the title, and make a prediction about the story. On the bottom fold, have him complete and illustrate the sentence "I think _____."

After reading the book, instruct each child to open the paper and to write and illustrate what really happened in the story. Encourage him to share his project at home and peek inside to prompt a detailed retelling of the author's version. **Making predictions**

Students as the Authors

Heighten student interest in your current literature with this prediction activity. Read aloud a story to your students, stopping before the conclusion. On a piece of story paper, have each student write and illustrate a prediction of what will happen next. Encourage students to share their predictions with their classmates; then read aloud the conclusion of the book. If desired, bind your students' predictions into a book and place it and the actual book in your reading area for students to compare. **Making predictions**

All Mixed-Up!

Cooperative learning takes place with this small-group activity. To prepare, write a main idea statement on a sentence strip for one group member. Then, for each remaining group member, write a different corresponding detail sentence on an individual strip. In turn, give each student a strip and ask him to read aloud his sentence. After each youngster has shared his sentence, challenge students to determine who has the main idea. Then discuss how the detail sentences support the main idea. If desired, make additional sentence strips for further practice. **Main idea and details**

I like dogs.

I like yellow dogs.

I like big dogs.

I like fluffy dogs.

We like to go to the zoo.

We can feed the animals.

We get to see lots of animals.

We can pet the goats.

2.

Nest Eggs

How "tweet" it is for youngsters to match the correct details to the main idea in this center activity. To prepare, cut out three copies of page 63. For each page, write a main idea sentence on the bird's strip and a supporting detail sentence on each egg. To make the center self-checking, number the nests and code the back of each egg with the number of the corresponding nest. Store the cutouts in a large resealable plastic bag and place the bag at a center. When a child visits the center, she reads the main ideas and matches each egg to the correct nest. When finished, she flips the eggs to check her work. **Main idea and details**

BOOK TITLES

Without telling your students the title, read aloud a book that they probably have not heard before. After reading the book, ask students to reflect on the events of the story and create a title for the book. Before revealing the book's title, encourage students to share the titles they chose. **Main idea**

PICTURE THE MAIN IDEA

Pair students and provide each pair with a picture (cut from an old magazine) that depicts an event or interesting situation. Have each pair discuss its picture and tell the main idea. For added practice have the pairs exchange their pictures. **Main idea**

Matching details to a main idea is a snap with this one-of-a-kind clothesline center. To prepare, write a different main idea sentence on each of three cards and cut out nine construction paper copies of the shirt pattern on page 64. For each main idea, write a different supporting detail on each of three shirts. Program the backs of the cards and the shirts with matching symbols for self-checking. Store the cards and shirts in a small basket with a supply of clothespins. Finally, suspend heavy string or yarn between two chairs at a center to make a clothesline and place the basket nearby.

When a child visits the center, he clips a main idea card on the clothesline. Then he clips the three shirts with supporting details next to the card. To check his work, he looks on the back of each shirt. If correct, he removes the items from the line and hangs a new card to continue. If incorrect, he re-sorts the shirts and begins again. **Main idea and details**

Scoops of Detail

Here's a banana split project that can be used with just about any story. At the conclusion of a chosen book, give each student a copy of the banana split patterns on page 65. Have each child write the title of the book on the dish and the main idea on the banana. Then have her write or draw a different story detail on each ice-cream scoop. If desired, provide extra copies of the scoop pattern to add more details. Instruct her to cut out the patterns and glue them together to resemble a banana split. Finally, encourage her to use her sweet treat to prompt a retelling of the story! **Main idea and details**

Detail
He is sad.

Detail
He makes a friend.

Detail
He sees more cracks.

Main Idea You shood be happy wif yrsef even if yr difrent

Title Eggbert

It's in the Bag!

This kid-pleasing collection helps youngsters recall details in stories read throughout the year. Place a gift bag in an easily accessible area along with a supply of blank cards. After a chosen reading selection, help youngsters determine the main idea. Write the title of the book and the main idea on a card. Then invite students to share story details that support the main idea as you write each one on the card. If desired, select a volunteer to add an illustration on the back. Have a student drop the completed card in the bag. Continue in this manner with other stories. From time to time, have youngsters use the cards to review stories. **Main idea and details**

Bunny Money
Max and Ruby learn the value of money when they go out shopping for Grandma's birthday.
* ~~~~~~~~~~~~~
* ~~~~~~~~~~~~~
* ~~~~~~~~~~~~~

Ducks in a Row

Children sequence the events of a familiar story with this small-group activity. To prepare, cut out a construction paper copy of the duck pattern on page 64 for each group member. Select a story and program each of the ducks with an important event from the story. If desired, add a related illustration. Also cut out a pond shape from blue bulletin board paper.

To begin, read the story aloud. Then give each group member a duck. In turn, encourage her to share her story event. Finally, help youngsters work together to place their ducks in order on the pond. **Sequencing**

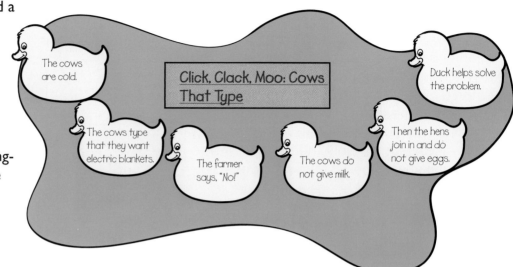

The cows are cold.

The cows type that they want electric blankets.

The farmer says, "No!"

The cows do not give milk.

Then the hens join in and do not give eggs.

Duck helps solve the problem.

Click, Clack, Moo: Cows That Type

Picture-Perfect Events

Here's a great way to make a real-world connection in sequencing. When preparing to go to recess, take a picture of your youngsters lining up. Take another picture of the children standing in line ready to go. While walking by an obvious location on the way to play, take a third picture. Take a final picture of your youngsters' jubilation as they are released to the playground. Mount each photo on construction paper and number the backs in the correct sequence. Encourage students to put the pictures in chronological order. They will be delighted by the opportunity to look at classmates while learning to sequence events! **Sequencing**

ALL IN ORDER

Improve reading comprehension with this sequencing activity. After reading a book aloud to youngsters, write a sentence about a different story event on each of five cards. Number the backs of the cards for self-checking and store them in a large resealable bag with the book. A child puts the cards in order, referring to the story as needed. Then she flips the cards to check her work. For added practice, make cards for other familiar books. **Sequencing**

A Day at the Park

We went on the slide.

Chapter Book Trains

If your students enjoy listening to chapter books at storytime, then try this sequencing activity! Write the title and author of a selected chapter book on a copy of the engine pattern on page 66. Also, make a copy of the train car pattern on page 66 for each chapter. After reading aloud the first chapter, have students summarize the important events as you write their responses on a train car. If desired, display the engine and car on a paper railroad track. Continue in this manner with the remaining chapters. When the train is complete, reread the cars to review the sequence of events. **Sequencing**

Beneficial Bookmarks

Improve reading comprehension with this unique bookmark idea. Give each student a construction paper copy of the bookmark on page 67. Encourage him to use the bookmark as a reference as you lead a discussion about making connections to text. Following sufficient practice with each connection, read a selected story aloud. Then encourage each youngster to use his bookmark as needed to make his own connections to the story. Now that's a simple reading strategy reminder at each child's fingertips! **Making connections**

A Chain of Connections

Make students more aware of text connections with this chain activity! To prepare, make a display similar to the one shown. Then read a story aloud and have each child write or draw a text connection on a strip of paper. Invite each youngster, in turn, to share her strip, identify the connection, and glue her paper in a loop to extend the matching chain on the chart. When each student has had a turn, compare the length of the chains. If desired, challenge youngsters to extend the length of the shorter chains after future readings of a story. **Making connections**

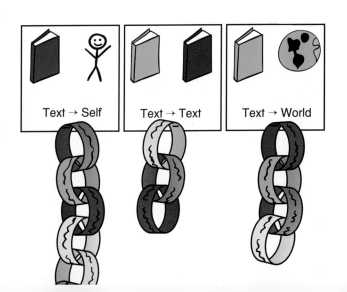

The Domino Effect

Use dominoes to engage students in cause-and-effect relationships with this activity. Set up a line of dominoes to demonstrate what happens when an end domino falls toward the rest of the line. After the demonstration, guide youngsters to discover how dominoes and stories are alike—one event can cause something else to happen.

Next, have each student glue black circles to each half of a large white rectangle to resemble a domino. On the reverse side, instruct her to write an "if" statement on the top half. (Provide prompts to help her get started if needed.) To tell what happened next, have her complete the sentence with a "then" statement on the bottom half of her paper. To complete her project, encourage her to add illustrations. Then invite youngsters to share their dominoes with their classmates. **Cause and effect**

If it rained all day,
then I would read a book.

Freeze-Frame

Use the captured image in a photo as a springboard for a multitude of cause-and-effect events! Give each student a photograph or a picture from a magazine. Have her use her imagination to draw on a sheet of paper what might have happened right after the picture was taken. When students are finished with their work, invite them to share their images and pictures with the class. For added interest, give each student the same image and see how different the effects are from each other. **Cause and effect**

Then What Happened?

Children will be eager to match an event (cause) to the result (effect) with this small-group activity. Write the word *cause* on a paper lunch bag. Then write several related events on individual cards and store them in the bag. For each cause, write an effect on an individual sentence strip. Display the strips in a pocket chart. To begin, have students read the sentence strips. Then invite a youngster to remove a card from the bag. Help him match the cause of a situation to the correct result. Continue in this manner with other students until the cause of each effect has been revealed. **Cause and effect**

The mouse escapes from its cage.

The mouse is scared.

The mouse is thirsty.

cause

The mouse is sitting on your desk.

The mouse eats food.

The mouse takes a nap.

The mouse drinks water.

The mouse hides in the tunnel.

Showing Emotion

Here's an opportunity to incorporate story characters' emotions into your lessons on making inferences! To begin, discuss with students the many feelings people have in different situations. Each time an emotion is mentioned, have students share what it might look like. For instance, when a person is happy, he might smile; when he is scared, he may shiver. Then, as you read a story, stop along the way to have students infer how the character is feeling and then act out the emotion. **Making inferences**

1. It is yellow.
2. You sharpen it.
3. You use it every day.

Inference Bags

Here's a fun yet simple way to provide your youngsters with practice making inferences. Have each student secretly place an object or a picture of an object in a paper lunch bag. Each student then writes three clues about his item on an index card, folds his bag, and tapes the card on the outside. In turn, invite each student to read his clues to the class and call on a volunteer to infer the bag's contents. **Making inferences**

Reality vs. Fantasy

Introduce your students to the difference between reality and fantasy with this literature-related activity. Label one half of a sheet of chart paper "Could Be" and the other half "Could Not Be." Then mount the chart in a prominent location. After reading a story aloud, have students name examples of story events that are fantasy and some that could be reality. List students' responses under the correct heading on the chart. To follow up, have students replace the fictional parts of the story with things that could happen in reality. Or have students try turning the nonfiction parts of the story into fantasy. **Reality and fantasy**

Could Be	Could Not Be
• Cinderella has two mean stepsisters.	• Cinderella has a fairy godmother.
• Cinderella has to do all the chores.	• A pumpkin turns into a coach.
• She loses her slipper.	• The mice turn into horses.
• The prince finds her slipper.	• Cinderella's torn dress turns into a beautiful gown.

Is It Real?

Illustrations for this whole-group activity are sure to keep your students guessing. Copy and cut out a class supply of the reality and fantasy cards on page 68. Give one card to each child. Have him secretly look at the card and draw a corresponding picture on the back. When everyone has finished, invite each youngster, in turn, to share his drawing. Encourage his classmates to guess whether the illustration is reality or fantasy. Then have the child flip his paper to reveal the answer. **Reality and fantasy**

Crack the Code

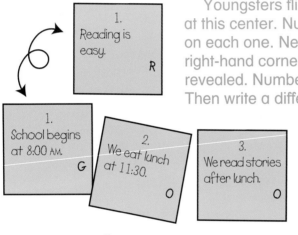

Youngsters flip to the facts to reveal a secret message at this center. Number eight cards and write a different fact on each one. Next, sequence the cards and label the lower right-hand corners so the hidden message "Good job!" is revealed. Number the back of each card to match the front. Then write a different opinion on each one. Code the opinions with letters that do not appear in the hidden message. Store the cards in a resealable plastic bag and place the bag at a center. A student arranges the cards in numerical order, fact side up. If her work is accurate, the hidden message can be read! **Fact and opinion**

Looking for the Facts

Review fact and opinion with this daily activity. Have each student use a crayon to program one side of an index card "Fact" and the other side "Opinion." Have students store their cards in their desks. Each day secretly record five student-generated statements—some facts, some opinions. Then, at the end of the day, read a statement from the list. If a student thinks the statement is a fact, she displays the fact side of her card. If she thinks the statement is an opinion, she shows the opinion side of her card. Continue in this manner until all the statements have been read. Next, reread each statement and reveal its answer. Students can't help but be amazed at the interesting statements they say throughout the day! **Fact and opinion**

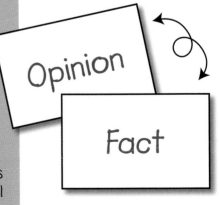

Third Time's a Charm!

Need a way to promote rereading text in the classroom? A classroom puppet can help! Select a short passage for the puppet to read in front of the class. As he reads, model good reading strategies such as chunking word parts, sounding out words, and using picture clues. After the first reading, be sure to let the puppet tell the children that he thought the reading was difficult. Make comments to help him feel better and then ask the puppet to read the passage again. When finished, encourage youngsters to comment on his improvements! Next, have the puppet read the passage one more time with expression. Your youngsters will surely notice this last confident reading! To follow up the activity, invite volunteers to read similar passages two or three times, recognizing all of the improvements made along the way. **Fluency**

The tr...truck is in the m...u...mu...d...mud.

Penguin Pointers

These chilly critters are perfect for improving youngsters' fluency skills. Have each child color and cut out a copy of a penguin pattern on page 62. Then direct him to glue the cutout to a large craft stick as shown. Instruct him to point the penguin's beak to each word as he reads. Youngsters will have fun tracking words, and you'll have a great way to monitor student progress at a glance. Fluency

Variety of Voices

Improving fluency is a matter of voice with this rereading idea. Brainstorm a list of voices with your students, such as a squeaky mouse, a baby, or an energetic voice, and write them on a chart. After a youngster reads a passage for the first time, encourage him to choose a new voice from the chart each time he rereads the text. There's no doubt your students will read and reread their favorite texts over and over again! **Fluency**

Reader of the Week

Your youngsters will look forward to rereading a story with this opportunity! Each week, select a student to read to a class of younger students, and name her Reader of the Week. On Monday, have her choose a book and practice reading the story to herself. On Tuesday and Wednesday, help her with any troubling words and discuss how to read in front of a group. Encourage her to take the book home and read it to her family. On Thursday, invite her to read the story to her own class. Lead youngsters to praise her effort and then invite them to offer suggestions on ways to improve her oral reading. By Friday, not only is the Reader of the Week well prepared to read her selection, but the younger students are anxiously awaiting their special guest reader too! **Fluency**

Favorite Character

Students are sure to enjoy adding their favorite character to a class graph! To prepare, write the title of a selected story on a sentence strip and the names of each story character on separate cards. Place the cards and strip in a pocket chart as shown. After reading the story aloud, use the cards to identify the characters in the story. Then have each youngster draw her favorite character on a four-inch square and place her square in the corresponding row in the pocket chart. After everyone has had a chance to vote, lead youngsters in interpreting the completed graph. **Story characters**

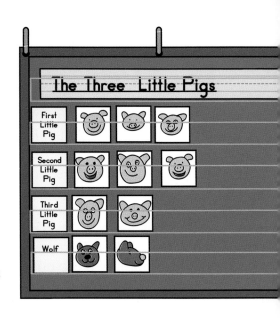

Character Cars

Display character-related details with this small-group activity. Use a white crayon to write the title of a book on a black strip of paper to resemble pavement. To begin, have students name each of the characters in the selected story. Assign one character to each child (grouping students as needed). Then encourage each youngster or group of youngsters to write or draw details about the character on a car cutout. To complete the project, have students glue the cars to the pavement to create a roadway review of characters! **Character details**

Flip and Find

Students review a story's plot from cover to cover with these mini flip books. Each student cuts a white sheet of paper in half to make two strips (5½" x 8½"). He stacks the strips and positions them vertically. He slides the top strip upward about one inch and then folds the top of the stack forward, creating four graduated layers. He staples the stack along the fold to make a booklet. Next, he writes the title on the cover and labels the tabs as shown. Then he writes and illustrates the beginning, middle, and end of a selected story on the corresponding pages. He adds details as desired to complete the project. Beginning, middle, and end

Stir the Story

This story stew is a great way to review your latest shared reading! In advance, trim a large recipe card from a sheet of bulletin board paper and label it with the book title and four story elements as shown. Also write the story's setting, the name of each character, the problem, and the solution on separate blank cards or sentence strips. Place the cards in a pot along with a wooden spoon. After reading the selected story aloud, choose a volunteer to scoop up an ingredient from your pot and read the text aloud. Then have her tape the card near the corresponding story element on the recipe card. Continue in this manner until each of the ingredients has been identified. If desired, repeat this activity with several books to create a class cookbook of stories! **Story elements**

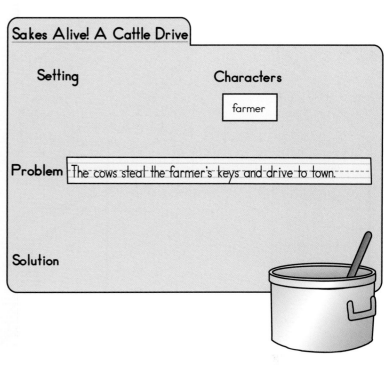

Sakes Alive! A Cattle Drive

Setting   Characters

farmer

Problem   The cows steal the farmer's keys and drive to town.

Solution

Story Alterations

Youngsters change a story element to explore new endings with this whole-group activity. After reading a story, identify a story element that could be changed, such as the setting or the characters. Then ask individuals to share their thoughts; record each change on the board. For example, a story setting that features a quiet country park could be changed to a large city. Then explore how each change might affect the story's ending and record the new endings next to their corresponding changes. **Story elements**

Change
The bears go to the city.

New Ending
The bears move into an apartment.

Teddy Bear Story Map

This unique idea is a "bear" essential when it comes to assessing your students' reading comprehension. On light brown bulletin board paper, cut out an enlarged copy of the bear pattern on page 69. Laminate the cutout for durability before mounting it in a prominent location. After reading a story aloud, use a wipe-off marker to write the story's title and author on the bear's tummy. Next write student-generated responses to the four story parts listed on the bear's limbs. When it's time to review another book, simply wipe away the programming, and the story map is ready to use again! **Story elements**

Main Characters:
Title:
Setting:
Author:
Problem:
Solution:

Pencil Pattern
Use with "Pencils With a Purpose" on page 50.

Penguin Patterns
Use with "Penguin Pointers" on page 59.

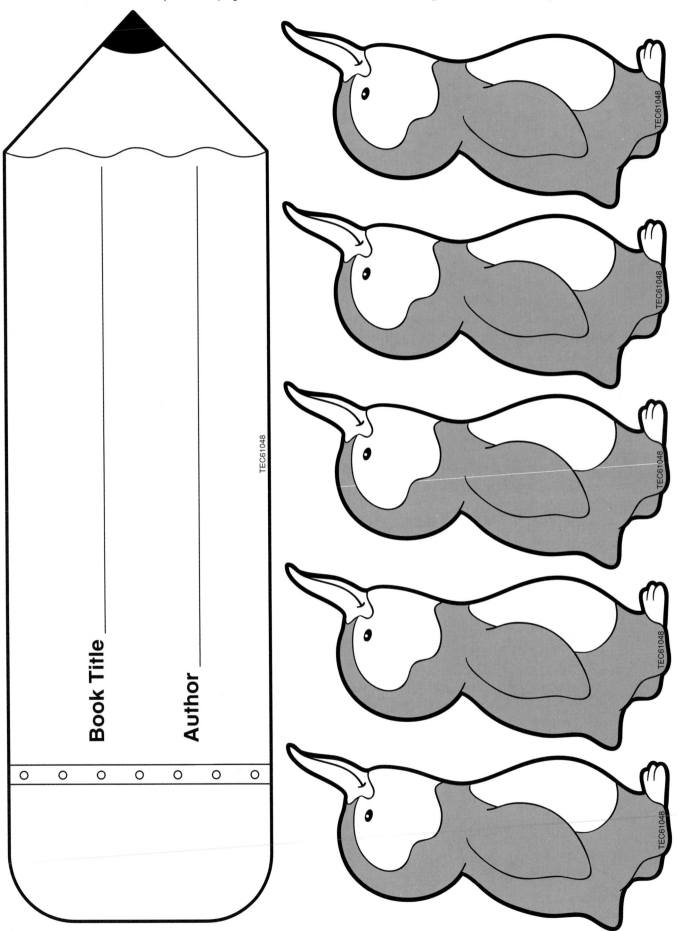

Book Title

Author

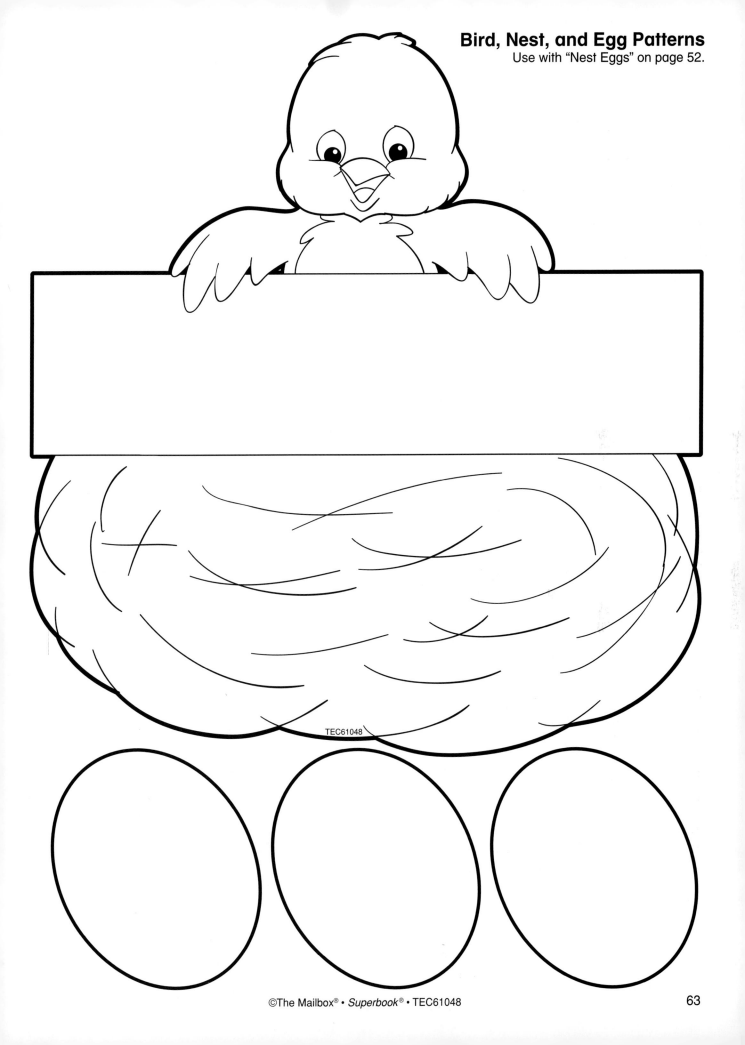

TEC61048

Shirt Pattern
Use with "Laundered Stories" on page 53.

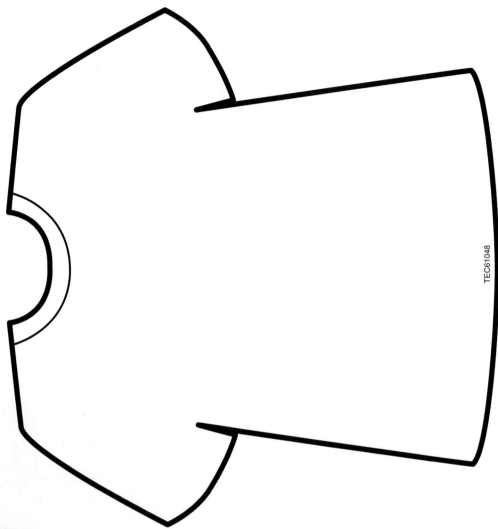

TEC61048

Duck Pattern
Use with "Ducks in a Row" on page 54 and "Just Ducky!" on page 129.

TEC61048

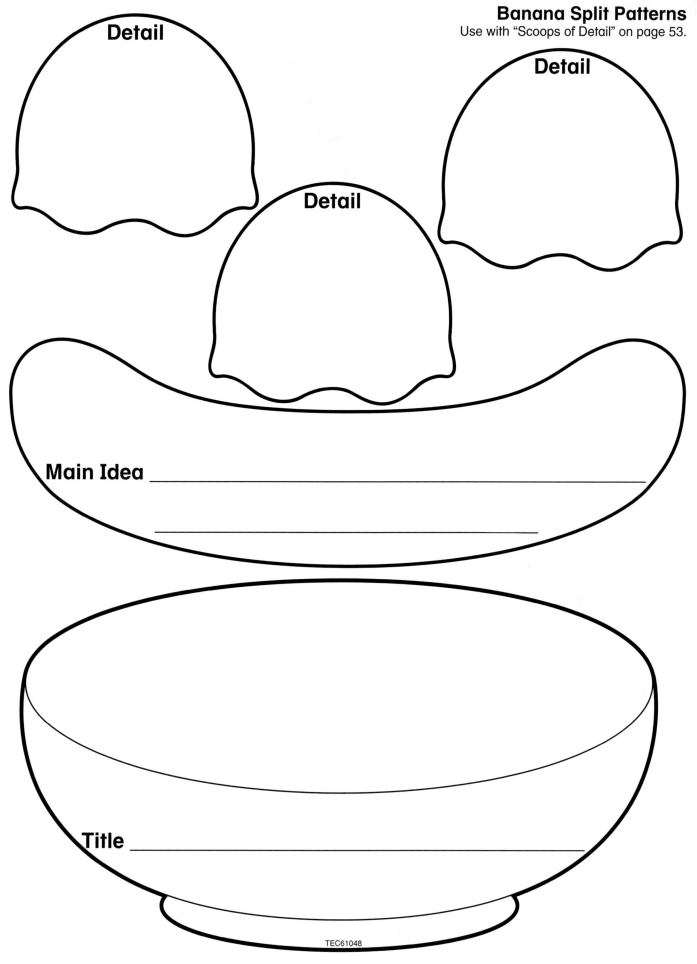

Detail

Detail

Detail

Main Idea _____

_____

Title _____

TEC61048

Engine and Train Car Patterns
Use with "Chapter Book Trains" on page 55 and "Peace Train" on page 306.

TEC61048

I am making connections!

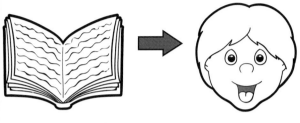

Text to **Self**

This story reminds me of when I…

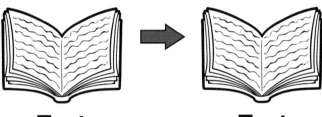

Text to **Text**

This story reminds me of another story that…

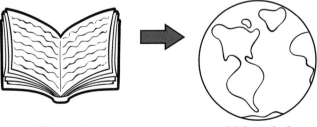

Text to **World**

Since I know that…, this story…

©The Mailbox® • *Superbook*® • TEC61048

I am making connections!

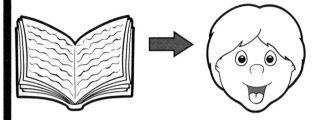

Text to **Self**

This story reminds me of when I…

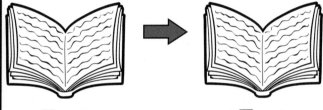

Text to **Text**

This story reminds me of another story that…

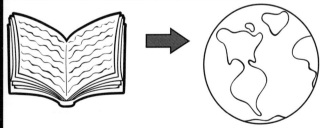

Text to **World**

Since I know that…, this story…

©The Mailbox® • *Superbook*® • TEC61048

Reality and Fantasy Cards

Use with "Is It Real?" on page 58.

TEC61048

TEC61048

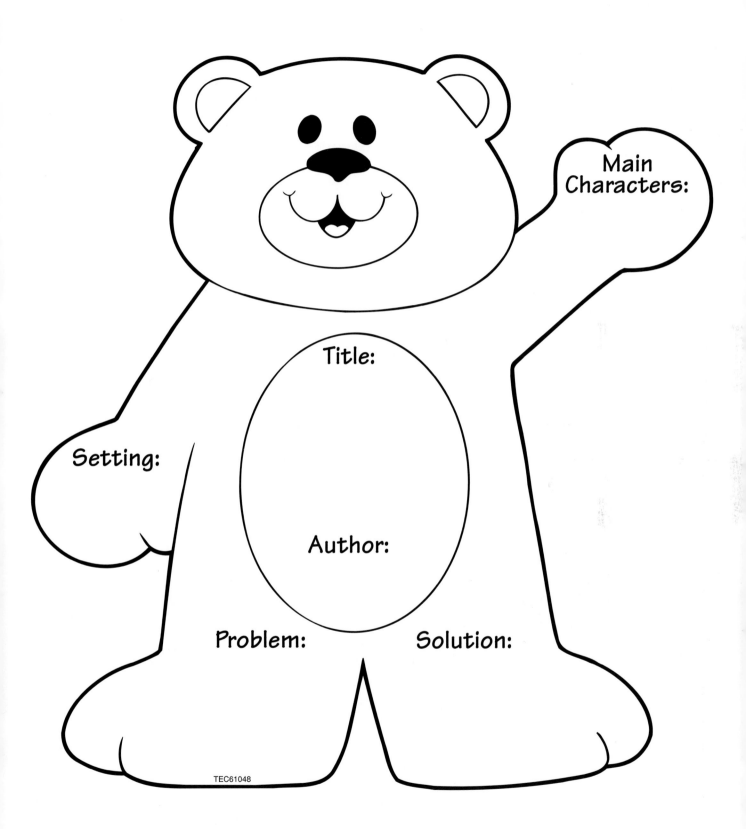

Main Characters:

Title:

Setting:

Author:

Problem:

Solution:

TEC61048

Literature Links

Motivate students to read and encourage a love of literature with these kid-pleasing ideas that can be used with any book.

Honorary Book Awards

Students are sure to pour their creativity into making book awards to honor books they've read. Have each student select a book to read. Then have him create an award to honor a certain aspect of his book, such as best character, best setting, best plot, or best ending. Encourage students to use a variety of materials to construct their awards. If desired, have each student fill out a certificate similar to the one shown, explaining why the award was presented to the book. This project is sure to create lots of excitement for reading in your classroom!

1st FIRST PLACE

Title: Clifford
Author: Norman Bridwell
Best Animal Character:
I like Clifford because he tries to be helpful.

Best Animal Character

Seasonal Reading

Try these seasonal displays to motivate your youngsters to read! Each month mount the designated character (or object) on a classroom wall. Then have students write on the smaller designated cutouts titles of books they have read. Mount the cutouts on the wall along with the title.

→ September—tree, apples, "A Bushel of Good Books"
→ October—scarecrow, pumpkins, "Reading at the Pumpkin Patch"
→ November—turkey, feathers, "Books to Gobble About"
→ December—Christmas tree, ornaments, "'Tis the Season to Read"
→ January—snowpal, snowflakes, "A Blizzard of Books"
→ February—cupid, hearts, "We Love to Read"
→ March—leprechaun, shamrocks, "Get Lucky and Read"
→ April—rabbit, eggs, "Hop Into These Great Books"
→ May—cowboy, horses, "Rounding Up a Great Year of Reading"

The Growing Caterpillar

Motivate students to read independently by challenging them to achieve a group reading goal. To create this display, cut a supply of large construction paper circles. Add pom-pom eyes, a yarn mouth, and pipe cleaner antennae to one circle to resemble a caterpillar's head. Mount the caterpillar's head on a classroom wall. Tell students that for every book a student reads, a segment will be added to the caterpillar. The student must write his name, the author's name, and the title of the book on a construction paper circle. Your students will be amazed at how fast the bookworm grows!

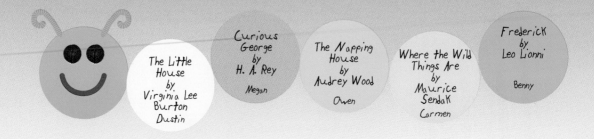

Author Quilts

Looking for a way to familiarize your students with several books by the same author? Have your youngsters make an author quilt. After sharing several stories written by a selected author, ask students to illustrate their favorite scenes from the stories. Provide each student with a sheet of drawing paper and an assortment of art materials, such as markers, construction paper, fabric scraps, and glitter. Have the storybooks handy for students to refer to as they draw. Arrange the completed illustrations on a bulletin board to resemble blocks on a quilting pattern. Use a marker to add stitch marks around each square. Just imagine the variety of quilts you'll see by the end of the school year!

It's in the Bag

This reading homework assignment is sure to bring squeals of delight! Ask each student to find an object at home that reminds him of a designated story that was recently read in class. Have students bring their mystery objects to school in paper bags. On the following day, have each student give clues to the contents of his bag while his classmates try to guess his mystery object. When a student reveals his object, have him explain why the object reminded him of the story. What a great way to expand each student's understanding of a story!

All Aboard!

All aboard for this reading-incentive program! Mount a construction paper engine on a classroom wall. Provide each student with several colored copies of the boxcar patterns on page 72. Each time a student reads a book, have her complete the information on the boxcar, and cut it out. Mount the boxcars on the wall to create a train. As the train grows throughout the year, so will your students' reading abilities!

Check out the skill-building reproducible on page 73.

Boxcar Patterns

Use with "All Aboard!" on page 71.

Name _____

Title _____

Author _____

Rating ☆ ☆ ☆ ☆

☆☆☆☆ = Best

TEC61048

Name _____

Title _____

Author _____

Rating ☆ ☆ ☆ ☆

☆☆☆☆ = Best

TEC61048

Read All About

_____
book title

Written by reporter _____ **Date** _____

Characters

Setting

Portrait of the Main Character

Plot

My Favorite Part

Note to the teacher: Duplicate for students. Use as a follow-up to a class read-aloud or to an individually read book.

Language Conventions

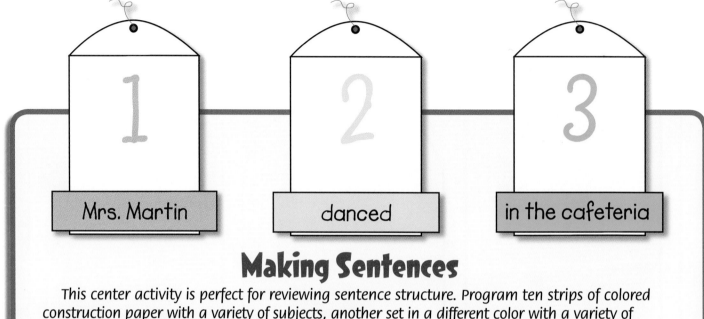

1	2	3
Mrs. Martin	danced	in the cafeteria

Making Sentences

This center activity is perfect for reviewing sentence structure. Program ten strips of colored construction paper with a variety of subjects, another set in a different color with a variety of predicates, and another different-colored set with a variety of prepositional phrases. Store each set of colored strips in a large envelope. Arrange the envelopes at the center with the subject on the left, the predicate in the middle, and the prepositional phrases on the right; then use a marker in the same color as the strips to number each folder sequentially as shown. The student chooses one strip from each envelope and arranges the strips to create a silly sentence. He then copies the sentence on writing paper before returning the strips to their correct envelopes. The student continues in this same manner until he has written ten silly sentences. **Sentence structure**

Logan
1. Mr. Adams jumped in the library.
2. Mrs. Martin danced in the cafeteria.

Complete-Sentence Challenge

Reinforce the concept of complete sentences with this whole-group activity. Gather students in a circle and announce a word such as "We" or "I" that could start a sentence. Then choose a student to say another word that could come after the first word in a sentence. The child then "passes" the phrase to the student on his left to continue. Students continue in this same manner until a complete sentence is formed. Then write the completed sentence on the board for everyone to see. Using a new beginning word each time, repeat this activity until each student has had a turn to contribute to a sentence. **Complete sentences**

Stop-Sign Periods

Your students will find that learning to use periods is a breeze with the help of stop signs. To prepare, cut several two-inch octagons from red construction paper and draw a period on each one. Explain to your students that a period is similar to a stop sign. Just as a stop sign tells a driver to stop, a period tells a reader to stop. If a period is missing, the reader will not know to stop, and the words in one sentence will "crash" into another sentence.

After sharing this information with your students, write a short story on chart paper, leaving a blank space for each period. Read the story aloud without periods. Then have volunteers tape the stop-sign cutouts where the periods should be. Invite students to join in as you reread the story, this time pausing where the stop signs have been placed. **Periods**

One day my dog and I went for a walk. We saw birds and cats. We also saw a big brown dog. He scared us, so we went home.

Questions, Questions!

When do you eat dinner?

When

To prepare for this class activity, write a different asking word such as *how, do, what, when,* or *why* on separate blank cards. Place the cards in a bag. Invite a student to remove a card and read the word aloud. Next, enlist students' help in incorporating the word into a question; then write it on the board. Then ask a student to add a question mark to the end of the sentence. For more advanced students, give each child a word card and have her use it to write a question on a sheet of paper. **Question marks**

Ask and Tell

This picture-perfect partner activity gets to the point of punctuation! Assign one student in each twosome to ask a question and the other one to answer it. Then have each child write his sentence on a white speech-bubble cutout, making sure to use proper punctuation. Display each pair's speech bubbles with student photos or self-portraits as shown. **Periods and question marks**

What is your favorite food?

My favorite food is pizza.

Punctuation Pointers

To make a punctuation pointer, label a blank card with a period and tape it to one end of a large craft stick. Make a pointer in this manner for an exclamation mark and a question mark. Write several unpunctuated sentences on a sheet of chart paper. Display the chart within students' reach and place the pointers nearby. Lead students in reading the first sentence aloud. Then invite a volunteer to choose the appropriate pointer and hold it up at the end of the sentence. After the class confirms his choice, repeat the activity with each remaining sentence. **Periods, question marks, and exclamation marks**

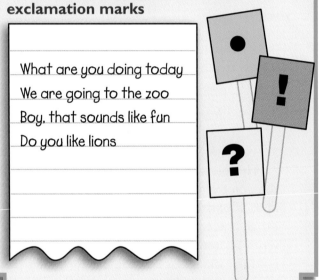

What are you doing today
We are going to the zoo
Boy, that sounds like fun
Do you like lions

A Comma, Please!

To prepare, invite a student to dictate a sentence that includes a series of objects, a date, or a city and state; then write the sentence on a tagboard strip. Cut the strip apart between each word and cut off the commas. Give each resulting card to a different child.

To begin, have the students holding the comma cards stand to the side while the students with the word cards order themselves to form the original sentence. Lead the remaining students in reading the sentence aloud. When students come to a word that needs a comma after it, have them announce, "A comma, please!" Then ask a youngster with a comma card to position himself in the sentence. After each comma has been placed, have the class reread the sentence to verify the placement of the commas. **Commas**

Pause for Pasta!

Here's a tactile way for youngsters to practice using commas! After reviewing comma usage in sentences, give each youngster a sentence strip and a marker. Have her write a sentence that includes a series of items or a date, omitting all commas. Then instruct each child to trade strips with a partner. Ask her to read the sentence and place a piece of elbow macaroni on the strip to represent each missing comma. After her partner confirms her work, direct her to glue the macaroni in place. If desired, invite each youngster to read her original sentence to the class. **Commas**

My birthday is May 14, 2000.

I like red, blue, and green balloo

Magnetic Capitalization

You're sure to attract students to this capitalization activity! Each morning write several sentences on a magnetic board, omitting all capitalization. Challenge student volunteers to correct the sentences by positioning magnetic capital letters atop the appropriate lowercase letters. What an easy way to improve students' capitalization skills! **Capitalization**

Pick a Posy

This center is sure to be youngsters' first pick for practicing capitalization! To prepare, write a different sentence, omitting capitalization, on each of several jumbo craft sticks. Then glue a construction paper flower blossom to the end of each stick to resemble a flower. Place the flowers in a plastic flowerpot at a center stocked with paper and pencils. When a child visits the center, she picks a flower, looks for the capitalization errors, and writes the sentence correctly on her paper. She continues in the same manner for each remaining flower. **Capitalization**

A Capital Display

Help youngsters remember to capitalize proper nouns with this center! Collect a variety of objects or pictures that represent proper nouns such as photos of people, postcards of places, or empty food cartons. Label a blank card for each item that does not have its title printed on it. Display the items and their corresponding labels at a center stocked with writing paper. A center visitor uses one or more of the displayed items in a sentence, using proper capitalization. If desired, display students' sentences near the center. **Capitalization**

Proofreading Detectives

Your junior supersleuths are sure to be on the lookout for capitalization and punctuation errors with this idea! Write a short passage on a sheet of chart paper, making several capitalization and punctuation errors. Have each child cut out a copy of the magnifying glass pattern on page 82; then help her cut out the center. After reviewing the rules on the pattern, enlist students' help in proofreading the text. Invite a child to "magnify" a mistake on the chart and then use a marker to correct it. Continue in the same manner to correct each mistake. Encourage youngsters to refer to their magnifying glasses to help them proofread their own writing. **Proofreading**

the little dog likes to play ball her

name is rosie rosie has a red blue

and green ball. rosie is very playful

Storybook Sentences

What better way to provide editing practice than with a favorite storybook! Choose two sentences from a favorite book and write them on the board, making several punctuation, capitalization, and spelling errors. Gather a small group of students and invite them to read the sentences aloud. Then invite volunteers to correct the mistakes. When the group is satisfied with its edits, have students read aloud the matching sentences from the book to verify their work. **Proofreading**

Point and Check

Have youngsters take the two-finger test to help them remember to check for punctuation and capitalization in their writing! To do this, a child holds up both of his pointer fingers. For each sentence, he places his left finger on the first letter of the sentence to check for a capital letter and his right finger at the end of the sentence to check for ending punctuation. If the sentence does not pass the test, the child corrects it as necessary. No doubt, students are sure to include capital letters and punctuation marks in all of their writing! **Proofreading**

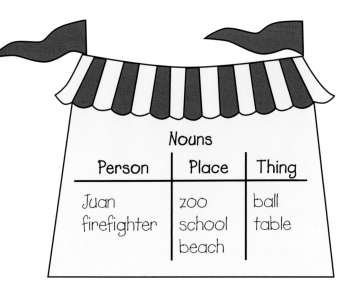

Nouns

Person	Place	Thing
Juan firefighter	zoo school beach	ball table

Nouns Under the Big Top

Hurry, hurry! Step right up to this class game, which reinforces the concept of nouns! Trim a piece of bulletin board paper to resemble a circus tent and program it as shown. In an open area of the classroom, place three Hula-Hoop toys (circus rings). Label each of three blank cards with one of the following words: *person, place,* and *thing.* Place each card in a different ring. Invite a child to toss a beanbag into one of the rings. Then have him name a noun in the corresponding category, while you write his response on the chart. Continue in the same manner until each youngster has a turn. Display the chart for future reference. **Nouns**

Search the Photo

At a center, display an old calendar picture or magazine photo that depicts a scene. Make a class supply of recording sheets similar to the one shown; then place them at the center. When a child visits the center, he looks at the picture for objects (nouns) and actions (verbs). Then he records his findings in the appropriate columns of his recording sheet. Nouns and verbs

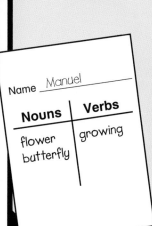

Name: Manuel

Nouns	Verbs
flower butterfly	growing

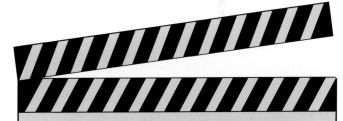

Acting Out Actions!

Get youngsters moving with this class activity! Cut out a copy of the action cards on page 83 and place them in a paper lunch bag. Invite a child to secretly remove a card and identify the action. Then have her act out her verb using movements or gestures but no words. Encourage the class to guess the verb she is performing. After the correct guess is made, invite a different child to choose another verb. *Verbs*

round
sweet
brown
crunchy

a cookie

Descriptive Stuffed Animals

In advance send a note home asking each student to bring a stuffed animal to school. On the day of the lesson, have each student share his stuffed animal. On a sheet of chart paper, write a student-generated list of adjectives that could describe the animal. Then have each child refer to the chart to write a description of her animal. **Adjectives**

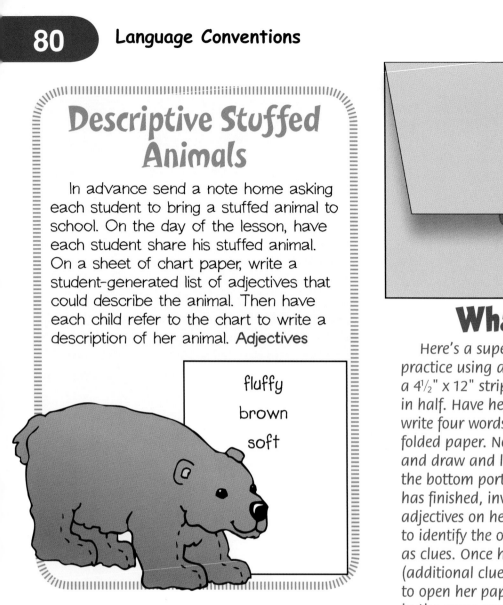

fluffy

brown

soft

What Could it Be?

Here's a supersimple way for youngsters to practice using adjectives! Help each child position a 4½" x 12" strip of paper vertically and fold it in half. Have her silently choose an object and write four words (adjectives) to describe it on the folded paper. Next, ask her to unfold her paper and draw and label the corresponding object on the bottom portion of the paper. When everyone has finished, invite a student to read aloud the adjectives on her paper. Encourage her classmates to identify the object using the descriptive words as clues. Once her object has been identified (additional clues may need to be given), ask her to open her paper to reveal the item. Continue in the same manner for each remaining student. **Adjectives**

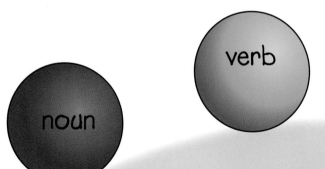

Pass It!

Review nouns, verbs, and adjectives with this action-packed class game! Label each of three balls with a different part of speech (noun, verb, or adjective). Seat youngsters in a circle and give the balls to three different students. Play lively music as they quickly pass the balls around the circle in the same direction. When you stop the music, ask each child holding a ball to name a word that corresponds with the part of speech on his ball. If desired, write each response on a chart for future reference. Continue in the same manner until each youngster has had a turn. **Nouns, verbs, and adjectives**

Plurals Practice

This hands-on activity provides your first graders with practice using singular and plural forms of words. Have each student visually divide a sheet of paper in half; then label one half of the paper "Singular" and the other half "Plural." Give each student several stickers or small cutouts of the same design. A student glues her stickers on her paper to show the meanings of *singular* and *plural*. Then she labels the resulting pictures with the appropriate singular and plural word forms. If desired, bind the completed papers in a class book for students to use as a reference. **Plural nouns**

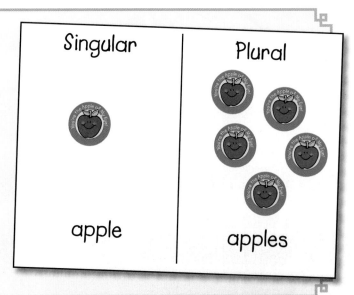

Practice With Possessives

For a fun introduction to possessives, have each student illustrate something she owns on a sheet of story paper. Then have her write a sentence that declares her ownership. Invite each child to share her completed work before displaying the projects on a classroom wall. Possessives

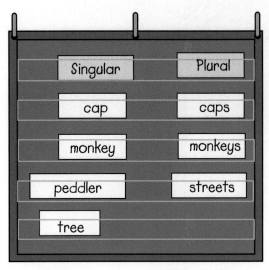

One, or More?

Follow up a favorite read-aloud with this idea to reinforce the concept of singular and plural nouns. After sharing a story with youngsters, revisit the text and have students name nouns from the story. Write each noun on a separate blank card. Place the cards in a pocket chart and enlist students' help in sorting the cards by singular and plural. If desired, invite volunteers to underline the letter or letters that make each noun plural. **Plural nouns**

This is Morgan's teddy bear.

Check out the skill-building reproducibles on pages 84–87.

Magnifying Glass Patterns

Use with "Proofreading Detectives" on page 78.

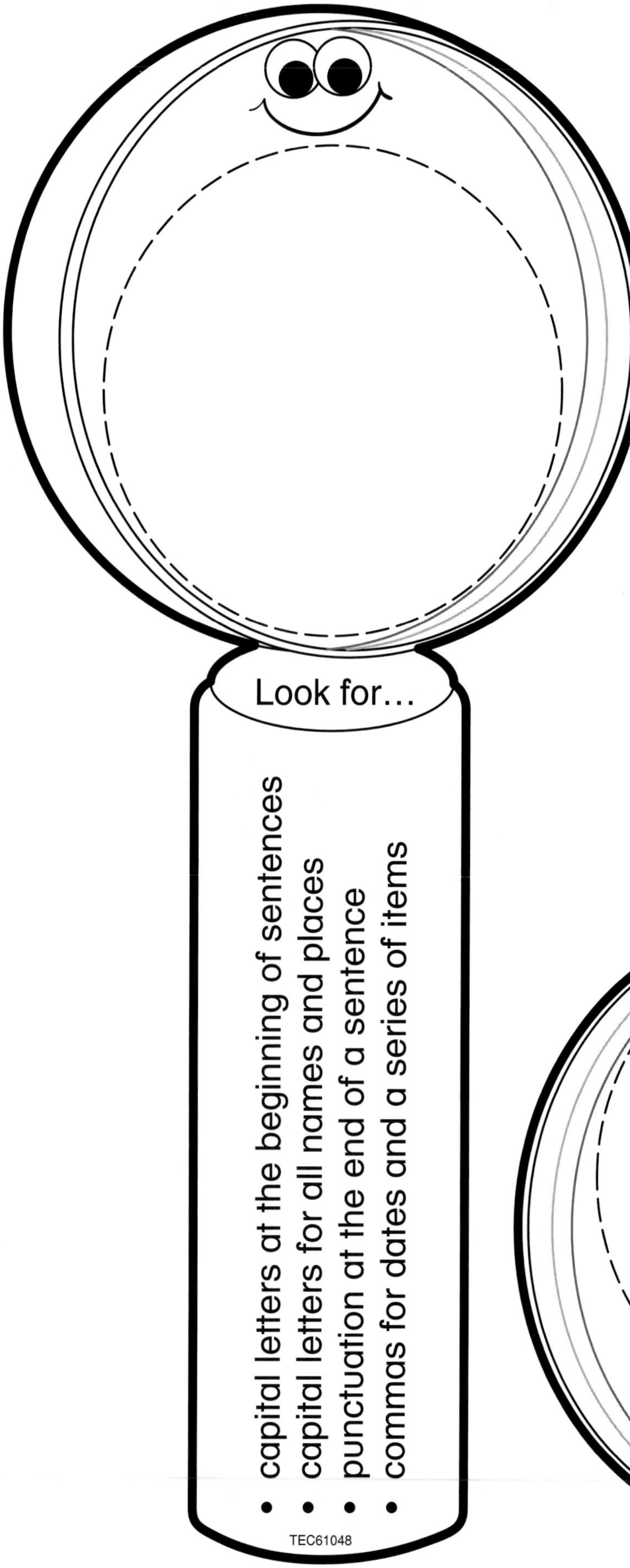

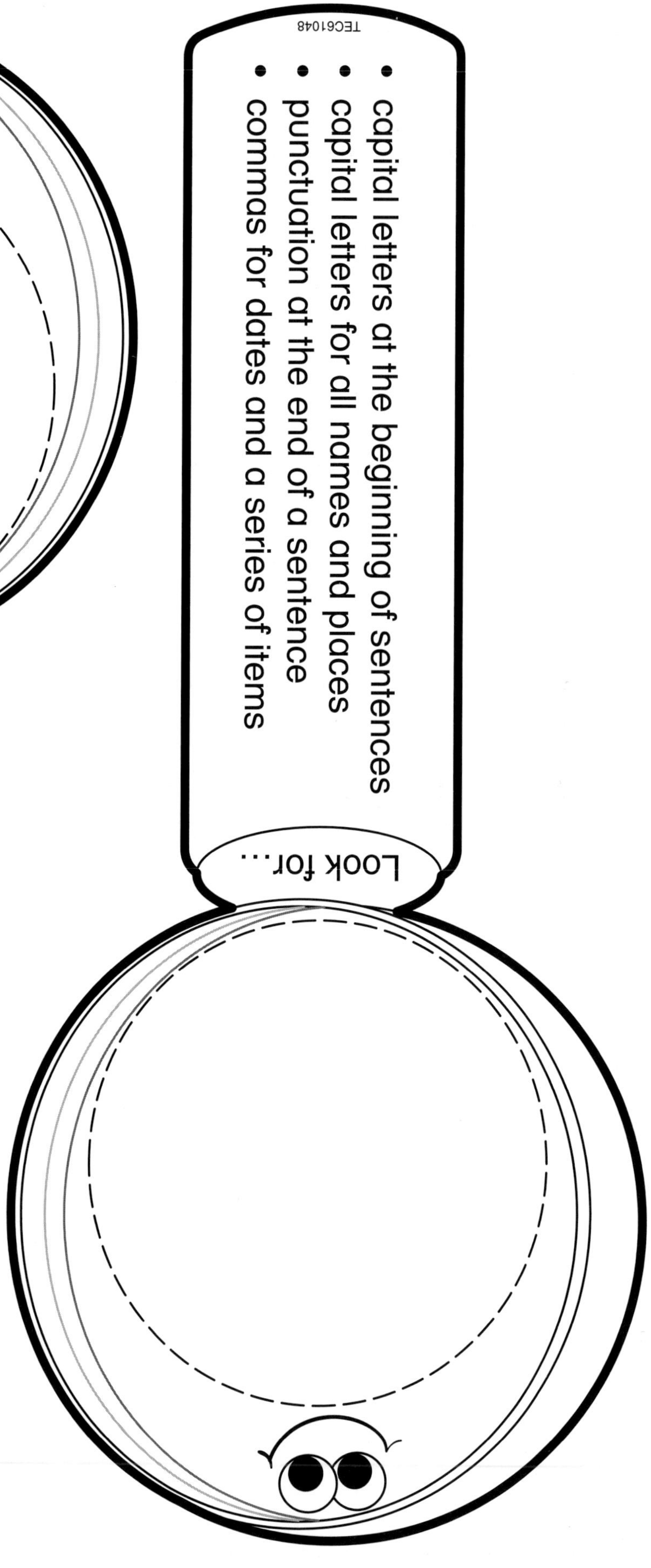

Look for...

- capital letters at the beginning of sentences
- capital letters for all names and places
- punctuation at the end of a sentence
- commas for dates and a series of items

TEC61048

Look for...

- capital letters at the beginning of sentences
- capital letters for all names and places
- punctuation at the end of a sentence
- commas for dates and a series of items

TEC61048

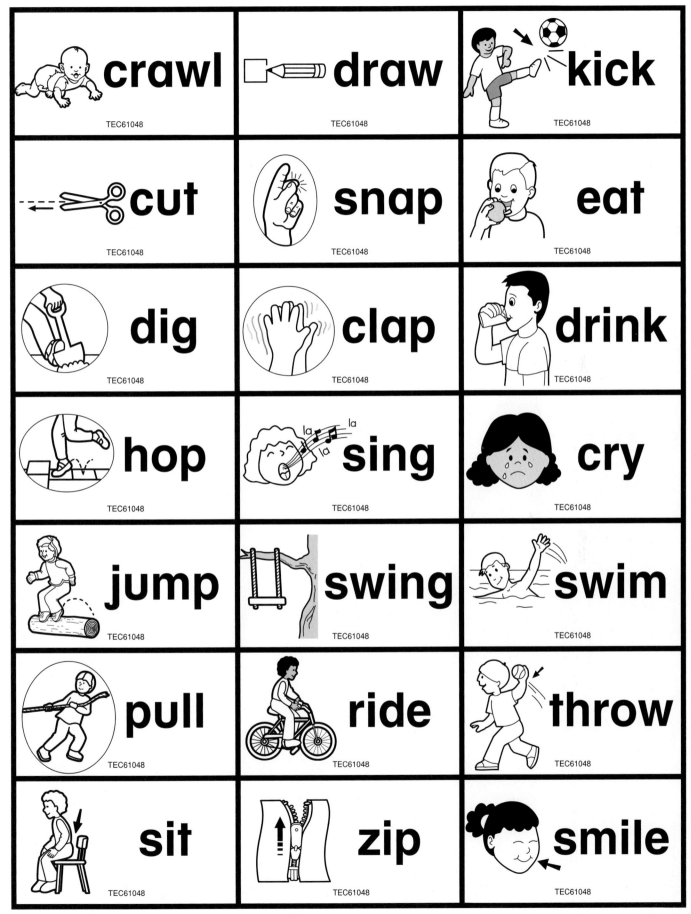

crawl	draw	kick
cut	snap	eat
dig	clap	drink
hop	sing	cry
jump	swing	swim
pull	ride	throw
sit	zip	smile

Batter Up!

Read each group of words.

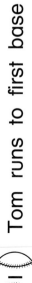 Color the baseballs by the code.

Add a . or **?** to each **complete** sentence.

① Tom runs to first base

② on my cap

③ Do you see my mitt

④ a lot of baseballs

⑤ to see the game

⑥ Does Tim throw the ball

⑦ Keep your eye on the ball

⑧ a fast pitch

Name _____

Busy Builders

✏️ Write a **.** or **?** or **!** to complete each sentence.

🖍️ Color the birdhouses by the code.

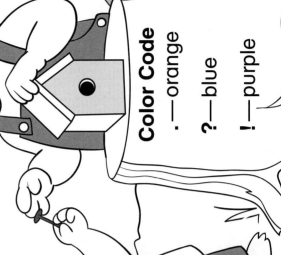

Color Code
.—orange
?—blue
!—purple

1 I like helping Dad ☐

2 We are making a birdhouse ☐

3 Will you give me a nail ☐

4 Let's paint it brown ☐

5 Where is my hammer ☐

6 I will get more wood ☐

7 Boy, my tool belt is heavy ☐

8 What should we build next ☐ ☐

©The Mailbox® • *Superbook*® • TEC61048

Name _____

Trash Collectors

Read each sentence.

Circle each word that needs a capital letter.

There are 13 mistakes in all.

1. The trash pickup is on monday.

2. is there a lot of trash?

3. june is a busy month.

4. i will drive the truck today.

5. Did rob drive the truck on friday?

6. rob picks up two trash cans.

7. we wash the truck every tuesday.

8. ron and i work hard

9. are we almost done?

10. it is time to go home.

Name

Pizza Toss

Add **s** or **es** to make each word plural.

Color by the code.

peach____

dress____

girl____

fork____

watch____

glass____

brush____

dish____

car____

box____

bag____

Color Code
es — orange

s — red

Writing

get (sky) (grass) (ground)

Handwriting Made Simple

Prepare your students for a handwriting lesson with this nifty idea. Teach handwriting placement as though letters lived outside. Refer to the area above the dotted line as the sky, below the dotted line as the grass, and below the bottom solid line as the ground. Students will easily recognize and remember correct placement with this method. **Handwriting**

Bend, Trace, and Write!

Here's a tactile way for young writers to practice letter formation! When a child is having trouble writing particular letters, help him shape pipe cleaners into the letters. Have him trace over each letter with his finger several times and then write the letters on a dry-erase board. Encourage the youngster to refer to his pipe cleaner letters as needed. **Handwriting**

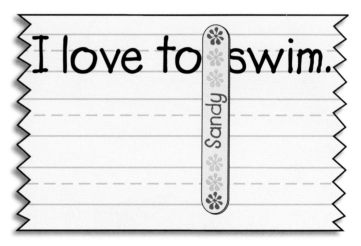

I love to swim. Sandy

Space Sticks

Help students remember to put space between their words with "space sticks." Give each student a craft stick and encourage her to personalize and decorate it as desired. To use the stick, the student places it on her paper to hold a space after each word. Before long you'll begin to notice neatly spaced papers! **Handwriting**

A Group Effort

Use this tip to ensure that all students participate in shared writing! Give each child a seasonal cutout to personalize and decorate. Laminate the cutouts, if desired, and store them in a large envelope. When composing a class story, give each youngster her cutout. As each child orally contributes to the story, have her place her cutout in the envelope. A quick glance at the remaining cutouts will let you know who has not had a chance to contribute. **Shared writing**

A Colorful Creation

Gather a small group of students around a sheet of chart paper for this interactive writing experience. Guide youngsters in choosing a writing topic (see page 111 for suggestions); then write the title on the chart paper. Enlist students' input in orally composing the first sentence and then have them repeat it aloud. Next, give each child a different color marker and then have the group work together to write the sentence on the paper. (Provide guidance as needed.) Continue adding sentences in the same manner until students are satisfied with their writing. To complete the activity, have each child use his marker to sign his name at the bottom of the paper. When a youngster rereads the writing, he can look for his marker color to remember what he wrote!
Interactive writing

Freddie the Frog

Freddie the frog is green and purple. He eats flies for dinner. One day he turned into a purple prince.

Luis   Wendy

Nicco   Shelby

Details, Details!

For this group-writing activity, write a simple sentence without details on a sentence strip. Then cut the strip apart between each word and display the sentence in a pocket chart. Lead students in reading the sentence aloud. Next, have each child write on a blank card a descriptive word that would add a detail to the sentence. Invite each youngster, in turn, to arrange her word in the sentence and read the new sentence aloud. As a follow up, encourage youngsters to write their own detailed sentences. **Adding details**

Terrific Topics

Students sometimes need a jump start to come up with ideas for writing in their journals. Have each child write a journal starter on a piece of writing paper. After editing students' work, have each student decorate a 3" x 12" piece of light-colored construction paper so that it resembles a giant pencil; then instruct her to copy her edited journal starter on the pencil. Mount the pencils on the board. Now when a student is stumped for a writing topic, she can choose one from the board. **Journal prompts**

My favorite meal is...

Journal Topic Joggers

Inspire creative journal writing by having students bring in items to serve as writing topics. Encourage students to submit objects such as magazine pictures, ticket stubs, postcards, stickers, gift wrap, and greeting cards as journal-writing topics. Review each submission and place the approved objects in a container. Return the unapproved objects to students to take home. When a student can't think of anything to write about in his journal, have him draw an object from the container and use it as his writing topic. To keep student interest high, encourage students to periodically replace the items in the box. **Journal prompts**

Bright Ideas for Journal Writing

For writing motivation have students brainstorm writing topics. In advance laminate and cut out a large sun shape (with rays) from yellow poster board. Then use a wipe-off marker to write a journal topic on each of the sun's rays. To change the journal topics, simply wipe off the old topics and reprogram the rays with new topics. **Journal prompts**

Beatrice the Bunny loved carrots! She loved them so much that she would leave her home and hop over to Farmer Fred's yard to eat his carrots. One day Farmer Fred saw her eating the carrots. He told her to stop and chased her out of his carrot patch. Beatrice hid in the bushes until he went back inside.

Stuck on Journal Writing

Give each child a sticker that has a character on it. The student attaches the sticker to his paper and writes a story about the character. Each story's setting and plot must be related to the sticker. The child can include other characters in the story as well. What a great way to inspire students' writing! **Journal writing**

Newsworthy Journals

If your students have difficulty deciding what to write in their daily journals, try this approach. Near the end of each day, have students summarize the day's events as you write them on the board. Then have each student choose one of the events to write about in his journal. At the end of the school year, each student will have a keepsake journal that highlights some of the year's events. **Journal writing**

Today we:
- went to the library
- wrote a story about our class bear, Homer
- practiced our play
- worked on our subtraction facts
- read to our reading buddies

My Winter Journal

Name Jessie

'Tis the Season for Journaling

Looking for some fun and fresh seasonal journal prompts? Try these! Give each child a copy of the appropriate seasonal journal cover (pages 103–105) to personalize and color. Make this page the cover of each child's writing journal. Each month, have students respond to the following prompts in their journals. **Journal prompts**

September:
- How did you get ready for first grade?
- My first grade teacher…
- The biggest apple ever…

October:
- Tell about three things that you like to do in the fall.
- A day in a pumpkin patch…

November:
- Imagine you spent a day with turkeys. Describe that day.
- My favorite Thanksgiving foods…

December:
- Many animals sleep all winter long. Would you like to sleep all winter? Why or why not?
- A favorite holiday memory…

January:
- Write about something you would like to learn to do this year.
- The best thing that happened to me last year was…

February:
- Red is often worn on Valentine's Day. What does the color red remind you of?
- A good friend is…

March:
- On St. Patrick's Day many people wear green. If you could only wear one color every day, what would it be? Why?
- The March wind makes me think of…

April:
- What do you think you would find at the end of a rainbow?
- If I were a bird…

May:
- Think about how to stay safe while playing outside. List some important safety rules.
- The flowers grew so high that…

June:
- Describe some of your favorite school memories.
- The best vacation ever…
- A perfect picnic…

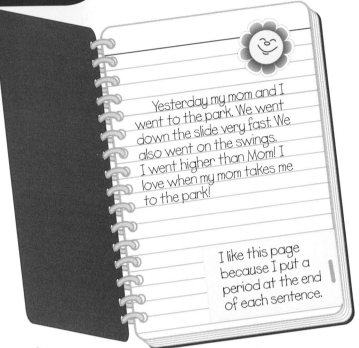

Yesterday my mom and I went to the park. We went down the slide very fast. We also went on the swings. I went higher than Mom! I love when my mom takes me to the park!

I like this page because I put a period at the end of each sentence.

Wonderful Writing

Youngsters review their journal writing with this self-assessment idea. Periodically allow students time to read through their journals. Give each child a decorative sticker and have him attach it to the entry that he feels shows his best writing. Have him write on a blank card why he chose the particular piece; then staple it to the corresponding page. A quick look at a child's journal will give you insight into his thinking. **Monitoring journals**

Reading Ribbons

Monitor students' journal writing with this rewarding idea! Establish a rotating schedule so that a few students can share a journal entry with the class each day. As children are writing in their journals, circulate around the room and give the assigned students a ribbon cutout. At a designated time, each child who received a ribbon takes a turn reading a selected journal passage aloud. After she reads, write a short message of praise on her ribbon and tape it to her clothing. Youngsters are sure to be proud of their reading and writing accomplishments. **Monitoring journals**

Your story was very funny! Great job!

Ms. Filler ☺

I <u>like</u> to play ball.
My favorite game to play is ball.

Highlight and Rewrite

Here's a tip that will help your young writers vary the word choice in their journals. In advance, scan students' journals for frequently used words. Choose one word and announce it to youngsters. Then have each child use a highlighter to highlight the word each time she spots it in her journal. After a predetermined amount of time, invite a volunteer to share a sentence that includes the word, as you write it on the board. Then enlist students' help in rewriting the sentence to replace the common word. Encourage each child to choose a sentence to rewrite in her own journal. **Word choice**

Sticker-Scene Stories

If you use stickers as incentives, this creative-writing idea is for you! Each time a student exhibits behavior worthy of a sticker, make a tally mark beside her name on a chart. At the end of each week, count the number of tally marks each child has and award her with that number of motivational stickers. Have the student use the stickers in place of words as she writes and illustrates a story. **Rebus writing**

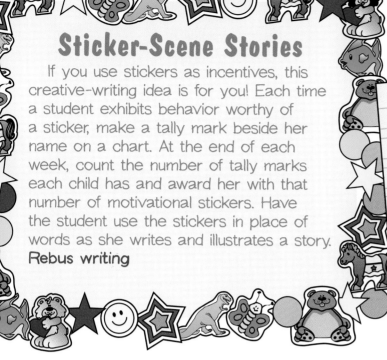

One day when the ☀ was shining. I saw a 🦋 on a ❀. I followed it. It led me to a **COOL!** lake full of 🐟. In the forest I saw a big fat 🐻 and big lizards that looked almost like 🦎s. It was fun!

Silly Animal Antics

To begin, enlist students' help in making lists on the board of animals, action words (in the past tense), and naming words. After writing at least ten words in each list, provide each child with a piece of story paper. Instruct each student to choose one word from each list; then use the words and any needed prepositions to create a sentence. Remind students to use the words in the order they appear on the board. After all students have written and illustrated their sentences, compile the pages between two construction paper covers. Add the title "Silly Animal Sentences" and display the book in your classroom library. **Writing sentences**

The cow sang in the shower.

Animals	Action Words	Naming Words
cow	played	park
dog	jumped	school
cat	swam	pool
bunny	skated	beach
lion	talked	phone
bear	jogged	pencil
elephant	sang	shower
tiger	climbed	bed
giraffe	ate	book
horse	rode	car

Picture Collection

Don't toss out old calendars and postcards! Use the pictures as unique story starters. Clip pictures from discarded magazines, calendars, and postcards. Display a picture from the collection and ask students to share their thoughts about it. Write students' ideas on the board. Then have each student use the ideas to help her write a few sentences about the picture. After students have completed their resulting stories, stack the pages and staple them together. If desired, send the stories and the picture home in a large envelope for students to share with their families. **Writing sentences**

One day my parents took me to the beach. We had fun. We went swimming. I saw a dolphin.

Sunshine Isle

Picture-Perfect Writing

Trigger creativity and writing enthusiasm with students' school photographs. In advance make a copy of each student's school photo. Trim each child's face from her photocopy; then give her the copy and a piece of story paper. Each child chooses an animal or a story character she would like to be. She then writes a story as if she were the animal or character. After completing the story, the child glues the photocopy of her face to her paper. She illustrates the rest of herself using the photocopy as the face of the animal or character. Display the completed papers for all to see. **Creative writing**

My name is Katie the Cat. I love to play with yarn. One day I got so tangled in a ball of yarn that I had to lie on the floor until my owner came in the room and used scissors to cut me free. That was very funny, and I still play with yarn.

Shapely Stories

Your students' writing will really take shape with this creative-writing activity! Provide each student with a sheet of colorful construction paper and instruct him to cut out any large shape. Next, have the student use construction paper scraps to transform his shape into a person, animal, or object. Challenge each student to write a story about his creation. After they complete their stories, invite your young authors to share their stories with their classmates. **Creative writing**

I turned my triangle into a parrot because I wish I had one. My parrot has wings and feathers made of hearts.

Story Sticks

Spark the imaginations of your youngsters with this crafty idea! Write story titles on several craft sticks; then place the craft sticks in a decorated can. Invite students to choose starter titles from the can whenever they have difficulty deciding on a writing topic. **Creative writing**

See the Ready Reference on page 111 for a list of story titles.

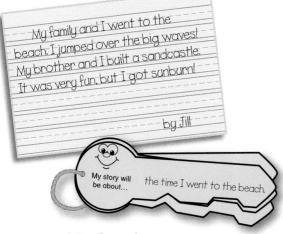

Unlock a Story

Prewriting is a key component of a well-developed personal narrative! Encourage youngsters to think about a personal experience to write about. Give each child a copy of page 107. Have her write the topic on the first key and a different related detail on each remaining key. After she cuts out the keys, help her hole-punch each key where indicated and connect them with a length of pipe cleaner to resemble a key ring. Then guide her in using the information on her keys to write a paragraph about the event. Display the completed papers along with the corresponding key rings and the title "The Keys to Writing." **Personal narrative**

A Sweet Story

Prewriting is a treat with this cool graphic organizer! To help each student plan her writing, give her a copy of page 106. Have her write a word or phrase on the cherry to represent the main idea. Then instruct her to write or draw a related detail on each ice-cream scoop and a concluding thought on the dish. Guide each student in using her organizer to write a story. **Prewriting**

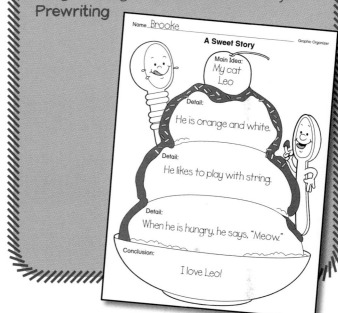

From Beginning to End

Youngsters write about familiar experiences with these clever caterpillars! Make a caterpillar labeled "Beginning," "Middle," and "End," similar to the one shown. Display it in a prominent location. Explain that a personal story has a beginning, a middle, and an end—just like the caterpillar. Give each child four five-inch construction paper circles in different light colors. Have him glue the circles together to resemble a caterpillar. Direct each youngster to title his first circle to reflect a personal event. Next, ask him to write about a different part (beginning, middle, and end) of his event on each remaining circle. To complete the project, instruct each child to decorate the first circle to resemble a caterpillar head. After students share their writing, display the projects along with your sample. **Personal narrative**

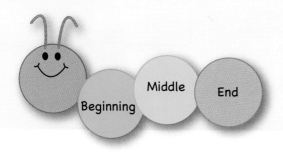

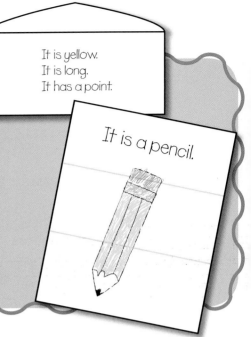

It is yellow.
It is long.
It has a point.

It is a pencil.

The Envelope, Please!

For this riddle-writing activity, ask each student to secretly choose a classroom item to describe. Encourage her to think about how the object looks, feels, smells, tastes, or sounds. Give each child an envelope and have her write three sentences that describe her object on it. Then instruct her to draw and label the object on a sheet of paper, fold the paper, and place it in the envelope. After each youngster trades envelopes with a partner, she reads the clues, makes a guess, and then removes the paper to check her guess. Continue having students trade envelopes with each other as time allows. **Descriptive writing**

My hat is tall. It has yellow and red skwares on it. There are two pink flwrs. There are eight gray dots on the botum.

Top Hats

A hat shop full of one-of-a-kind hats is the result of this descriptive-writing project! For each child, trim a sheet of construction paper and a sheet of writing paper into identical top-hat shapes. Ask each child to decorate the construction paper hat as desired. Then have her write on the other paper a description of her hat. After she is finished writing, secure a tagboard strip to fit around her head. Next, direct her to glue each hat to opposite sides of the resulting headband. Invite youngsters to read their writing to the class and then don their hats. When all youngsters have shared, have them remove their hats and place them on a table display with the title "Hats for Sale! Read All About Them!" **Descriptive writing**

How to...

For this writing idea, give each child a copy of the graphic organizer on page 108. Have him think about several things that he knows how to do and write them on his paper where indicated. After he reviews his list, ask him to circle the task that he would like to write about and then complete the sentence starter. Next, direct him to list any materials needed and the steps to complete the task.

After reviewing his organizer, give him a $4\frac{1}{2}$" x 6" piece of paper for each required step along with a construction paper cover. Direct him to write each step on a separate piece of paper and title the cover as desired. After stapling the sequenced pages behind the cover, encourage him to illustrate the cover and booklet pages. Invite youngsters to share their booklets with their classmates before taking them home. **Expository writing**

Name Riley   Expository writing

"Paws" and Plan

I know how to...
play baseball
make toast
catch a fish
ride a bike

I will write about how to make toast.

I need...
bread
a toaster
butter
a plate
a knife

Steps:
1. Get a slice of bread.
2. Put it in the toaster.
3. Put it on a plate.
4. Spread butter on it.

How to Make Toast by Riley

Planning	First Draft	Revision	Edit	Final Draft
Cara	Mike	Lisa	Penny	
Mary	Lori	Jerry		
Baron	Eugene			
	Calvin			

☑ My name is on my paper.
☑ My story has a title.
☑ My story has a beginning, a middle, and an ending.
☑ I used complete sentences.
☑ Each sentence begins with a capital letter.
☑ Each sentence ends with a . or ? or !.
☑ I used my neatest handwriting.

Editing Checklist

Even young writers can benefit from a writer's checklist. Give each student a copy of page 109. Instruct each student to check off each guideline as she evaluates her writing. By adding this writing step to the editing (proofreading) step, students are sure to eliminate careless mistakes. **Writing process**

Managing Classroom Editing

Try this simple technique to keep track of where each student is in the writing process. Write each child's name on a decorative construction paper cutout. Laminate it and attach a piece of magnetic tape to the back. Then divide the board into five columns: planning, first draft, revision, edit, final draft. Each student begins a writing assignment with his name under the planning column and moves his marker as he progresses through the writing process. When the student reaches the editing phase, meet with him individually. Now you will no longer have a line of students at your desk waiting for help. **Writing process**

Proofing Buddies

Have students work as editing partners. After a student has edited his partner's work, have him share at least one positive comment about the writing and one writing suggestion. Also, encourage students to work together to correct spelling and punctuation errors. **Editing**

Check Five!

Here's a handy tool for students to use as an editing reminder! Enlist students' input in compiling a list of the five most important things to look for in a piece of writing. Write the list on the board. Have each student trace her hand on a sheet of construction paper and cut it out. Next, direct her to copy each word or phrase from the board onto a different finger of her cutout. Encourage youngsters to refer to their hands before turning in a writing assignment. **Editing**

spaces
neat writing
spelling
punctuation
Check five
capitals

I have a dog named Hobbes.

He loves to go for walks.

He sleeps at the foot of my bed.

He barks at strangers.

He is the best dog in the world.

Flip Books

Provide students with easy-to-make flip books to use in publishing their work. To make a booklet, stack three 8½" x 11" sheets of white paper and hold the pages vertically in front of you. Slide the top sheet upward one inch; then repeat the process for the second sheet. Next, fold the paper thicknesses forward to create six graduated layers or pages. Staple close to the fold. A student writes the title of his story and his name on the cover and then writes sentences on the bottoms of the booklet pages as shown. Then the student illustrates the sentence on each page. Publishing

Pop-Up Cards

Have each student publish a favorite writing piece in a self-made pop-up card. **Publishing**

To make a pop-up card:

1. Fold in half a 9" x 12" sheet of white construction paper.
2. Cut two two–inch slits in the center of the fold about 1½ inches apart. Open the card and rewrite your story near the bottom of it.
3. Illustrate the main character in the story on a three-inch square of white construction paper. Cut out the illustration.
4. Pull the narrow strip in the center of the opened card forward and crease it in the opposite direction from the fold. Glue the cutout to the lower half of the strip; then illustrate the inside of the card to show the setting.
5. Close the card, making sure the strip stays inside.
6. To complete the project, write the title of the story on the outside of the card.

One day I was walking in the forest when I met a bear named Bessie. We became friends. I took her food and taught her to read.

Paper-Plate Books

With this method of publishing, students can easily share their favorite literary pieces. Provide each student with two paper plates, lined paper to fit inside the paper plates, and various art materials—such as construction paper, pipe cleaners, glue, and scissors. To make a plate book, a student decorates one paper plate as desired and then staples the lined paper between the front cover and the back cover. The student then writes her story on the lined paper. What a great way to get students wild about writing! Publishing

Sturdy Class Books

If your class books do not hold up to heavy use, try this tip. Purchase clear, plastic sheet protectors from an office-supply store. Place the protectors in a three-ring binder. Insert pages for a class book in the protectors back-to-back. If you have a binder with a clear pocket on the cover, just slip your book cover inside. These sturdy class books will hold up for the entire year. At the end of the year, simply pull out each child's pages and return them. Then reuse the binder and sheet protectors next year. **Publishing a class book**

Easy Book Binders

Looking for alternatives to metal ring binders? Then try these tips! **Publishing tips**

- Use plastic shower-curtain rings to bind your classroom-published books instead. Not only do they come in a variety of colors, they're also less expensive and easier to open and close.
- Use a hole puncher to make holes in each book; then insert a twist-tie through each hole and twist the ends of the ties together. Wow, bookmaking has never been so easy!

Plastic Class Books

Make classroom-published books more durable with gallon-size, resealable plastic bags. To make a book using this method, have each child insert his page into a resealable plastic bag. Staple all of the bags together along the sealed end. Cover that end with colored tape and you've got a bound book that will stand up to your youngsters' hands. **Publishing a class book**

Author Photos

This tip makes it easier for a student to identify which of his classmates created a specific page in a class-made book. Photocopy a picture of each of your students. Glue each copy to the back of that student's book page. Then youngsters can tell at a glance which page belongs to which student. **Publishing tip**

Letter-Writing Center

Motivate your first graders to become independent letter writers with these center ideas. They're guaranteed to deliver letter-writing fun! **Letter writing**

- Provide greeting cards, leftover stationery pages, and postcards for students to use.
- Provide art supplies—such as markers, glitter, rubber stamps, stamp pads, and envelopes—for students to use in creating their own stationery.
- Purchase a premade mailbox center (or make one from shoeboxes), and label a mailbox for each student and yourself. Encourage students to write letters to their classmates and then deliver the letters to their classmates' mailboxes. Be sure to remind students to respond to the letters they receive!
- Collect free offers from magazines and highlight the addresses. Place the offers at the center and encourage students to write letters asking the companies to send their free products. Assist students in addressing the envelopes.

Label the Letter

You can count on this idea to help students remember the parts of a friendly letter! On a sheet of chart paper, write a short friendly letter, making sure to leave space in the margins. Label each of five blank cards with one of the following words: *date, greeting, body, closing,* and *signature.* Read the letter aloud with students and then display a card. Invite a volunteer to tape the card to the chart near its corresponding part and draw a connecting line. Continue in the same manner for each remaining card. If desired, have each child complete a copy of page 110 for additional skill practice. **Friendly letter**

April 3, 2007

Dear Megan,

Today was another rainy ← body
day. I played in the puddles.
It was so wet!

closing → Your friend,
Mike

Fairy-Tale Mail

Heighten student interest in letter writing with the help of fairy-tale characters. Have each student write a letter to his favorite fairy-tale character telling the character why he or she is his favorite. After he completes the letter, have each student illustrate his chosen character. Post the letters and the illustrations on a bulletin board for everyone to see. **Friendly letter**

Sweet Similes

Entice your first graders to write a class simile poem with the help of chocolate-chip cookies. To begin, give each student a cookie. Ask students to name words that describe their cookies. Write students' descriptions on a piece of chart paper. Next, reread the first word on the list and have students think of an object that has a similar feature. Write that word beside the descriptive word; then add the needed words (*as* or *like*) to create a simile. Continue in this manner with the other descriptive words on the list. To complete the poem, simply add the title "A Chocolate-Chip Cookie Is..." Invite students to munch on their cookies as you read the completed poem. Now, that's sweet success with poetry! **Poetry**

A Chocolate-Chip Cookie Is...

As sweet as a piece of candy,
As delicious as a birthday cake,
As brown as a camel,
As round as the sun.

Poem Puzzler

An unfinished poem is sure to inspire youngsters to write some poetry of their own! Write a favorite short poem on a sheet of chart paper, omitting the last line. Challenge students to complete the poem by copying it onto a sheet of paper and writing their own version of the last line. Invite youngsters to share their poems. Then read the original poem in full for youngsters to compare their writing to the original! **Poetry**

Seasonal Poems

Students are sure to remember that not all poems need to rhyme when you use this idea! Trim a sheet of bulletin board paper into a shape that corresponds with the current season. Then have students brainstorm seasonal words. Write the words on the cutout and display it in a prominent location. Model for students how to use the words to write a seasonal poem similar to the one shown. Then ask each child to write a poem of his own and add desired illustrations. After students share their writing, display their papers around the seasonal cutout. **Writing a poem**

winter
mittens
snow
sled
snowman
ice
snowball
hat
scarf
gloves
hot chocolate
cold

Winter
Warm mittens.
Cold snow.
Silly snowmen.
Yummy hot chocolate.
I like winter!

So Lovable!

This kid-pleasing poetry activity is sure to boost youngsters' self-esteem! Encourage students to name positive qualities about themselves as you write their responses on the board. To begin his poem, a child writes his name as the title and the sentence "I am lovable!" as the first line. Then he refers to the list to write several sentences about his positive qualities. He concludes his poem with the line "Yes! I am lovable!" After each child adds decorations to his poem, display the poems with the title "We're So Lovable!" **Poetry**

Ethan
I am lovable!
I am kind.
I am a good helper.
I love animals.
I like to laugh.
Yes! I am lovable!

Colorful Prose

For this poetry-writing activity, have each child choose a family member to write about. On a sheet of paper, direct her to write the name of the chosen person as the title. Next, direct her to write a color word, the word *like*, and an object of that color to create a simile. Have her continue in the same manner for several colors and then write the name of the person to conclude the poem. After adding an illustration, invite each child to share her poem with the class before presenting it to her loved one. **Poetry**

Nana
Red like a heart.
Yellow like the sun.
Purple like sweet grapes.
White like a cloud.
Nana

by Mia

Piggy Poems

Here's a toe-tapping way for youngsters to write a rhyming poem! Enlist students' help in compiling a list of rhyming word pairs. Then recite the familiar poem "This Little Piggy." Ask each child to choose two rhyming pairs from the list and incorporate them into a rewriting of the poem. After she edits her work, direct her to copy her poem onto a large construction paper foot cutout. Invite each student to decorate the toes on her cutout to resemble pigs. Display the completed poems for all to see! **Poetry**

This little piggy played ball.
This little piggy went to the mall.
This little piggy had a hat.
This little piggy had a bat.
And this little piggy went
wee, wee, wee all the way home!

My Fall Journal

Name _____

My Winter Journal

Name _____

Note to the teacher: Use with " 'Tis the Season for Journaling" on page 91.

My Spring Journal

Name _____

A Sweet Story

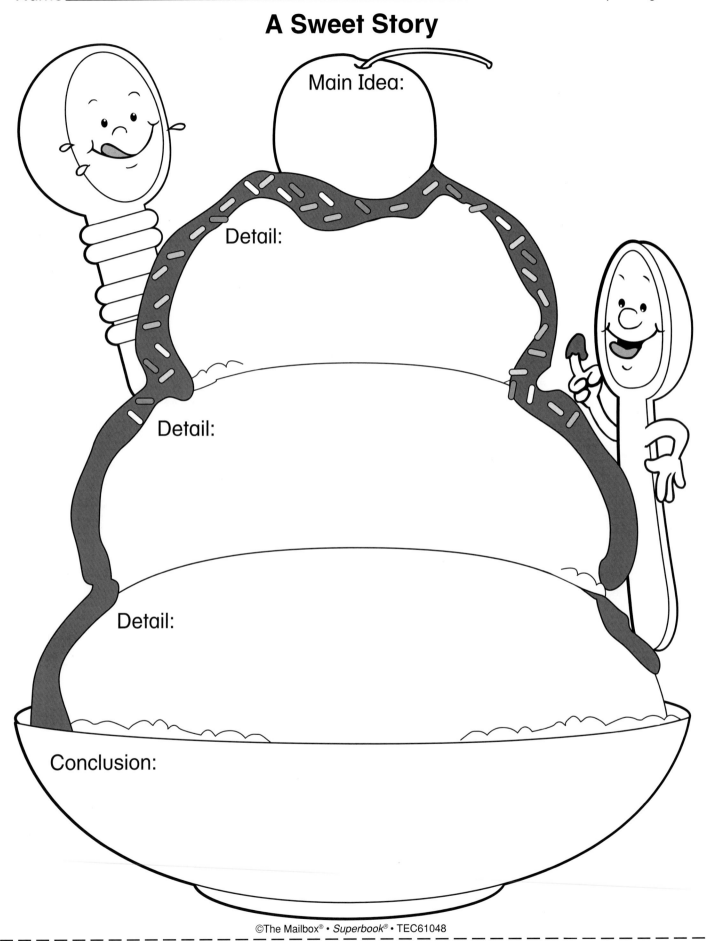

Main Idea:

Detail:

Detail:

Detail:

Conclusion:

Note to the teacher: Use with "A Sweet Story" on page 95.

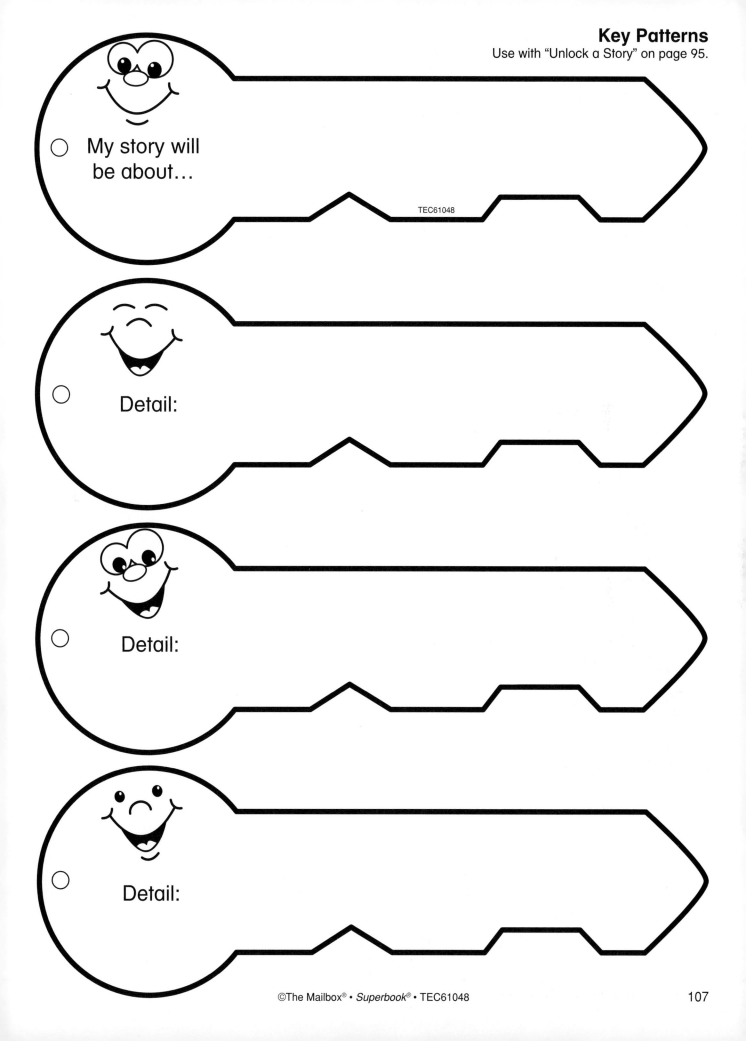

My story will
be about…

TEC61048

Detail:

Detail:

Detail:

"Paws" and Plan

I know how to...

 I will write about _____

_____

I need...

Steps:

Note to the teacher: Use with "How to..." on page 96.

Did You Reach the Finish Line?

Check each box as you read your story.

- [ ] My name is on my paper.

- [ ] My story has a title.

- [ ] My story has a beginning, a middle, and an ending.

- [ ] I used complete sentences.

- [ ] Each sentence begins with a capital letter.

- [ ] Each sentence ends with a **.** or **?** or **!**.

- [ ] I used my neatest handwriting.

**If you checked each box, color the turtle.
Congratulations! You reached the finish line!**

Note to the teacher: Use with "Editing Checklist" on page 97.

Birthday Thanks

✂ Cut.

Glue to match each part of the letter.

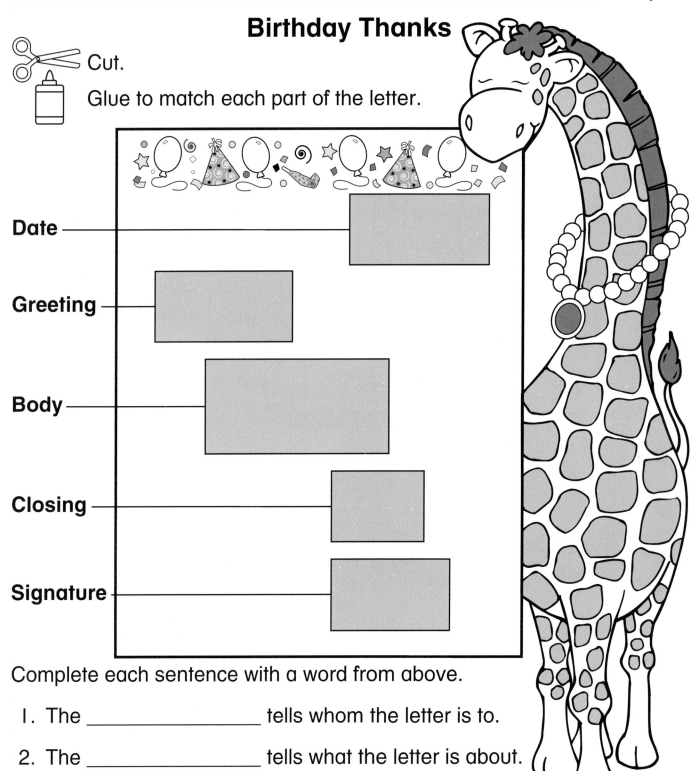

Date ————

Greeting ————

Body ————

Closing ————

Signature ————

Complete each sentence with a word from above.

1. The _____ tells whom the letter is to.

2. The _____ tells what the letter is about.

3. The letter is from _____.

| Thank you for the pretty necklace. I will wear it every day. | Love, | Gina | Dear Julie, | March 10, 2007 |

Story Starters

Lost at Sea
The Magical Mirror
The Vanishing Footprints
Race Against the Clock
Visitor From Another Planet
Stranded on a Desert Island
The Big Escape
The Ice-Cream Gang
Monster on the Loose
The Secret Formula
The Empty Cage
The Case of the Stolen Key
My Day as a Giraffe
The Perfect Birthday Party
The Runaway Sled
Stuck in the Snow
Magical Mittens
A Visit From the Snow Fairy
The Valentine Surprise
The Race Begins!
Whispers in the Forest
The Runaway Bus

Footsteps in the Mud
The Talking Bear
The Mystery in the Schoolroom
Surprise!
Freddie the Frog
The Giggling Gorilla
The Puppy in Trouble
The Mountain Rescue
Trapped!
The Day the Sun Disappeared
The Talking Cloud
The Pig That Kept Growing
The Lost Penguin
The Magical Wizard
The Surprise Package
The Secret of Candy Cave
The Winning Goal
A Field Trip to Mars
Danny Dinosaur Saves the Day
The Perfect School Playground
The Day a Monster Ate My Homework
The Camping Trip

NUMBER CONCEPTS

That's the Number!

Looking for ways to help students recognize, write, and read numbers? Check out the following ideas for some great suggestions. **Reading numbers, writing numbers, and counting to 100**

* Have your youngsters practice writing numerals using fingerpaints, instant pudding, shaving cream, or sand.

* Play a recording of some lively music with a steady beat. As the music is playing, announce directions such as "Tap your head 20 times" or "Hop up and down ten times." Have students count aloud as they follow the directions.

* Divide a piece of poster board into nine squares; then write a numeral from 1 to 100 in each square. In turn, have students toss a beanbag, name the numeral the beanbag lands on, and clap that number of times.

Tally–Numeral Match

Do your students have difficulty making the connection between tallies and numerals? If so, try this activity. Make tally index cards for half of your class and matching numeral index cards for the other half. At your signal, encourage each student to find the classmate who is holding his card's match. Have each pair of students sit down after verifying their match. To repeat the activity, simply have students exchange index cards with classmates. Reading numbers to 100

Guess the Number

Divide the class into small groups and secretly assign each group a different number up to 100. Encourage each group to decide on a unique way to represent its amount to the rest of the class. For example, youngsters could draw shapes on a poster to match the featured number or do as many jumping jacks as the featured number. Once the groups have their ideas prepared, invite each group, in turn, to present its idea to the class as the remaining students try to guess the featured number.
Counting numbers to 100

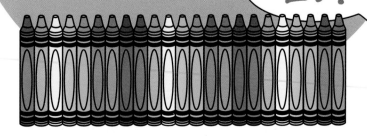

23!

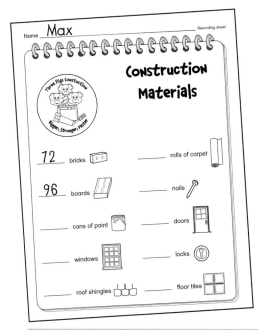

Three Pigs Construction

Youngsters help the three little pigs prepare for house building with this number-writing activity. After sharing your favorite version of the story *The Three Little Pigs,* give each youngster a copy of the construction materials list on page 120. Explain that the three pigs have decided to build a stronger house and that this list shows the construction materials they will need. For each material on the list, announce a predetermined number between 1 and 100. Then have each child write the numeral in the corresponding blank on her list. If desired, invite students to draw houses to correspond with their lists. **Writing numbers to 100**

Stamping Numbers

Reinforce students' counting skills with this class book. Place a class supply of index cards, each labeled with a different number between 1 and 100, in a resealable plastic bag. Set the bag on a table along with a variety of stamps, ink pads, and a supply of paper. A child draws a card from the bag and copies the number onto a piece of paper. Next, he makes a corresponding number of stamps on his paper and sets it aside to dry. When each child has completed a page, bind the pages between two construction paper covers and add a title. **Reading and counting numbers to 100**

Order, Please!

To prepare for this whole-group activity, label a sheet of paper with a numeral for each student. (Start with one and do not skip any numerals.) Give each student a labeled piece of paper and have him read his numeral. As a class, determine which students have the highest and the lowest numerals. Have these two students hold their numerals as they stand at the front of the room facing their classmates. Position one student to the far right and the other to the far left. Then have the remainder (or a designated group) of the students line up in sequential order based on the numerals on their pieces of paper. **Ordering numbers**

Top It Off

Youngsters top off their number-ordering skills by making these seasonally themed head-bands. For this center, randomly label a supply of cards with numbers from 1 to 100 and place them in a resealable plastic bag. Die-cut a set of five seasonal shapes for each child and place them at a center along with the bag of cards and a class supply of tagboard strips.

A child visits the center and takes five cards from the bag and five die-cut shapes. He copies each of the numbers from his cards onto a separate shape. Next, he orders the shapes from least to greatest and glues them onto the strip. Size each child's headband and secure it. Encourage young-sters to wear their headbands home to share their number knowledge with their families. **Ordering numbers**

Orderly Cups

Ordering numbers is a snap with this small-group activity. Using a permanent marker, label a supply of 20 plastic cups, each with a different number up to 100. Mix up the cups and randomly place them into stacks of five. Gather four students and give each a stack of cups. Have him unstack the cups and order the numbers on the cups from least to greatest. For added fun, direct each student to trade an equal number of cups with another student and then order her new stack of cups. *Ordering numbers*

Rolling Along

Here's a quick and easy partner game to help youngsters compare numbers. In advance, create a recording sheet like the ones shown and copy to make a class supply. Give each child in a twosome a recording sheet and a die.

To play, Player 1 rolls his die twice, writes each number in the corresponding column on his recording sheet, and then uses the numbers to create a two-digit number. Player 2 takes a turn in the same manner. Then the players compare the two-digit numbers and determine which is larger. The player with the larger number circles his number. Play continues in this manner as time allows. **Comparing numbers**

First Roll	Second Roll	Number
4	2	(42)
3	3	33

First Roll	Second Roll	Number
1	5	15
6	4	(64)

Dog Treats

Color and cut out a copy of the dog pattern on page 263 and attach it to a lunch-size paper bag. Also, copy and cut out a class supply of the bone patterns on page 263. (Prepare a cutout for yourself if there is an odd number of students.) Randomly program each bone with a different number and store it in a dog bowl or a clean, empty dog-bone box. Then set the bowl and bag in your group area.

To begin, ask two volunteers to each take a bone and hold it up for the class to see. Have each student read his number aloud and then invite the class to help determine which of the two numbers is larger. The student holding the bone labeled with the larger number drops his bone into the bag, and the other youngster sets his bone aside. Repeat with a new twosome until each student has taken a turn. **Comparing numbers**

Round and Round

Put a spin on comparing numbers with this whole-group activity. Randomly program a class set of blank cards with numbers appropriate for your class. Divide students into two equal groups and give each student a card. (Plan to participate if there is an odd number of students.) One group stands in an inner circle, facing outward. The other group stands in an outer circle with each person facing a partner from the inner circle. Then each student in a twosome reads aloud her number to compare it to her partner's. Together they decide which number is larger, and the partner with the larger number raises his hand. Quickly scan for accuracy. Then at your signal, members of the inner circle take one step to the right and the new pairs compare their numbers in the same manner. Continue for a desired number of rotations.
Comparing numbers

Skip-Counting Tools

Students always have manipulatives on hand to practice skip-counting—their body parts! To begin, ask each student in a small group to count the ten fingers on her hands. Then choose a child to start the group off counting by tens. Ask the next child to use her ten fingers to continue counting by tens and say the next consecutive number. Continue in this manner until each student has had a turn. For a variation, have students use their mouths, noses, or heads to count by ones; their eyes, ears, or arms to count by twos; or their toes (on one foot) to count by fives. **Skip-counting by twos, fives, or tens**

Five-Point Stars

Looking for an easy way to help your young-sters practice skip-counting by fives? Try stars! Make a supply of star cutouts and punch a hole in each. Give a supply of the stars to each student. Then have each student use the points of the stars to help him practice counting by fives. Ask him to label each star with the corresponding number and slide his labeled stars onto a metal-ring binder. When he has some extra time, he can use his ring of stars to practice counting by fives. **Skip-counting by fives**

Counters and Skippers

To provide practice counting by twos, divide your class into two groups and designate one group to be the "skippers" and the other group to be the "counters." Explain that the numbers used to count by twos will be said aloud by the counters and the numbers that are skipped when counting by twos will be whispered by the skippers. Ask the skippers to begin by whispering, "One." Then have the counters say aloud "Two." Continue having the two groups skip-count back and forth in this manner until a predetermined number is reached. *Skip-counting by twos*

What's the Task?

Give students a chance to pair up and practice skip-counting at this center. To prepare, program blank cards with skip-counting tasks similar to those shown. Set the resulting task cards at a center along with two hundred charts. To begin, have each youngster take a chart. Player 1 chooses a task card and reads it aloud for Player 2. Then Player 2 completes the task on the card aloud, using his chart as needed. While Player 2 completes his task, Player 1 uses his chart to check Player 2's response. The twosome then switches roles and repeats the activity. **Skip-counting by twos, fives, and tens**

Task 1

Start with 2.
Count by twos.
End at 20.

Task 2

Start with 25.
Count by fives.
End at 75.

Following Directions

Write the ordinal numbers "first" through "tenth" on the board and direct one student to stand beneath each number. In turn, have each seated child give another seated child a direction to follow, such as "John, please tap the fourth person on the head." When all the seated students have had a turn to follow a direction, have them switch places with the standing students and repeat the activity. **Ordinal numbers**

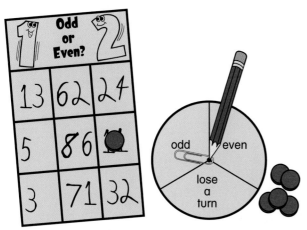

Odd or Even Lotto

Playing this partner game helps students identify numbers as odd or even. Make a copy of the lotto board on page 121 for each student, and make one copy of the spinner on page 121 for every two students. Have each student prepare her board by writing a different number from 1 to 100 in each square.

To begin, give each student pair a spinner, a large paper clip, and a supply of game markers. Player 1 uses the paper clip and a pencil to spin and announces whether the paper clip stops on the odd, even, or lose-a-turn section of the spinner. Then either she places a marker on a corresponding number on her board or her turn is over. Her turn is also over if she does not have a corresponding number. Player 2 takes a turn in the same manner. Play continues until one player covers three numbers in a row and calls out, "Three in a row!" **Even and odd numbers**

Even or Odd?

Here's a hands-on approach to identifying even and odd numbers. Give each student pair a plastic bag of manipulatives, such as dry cereal or counters. Name a number; then have the student pairs count a corresponding number of manipulatives. To determine whether the number is even or odd, have the students attempt to share their manipulatives by dividing their counted manipulatives into two equal groups. If the groups are equal in number, the number is even. If the groups are not equal in number, the number is odd. Repeat the activity several times, using a different number of manipulatives each time. **Even and odd numbers**

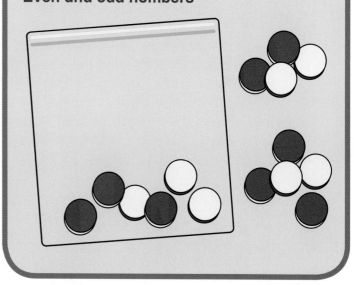

Musical Plates

To prepare this small-group game, write the ordinal numbers "first" through "tenth" on separate paper plates. Then place the plates in random order in a circle on the floor. Play soft music and invite ten youngsters to slowly walk around the outside of the circle. When you stop the music, instruct each youngster to pick up the nearest plate. Then have youngsters arrange themselves in the order that corresponds with the plates they are holding. Repeat this process with a new group of students until each child has had a turn. Ordinal numbers

Estimation Questions

Display a chart in the classroom that features the following questions. Refer to the chart when discussing whole-group estimating activities with your students. **Estimation**

? What is the smallest estimate?

? What is the greatest estimate?

? What is the difference between your estimate and the actual result?

? Did you make a reasonable estimate?

? Which estimates are closest to the actual result?

? Are most of the estimates too high, too low, or just right?

Estimation Station

Challenge students to work on their estimating skills with this ongoing activity. At the beginning of the week, fill a clear plastic jar with items for students to count. Items such as macaroni, dried beans, buttons, and jelly beans work best. Secure the lid on the jar; then display the jar for all students to see. At the end of the week, provide each student with an opportunity to estimate how many things are in the jar. If desired, write all of the guesses on the board and circle the highest and the lowest guesses. Then, as a class, count the items in the jar and discuss the results. Change the items in the jar each week and continue in the same manner. **Estimation**

How many jelly beans are in the jar?

Math to Munch

This yummy estimation activity is sure to please your students and their taste buds! Give each child a plastic bag of cereal pieces and a napkin. Before students open their bags, have each child estimate how many pieces of cereal are in her bag; then have her write that number on a piece of paper. Next, have each student open her bag and eat one piece of cereal at a time while tallying each one on the paper. Once students have finished eating and tallying their cereal, have each student determine her total number of cereal pieces. Then have students compare their estimates to their actual numbers. **Estimation**

Estimate on a Plate

Place two different-size paper plates and a container of a food item, such as dried pasta, at a center. Once at the center, have the student choose a plate and estimate how many pieces of the food item are needed to cover it. After recording his estimate on a piece of paper, have the child count how many pieces of the food item are needed to cover the plate. Instruct the child to write down the actual number needed beside his estimate. Have the student continue in this same manner with the other plate at the center. **Estimation**

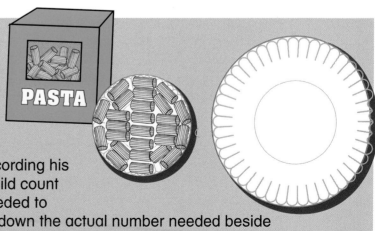

A Quick Peek

This whole-group activity gives students plenty of practice with estimation. Place a handful of manipulatives, such as beans or counters, on the overhead projector. Turn the projector on so that students can look at the manipulatives for about five seconds. Then turn the projector off and have each student write on a piece of paper an estimate of the number of manipulatives shown. Turn the projector on again and enlist students' help in counting the manipulatives to verify the estimates. Continue the activity in this same manner several more times. **Estimation**

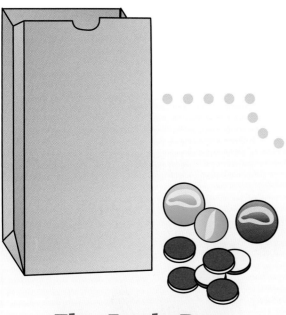

The Feely Bag

This small-group activity will get your students feeling good about their estimation skills! In advance, place a predetermined number of objects, such as counters or marbles, in a small paper or cloth bag. Gather a small group of students in a circle. Pass the bag to a student. Have the student quickly place her hand in the bag and feel the number of objects. Then have her record her estimate on a piece of paper (without anyone seeing it) and pass the bag to the student on her right. Have students continue in this manner until each child in the group has made an estimate. Then empty the objects from the bag and enlist students' help in counting them. Have each child compare her estimate with the actual number of objects. **Estimation**

Estimating More or Less

Strengthen your youngsters' estimating skills by having them answer the questions below. *Estimation*

- Are there fewer than 40 people in this room?

- Are there more than 50 books in this room?

- Are there fewer than 20 pieces of paper in this room?

- Would it take more than 20 steps to get to the cafeteria?

- Can you hold more than 25 pennies in your hand?

- Are there fewer than ten chairs in this room?

- Are there more than 15 boys in this room?

Check out the skill-building reproducibles on pages 122-124.

Construction Materials

_____ bricks

_____ boards

_____ cans of paint

_____ windows

_____ roof shingles

_____ rolls of carpet

_____ nails

_____ doors

_____ locks

_____ floor tiles

Note to the teacher: Use with "Three Pigs Construction" on page 113.

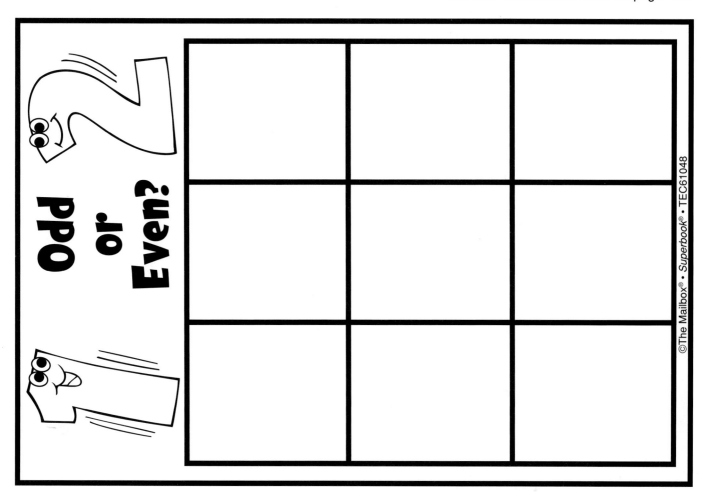

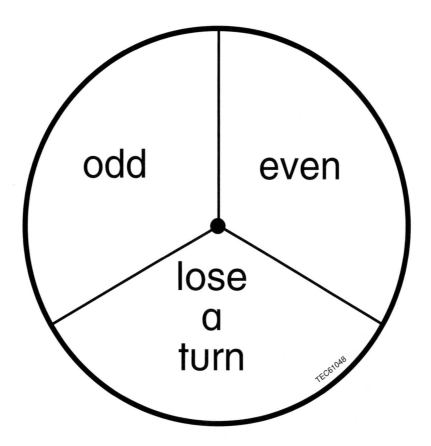

Name _____

122

Orderly Eggs

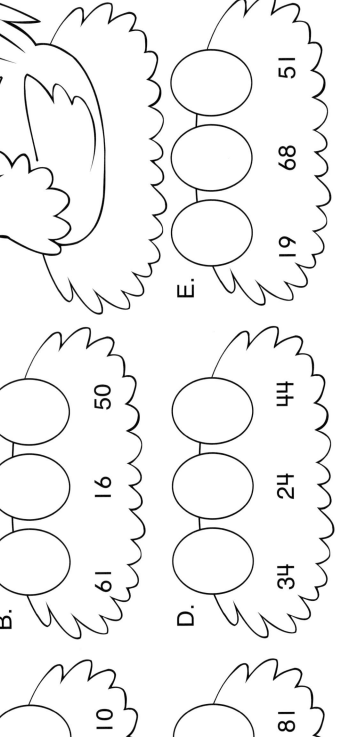

Write the numbers in order from least to greatest.

A.

38 14 10

B.

61 16 50

C.

80 82 81

D.

34 24 44

E.

19 68 51

F.

87 31 100

G.

15 73 26

H.

72 13 96

Name _____

Looking for Lunch

Count by twos or fives.

✏ Write how many.

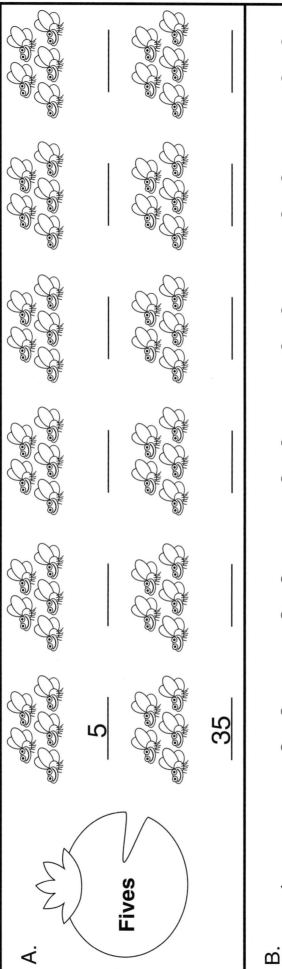

A.

Fives

5

35

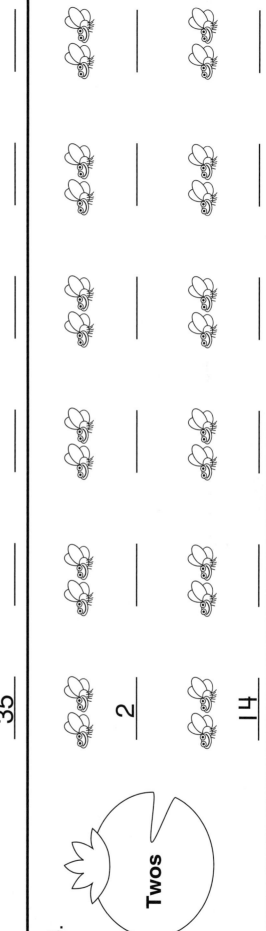

B.

Twos

2

14

Teatime!

Read and do.
Check off as you go.

☐ Color the **fifth** flamingo's hat yellow.

☐ Color the **fourth** flamingo's hat blue.

☐ Color the **third** flamingo's hat green.

☐ Color the **tenth** flamingo's hat brown.

☐ Color the **sixth** flamingo's hat red.

☐ Color the **eighth** flamingo's hat purple.

☐ Color the **ninth** flamingo's hat blue.

☐ Color the **first** flamingo's hat red.

☐ Color the **seventh** flamingo's hat orange.

☐ Color the **second** flamingo's hat black.

Feed the Critter

For this tasty addition activity, obtain a class supply of animal-themed paper plates with three sections. Give each child a plate and a supply of O-shaped cereal. Announce two numbers and direct each youngster to place a matching number of cereal in each of the smaller plate sections. Then have her pretend to feed the critter as she combines the cereal in the larger section and determines the sum. Continue in the same manner for several rounds. **Adding with manipulatives**

Math With Meatballs

On top of this plate of spaghetti is plenty of addition or subtraction practice! For an addition game, label each of nine cards with a different number from 1 to 9. For a subtraction game, label each of 18 cards with a different number from 1 to 18. Store the cards in a bag and place a supply of brown pom-poms (meatballs) in a bowl. Cover a paper plate with shredded red paper or red yarn to resemble spaghetti. Place the plate of spaghetti, the bowl, and the bag of cards at a center stocked with paper. Designate the center for the desired operation.

When a child visits the center, she chooses two cards. Then she places the corresponding number of meatballs on the plate to solve the problem. After determining the sum or difference, she writes the math fact on a sheet of paper. She returns the cards to the bag and continues in the same manner as time allows.
Adding or subtracting with manipulatives

Stand and Solve

Students become part of math sentences with this class activity. Invite a desired number of students to the front of the class. Announce an addition or a subtraction sentence that corresponds with the number of standing students. For example, for six students you could say, "Four plus two" or "Six minus five." Then have another child direct the standing students to group themselves to model the problem. After youngsters determine the solution, invite another group of students to stand for a different problem.
Adding or subtracting with manipulatives

Tasty Fish

For this subtraction activity, give each child a cup of fish-shaped crackers and a fishbowl cutout. Write a subtraction problem on the board, and have each child use his crackers to solve the problem. Invite a student to write the answer on the board. After completing several problems in this manner, invite youngsters to feast on their fish!
Subtracting with manipulatives

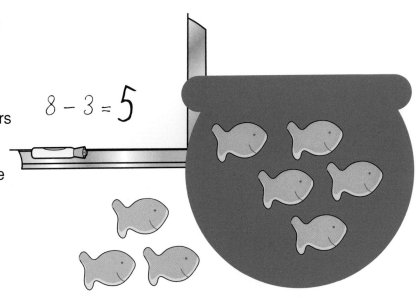

$$8 - 3 = 5$$

$$5 + 1 = 6$$

Roll 'Em!

Here's a fun way for students to improve recall of math facts without creating competition between classmates. Create a class supply of a recording sheet like the one shown; then distribute a recording sheet and a pair of dice to each student. Have each student roll the dice and add the two numbers. Then, starting at the bottom of the recording sheet, have the student color in the correct box depicting the sum rolled. Have students continue in this same manner until one number reaches the top of a column. **Basic addition facts**

Roll 'em!

Name _Randi_

| 2 | 3 | 4 | 5 | 6 | 7 | 8 | 9 | 10 | 11 | 12 |

Buzz, Buzz

To prepare for this honey of a partner center, make two gameboards with the numbers 2–12, similar to the ones shown. Place the gameboards, a supply of yellow pompoms (bees), and two dice at a center. When a twosome visits the center, one player rolls the dice, determines the sum of the two numbers rolled, and places a bee on the corresponding flower. If the appropriate flower is already covered, then her turn is over. Players take turns in this manner until one child has a bee on each flower. **Basic addition facts**

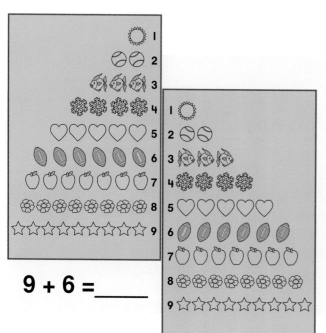

9 + 6 = _____

Addition Helper

These nifty cards help youngsters learn basic addition facts. Give each child a copy of page 133 and have her cut out the two cards. To use the cards, announce an addition problem up to 9 + 9. Each child lines up the two addends and then counts across the corresponding row to determine the sum. If desired, allow students to use the cards as an addition tool for independent work. **Basic addition facts**

Fast Facts

Youngsters bone up on basic facts with this partner center! Program a supply of bone cutouts (pattern on page 263) with different addition or subtraction problems. Label the back of each bone with the answer for self-checking. Also label several blank bones "Bowwow, stop now!" Mix up the bones and stack them faceup at a center. When a pair of students visits the center, the first player takes the top bone from the stack, answers the problem, and checks his answer. If he's correct, he keeps the bone and then takes another one from the stack. If he's incorrect or chooses the "Bowwow, stop now!" bone, it becomes the other player's turn. Students continue in this manner for the remaining bones. **Basic facts**

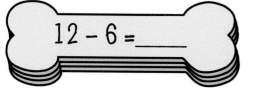

12 – 6 = _____

Popcorn Problems

For a quick way to engage youngsters in practicing math facts, try this! Program a class supply of popcorn cutouts with different math problems. Draw a simple popcorn box on the board. Give each child a cutout and write a sum or difference on the popcorn box. On your signal, each child with a corresponding fact pops up and takes a turn reading her problem. After students sit back down, erase the number on the box and write a different one. After several rounds, redistribute the cutouts for more practice! **Basic facts**

Math-Fact Fun

Help students memorize addition and subtraction facts with this partner game. Each student will need a deck of identical flash cards with the answers on the back. To play, each player shuffles his cards and stacks them faceup (problems showing). In turn, the players read and answer their top problems, then flip their cards to check. If both players answer correctly, the player with the larger solution wins and places both cards on the bottom of his card stack. If one player answers incorrectly, his opponent wins and keeps both cards. If both players answer incorrectly, they exchange cards. The player with more cards at the end of game time wins! **Basic facts**

Beach-Ball Math

This adaptable math activity is sure to become a class favorite! Use a permanent marker to write a different numeral on each section of an inflated beach ball. Toss the ball to a child. When she catches the ball, have her hold the ball without moving her hands and determine which two numerals are nearest her hands. Have the student use those two numerals to create an addition or a subtraction sentence. After announcing the sentence and answering it, the child tosses the ball to a classmate. Continue in the same manner until each child has had at least one turn to catch and toss the ball. **Basic facts**

Table Tents

This partner activity is a great review for addition or subtraction facts. For each student pair, fold a piece of construction paper into thirds. Unfold the paper, turn it over, and then program each outer section with different math facts. Then turn the paper back over and assemble it as shown.

To begin the activity, pair students and give a table tent to each pair. Have each student sit across from his partner with the table tent between them. Have students, in turn, announce the problems for their partners to answer. What a fun way for students to memorize their basic addition and subtraction facts! **Basic facts**

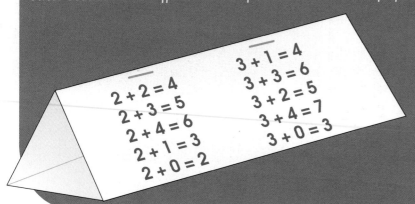

$3 + 1 = 4$
$3 + 3 = 6$
$3 + 2 = 5$
$3 + 4 = 7$
$3 + 0 = 3$

$2 + 2 = 4$
$2 + 3 = 5$
$2 + 4 = 6$
$2 + 1 = 3$
$2 + 0 = 2$

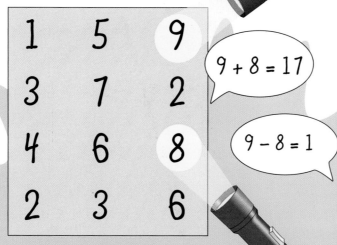

In the Spotlight

Shine light on basic facts with this bright idea! Randomly program a sheet of poster board with the numbers 1 through 9, repeating numbers as desired. Display the poster on a wall. To begin, give each of two youngsters a flashlight. Direct each child to aim the flashlight at a number on the poster and then turn it on. Invite a volunteer to state the sum of the two illuminated numbers, and ask another student to state the difference. Then instruct the students to pass the flashlights to two other classmates. Continue in the same manner until each child has used a flashlight. **Basic facts**

Toss Three

To prepare a game mat, visually divide a sheet of bulletin board paper into nine sections. Then label each section with a different number from 1 to 9. Obtain three beanbags (or fill each of three socks with beans and tie them closed). Place the beanbags and game mat in an open area of the classroom. Invite each of three students, in turn, to toss a beanbag onto the mat. Write the three numbers on the board in the form of an addition problem. Ask each child to solve the problem on a sheet of paper. After verifying the answer, clear the mat and invite three different students to toss the beanbags to play another round. If desired, have students complete a copy of page 137 for additional skill practice. **Adding with three addends**

Just Ducky!

Use the pattern on page 64 to make a class supply of construction paper duck cutouts. Program half of the ducks with correct math facts and the other half with incorrect math facts. Trim two sheets of blue bulletin board paper into pond shapes and label one "Correct" and the other "Incorrect." Gather students in a circle and place the ponds in the center.

To begin, give each child a duck and have her place it on the appropriate pond. After each youngster has had a turn, scan the ponds for accuracy and invite students to make any necessary changes. Then redistribute the ducks for another round of play. **Basic facts**

Domino Addition

Give a copy of page 134 and a domino to each student. Instruct each student to draw the arrangement of dots on her paper and then write the corresponding addition sentence. Next have the student turn her domino around (so that the dots are on opposite sides of where they were), copy the new arrangement of dots, and write its addition sentence. After each student has written two addition sentences for her domino, direct students to exchange dominoes and repeat the activity. Have students continue in the same manner until they have worked with five dominoes. **Commutative property of addition**

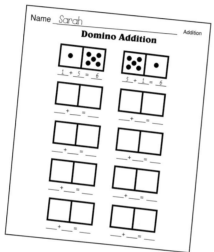

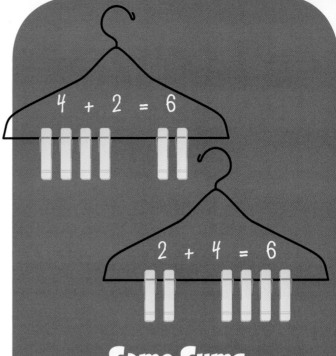

Same Sums

Clothes hangers and several clip clothespins are perfect manipulatives for demonstrating the commutative property of addition. Provide each child with a clothes hanger and ten clothespins. Display a number sentence. Have each student clip clothespins to his hanger to match the sentence. Without removing the clothespins, have students flip the hangers to show the inverse of the original number sentence. Discuss the fact that the sums are equal, illustrating the commutative property of addition. **Commutative property of addition**

Double the Fun

These student-made booklets provide a daily dose of doubles review! For each student, draw lines to divide a 12" x 18" sheet of construction paper into ten equal sections. Give each child a prepared paper and have her write the title "Seeing Double" and her name in the first section (booklet cover). Then direct her to write a different doubles fact up to 9 + 9 in each remaining section (booklet pages). Next, have her make sets of fingerprints to correspond with each fact, write each sum, and use a fine-tip marker to embellish the prints. After she cuts out the pages and stacks them from the smallest to the largest sum, staple the stack behind the cover. Invite youngsters to use their completed booklets to review doubles facts each day. **Adding doubles**

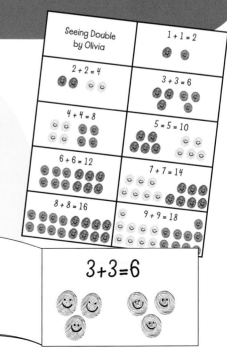

Subtraction Strips

Use this strategy to help students subtract by comparing sets. Program the left side of a supply of sentence strips with different subtraction problems. To model the strategy, post one strip on the board. Use a bingo dauber to make the number of dots that correspond with the minuend. Then use a different color dauber to make dots below the first set to correspond with the subtrahend. Explain that counting the dots that do not have a partner reveals the difference. Lead students in counting the appropriate dots and then write the difference on the strip.

Give each student a programmed strip and a supply of two-color counters. Have her use the counters to repeat the process that you modeled, using one side of the counters for the minuend and the other side for the subtrahend. After each youngster's answer is verified, have students trade strips and repeat the subtraction process. **Comparing sets to subtract**

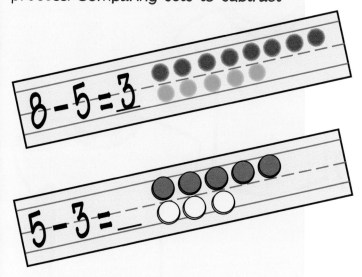

Hop to It!

Using a number line has never been so fun! In an open area of the classroom, adhere a long strip of masking tape to the floor and number it from 1 to 18 to make a number line. Invite a child to the number line and announce an addition or a subtraction problem. Have him stand on the starting number and hop in the correct direction the appropriate number of times. Then have him look at his final position on the number line to determine the sum or difference. Continue in the same manner until each child has had a turn. Using a number line

Four Corners

Students are on the move with a game that reinforces fact families! Label each of four corners of your classroom with the three numbers of a different fact family. Write on separate blank cards a corresponding number sentence for each fact family, repeating number sentences as necessary to make a class supply. To begin, give each child a card. On your signal, students proceed to the appropriate corner. After verifying each child's placement, collect the cards and play again.
Fact families

8, 4, 12

4 + 8 = 12

8 + 4 = 12

12 − 8 = 4

12 − 4 = 8

Fact Family Photos

To prepare, program a sheet of paper to resemble a picture frame and then copy it to make a class supply. Label each paper with the numbers of a different fact family. Give each child a prepared paper and a copy of the four small T-shirt patterns on this page. Have her cut out the patterns and write a corresponding addition or subtraction sentence on each T-shirt. Then direct her to glue the shirts to the paper and incorporate them into a family photo. Display the completed projects and encourage youngsters to refer to the photos as a fact family reference. **Fact families**

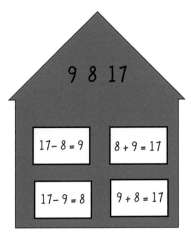

Building Houses

There's no place like the fact family homes at this center! Trim several sheets of construction paper into house shapes. Label the roof of each house with the numbers of a different fact family. For each house, program four construction paper rectangles (windows) with a corresponding addition or subtraction sentence. Place the windows and houses at a center. When a child visits the center, he sorts each window onto the house with the matching fact family numbers. **Fact families**

Check out the skill-building reproducibles on pages 135–138.

Small T-Shirt Patterns
Use with "Fact Family Photos" on this page.

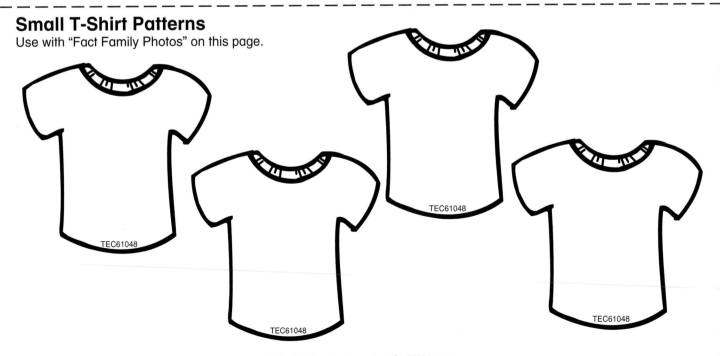

TEC61048
TEC61048
TEC61048
TEC61048

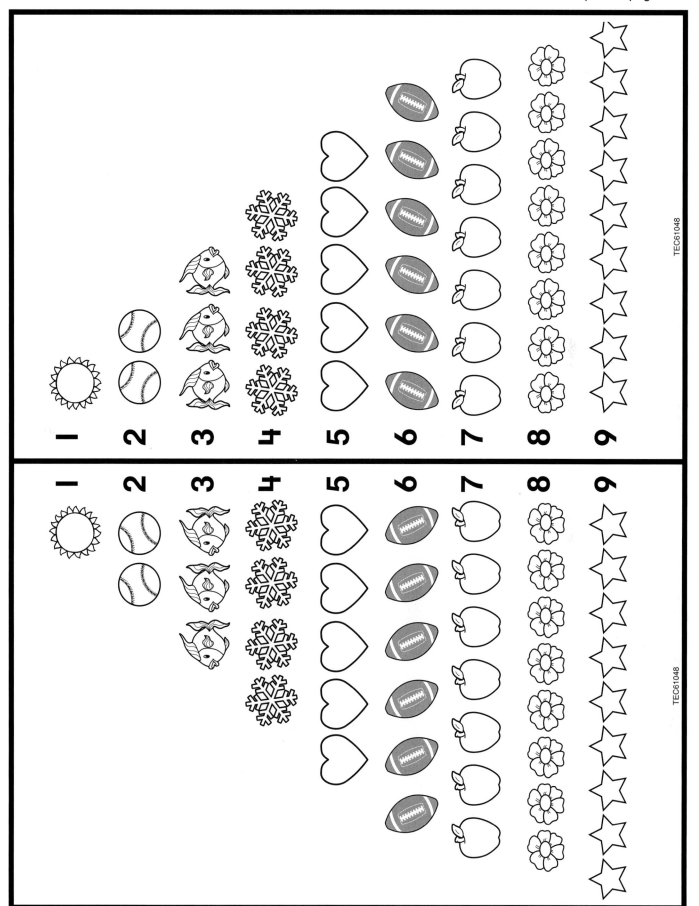

Domino Addition

_____ + _____ = _____

_____ + _____ = _____

_____ + _____ = _____

_____ + _____ = _____

_____ + _____ = _____

_____ + _____ = _____

_____ + _____ = _____

_____ + _____ = _____

_____ + _____ = _____

_____ + _____ = _____

©The Mailbox® • Superbook® • TEC61048

Note to the teacher: Use with "Domino Addition" on page 130.

Gone Fishing

Add.
Color by the code.

Color Code
7 or 8 — orange
9 or 10 — green
11 or 12 — yellow

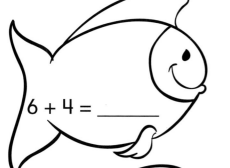
6 + 4 = _____

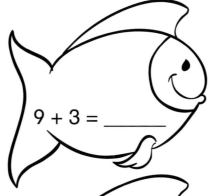
9 + 3 = _____

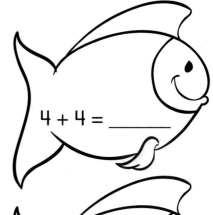
4 + 4 = _____

2 + 5 = _____

3 + 7 = _____

2 + 6 = _____

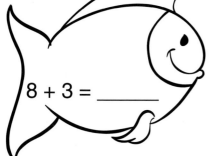
8 + 3 = _____

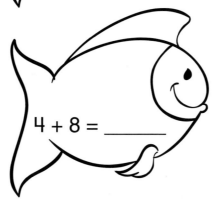
4 + 8 = _____

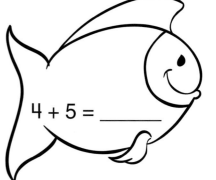
4 + 5 = _____

What a Spread!

Subtract.
Color by the code.

Color Code

4 and 5 — red   6 and 7 — purple   8 and 9 — blue

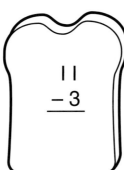

$$\begin{array}{r} 10 \\ -\ 6 \\ \hline \end{array}$$

$$\begin{array}{r} 11 \\ -\ 3 \\ \hline \end{array}$$

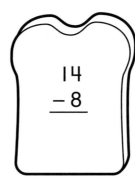

$$\begin{array}{r} 14 \\ -\ 8 \\ \hline \end{array}$$

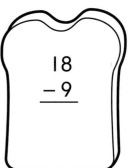

$$\begin{array}{r} 18 \\ -\ 9 \\ \hline \end{array}$$

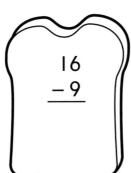

$$\begin{array}{r} 15 \\ -\ 6 \\ \hline \end{array}$$

$$\begin{array}{r} 16 \\ -\ 9 \\ \hline \end{array}$$

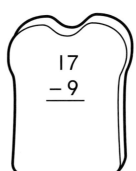

$$\begin{array}{r} 17 \\ -\ 9 \\ \hline \end{array}$$

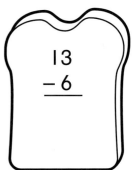

$$\begin{array}{r} 13 \\ -\ 6 \\ \hline \end{array}$$

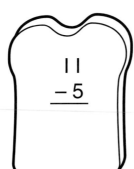

$$\begin{array}{r} 14 \\ -\ 9 \\ \hline \end{array}$$

$$\begin{array}{r} 11 \\ -\ 5 \\ \hline \end{array}$$

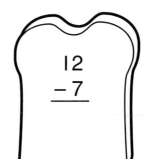

$$\begin{array}{r} 12 \\ -\ 7 \\ \hline \end{array}$$

$$\begin{array}{r} 12 \\ -\ 8 \\ \hline \end{array}$$

Name

Addition Site

Add.

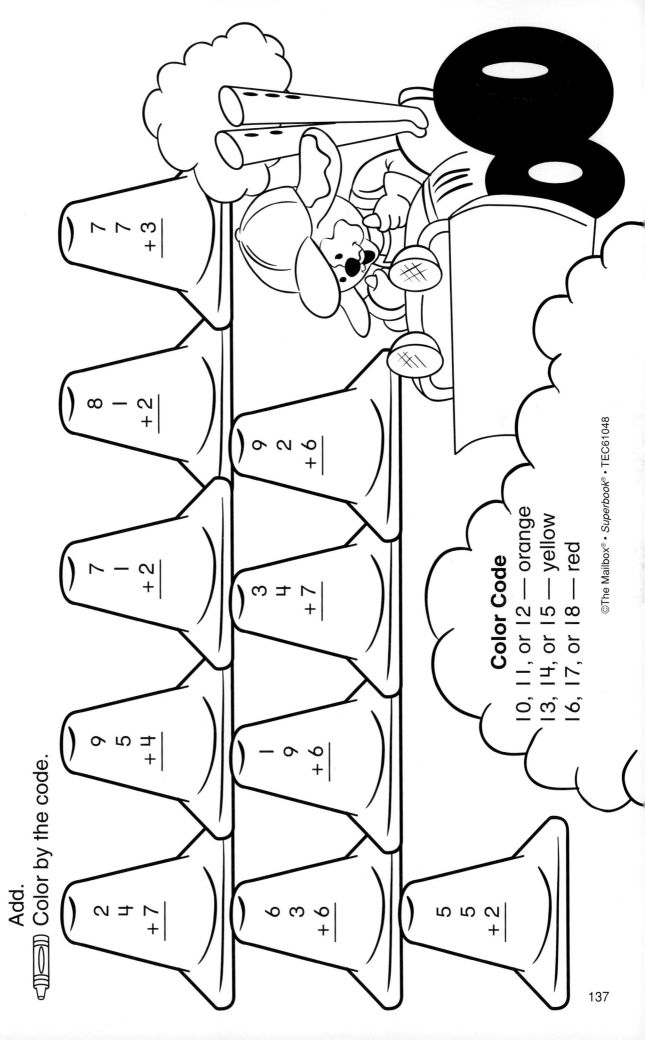

Color by the code.

$$\begin{array}{r} 7 \\ 7 \\ +3 \\ \hline \end{array}$$

$$\begin{array}{r} 8 \\ 1 \\ +2 \\ \hline \end{array}$$

$$\begin{array}{r} 7 \\ 1 \\ +2 \\ \hline \end{array}$$

$$\begin{array}{r} 9 \\ 5 \\ +4 \\ \hline \end{array}$$

$$\begin{array}{r} 2 \\ 4 \\ +7 \\ \hline \end{array}$$

$$\begin{array}{r} 9 \\ 2 \\ +6 \\ \hline \end{array}$$

$$\begin{array}{r} 3 \\ 4 \\ +7 \\ \hline \end{array}$$

$$\begin{array}{r} 1 \\ 9 \\ +6 \\ \hline \end{array}$$

$$\begin{array}{r} 6 \\ 3 \\ +6 \\ \hline \end{array}$$

$$\begin{array}{r} 5 \\ 5 \\ +2 \\ \hline \end{array}$$

Color Code
10, 11, or 12 — orange
13, 14, or 15 — yellow
16, 17, or 18 — red

Name _____

138

Add or subtract.

A Long Night's Sleep

$7 + 3 =$ _____

$3 + 7 =$ _____

$10 - 7 =$ _____

$10 - 3 =$ _____

$2 + 4 =$ _____

$4 + 2 =$ _____

$6 - 4 =$ _____

$6 - 2 =$ _____

$6 + 2 =$ _____

$2 + 6 =$ _____

$8 - 6 =$ _____

$8 - 2 =$ _____

$5 + 4 =$ _____

$4 + 5 =$ _____

$9 - 5 =$ _____

$9 - 4 =$ _____

PLACE VALUE

Place-Value Basics

A handy tens and ones chart is just what you need to introduce place value. Create a tens and ones chart, as shown, and then make a copy for each student. Also distribute a supply of base ten rods and cubes to each student. To begin, have students place one cube at a time on the ones side of the chart until they can exchange ten cubes for one rod (to place on the tens side of the chart). Continue in this same manner until students have a good understanding of exchanging ten cubes for one rod. For an added challenge, announce a number and have each student display the matching number on his place-value chart. If desired, have each student complete a copy of page 142 for additional skill practice.

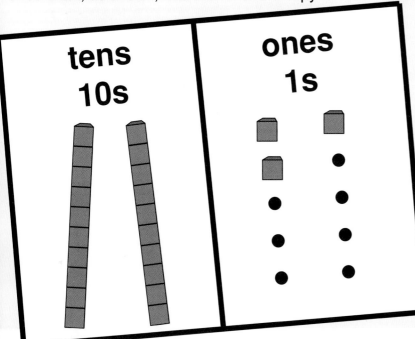

Tasty Place Value

Students are sure to enjoy this delicious place-value activity! Provide each student with a sandwich bag of toasted-oat cereal and a napkin. Instruct each student to organize her snacks into groups of tens and ones. Then have each student announce the number of tens and ones she made and the total number of snack pieces she has. Conclude the activity by inviting students to munch on their snacks!

2 tens + 4 ones = 24

I Spy the Number!

Use this variation of the game I Spy to reinforce your students' understanding of place value. Post a hundred chart (large enough for all students to view). Select one student to secretly choose a posted number. This student begins the game by announcing, "I spy a one- (or two-) digit number." The rest of the students try to identify the number by asking yes-or-no questions, such as, "Does the number have a three in the ones place?" or "Does the number have a five in the tens place?" The student who correctly names the secret number chooses the secret number for the next round of play.

Place-Value Lotto

To prepare, write any 25 numbers from 0 to 99 on a chart. Also make a copy of one of the lotto boards on page 141 for each student. Have each child randomly program each of the 16 squares with a different number from the chart. As students are programming their cards, write the 25 posted numbers on small pieces of paper and place the papers in a small container. Also distribute 16 game markers to each child. To play the game, draw a number from the container and announce each digit's value. For example, 43 would be announced as four tens and three ones. If a student has the announced number on her board, she covers it. The first student to cover all the numbers on her board announces, "Lotto!" To win the game she must read aloud the numbers on her board for verification.

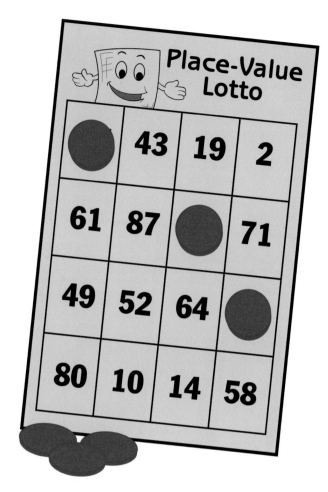

Race to One Hundred

Looking for a place-value game to use at a math center? Then try this two-player game! Place 20 cubes, 20 rods, and a pair of dice at a center. To play the game, the first player rolls the dice and collects a matching number of cubes. The second player then takes his turn. Play continues in this manner. When a player collects ten ones, he trades them for a ten (rod). The first player to collect ten rods wins!

Check out the skill-building reproducible on page 142.

Playing the Numbers

This two-player game of chance is a quick review of place value. Make two gameboards similar to the one shown. Remove all face cards and tens from a deck of playing cards. To play, each player draws two cards and strategically places each number in a column on her gameboard in hopes of making the largest possible number. Numbers may not be moved once they have been placed on the gameboard. The player with the larger number wins the round.

Place-Value Lotto

Place-Value Lotto

Name _____

Out of This World

Write how many tens and ones.

Write the number.

Color the matching star.

| | | | | | | | | |
|85|64|53|25|71|32|90|47|16|

A.

_____

B.

_____

C.

_____

D.

_____

E.

_____

F.

_____

G.

_____

H.

_____

I.

_____

Fractions

Fishing for Fair Shares

Get youngsters hooked on fractions with this center! Prepare a fishing pole by attaching one end of a length of yarn to an unsharpened pencil and tying the other end to a magnet. Program each of several fish cutouts (pattern on page 285) with different shapes divided into equal (fair shares) and unequal parts (not fair shares). Attach a paper clip to each fish and label two plastic pails as shown. Place the fish on a blue paper pond at a center along with the pails and the fishing pole. A child catches one fish at a time and places it in the appropriate pail. If desired, have her redraw each unequal shape on a sheet of paper so that it shows a fair share. **Fair shares**

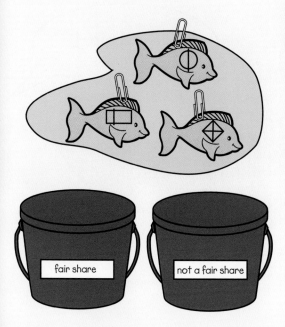

fair share   not a fair share

Slice by Slice

Anyway you slice it, this hands-on activity is just right for working with fractions. Give each child a small portion of play dough on a sheet of waxed paper and a plastic knife. Have him shape his dough into a square. Announce, "Fair share" or "Not a fair share." After each student cuts his dough accordingly, scan students' work for accuracy. Then instruct each child to reshape his dough into a different shape. Continue in the same manner for several rounds. For more advanced students, have them cut their shapes into fractional parts. **Fair shares**

Dinner for Two

Explore the concept of one-half with this taste-tempting idea! For each child, trim a large sheet of construction paper to resemble a serving platter, similar to the one shown. Arrange colorful pieces of construction paper for easy student access. Tell students that they are preparing a dinner for two. Have each child use the paper to cut out different foods that can be divided into halves. Direct her to draw a line to divide each item in half and label each part accordingly. Once she has prepared several food items, ask her to glue them to her platter. If desired, display the completed projects with the title "Dinner Is Served!" **Fraction:** $\frac{1}{2}$

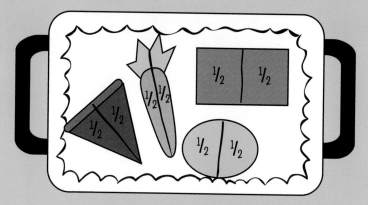

Pack the Bags

To prepare for this center, cut out a copy of the fraction cards on page 145 and program the back of each card for self-checking. Label each of three paper lunch bags with one of the following fractions: ½, ⅓, ¼. Place the bags and the cards at a center. When a child visits the center, she arranges the cards face-up and sorts them into the appropriate bags. To complete the activity, she unpacks each bag and checks the backs of the cards for accuracy. If desired, have each student complete a copy of page 146 for additional skill practice. **Fractions: ½, ⅓, ¼**

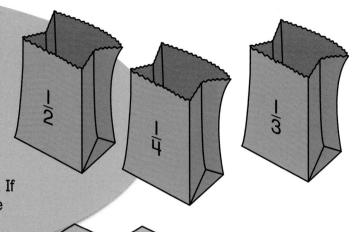

Sorting Socks

For this class activity, gather a supply of socks or sock cutouts in two different colors. Store the socks in a small laundry basket and place the basket near a clothesline suspended between two chairs. Announce a fractional statement, such as "One out of four socks is blue." Then invite a child to clip the socks to the clothesline to represent the statement. Encourage the class to verify his work; then ask another child to write the corresponding fraction on the board. Continue in the same manner for several different fractions. Parts of a set

A Bowlful of Fractions

Whet students' appetites for fractions with this partner activity! Give each child a simple bowl cutout, similar to the one shown, and a small cup of fruit-flavored O-shaped cereal. One student in a pair announces a fraction. The other child arranges cereal pieces on his bowl to represent the fraction and then describes the set. For example, if the fraction is one-third, a child could show one yellow and two green cereal pieces and say, "One out of three pieces is yellow." Have partners switch roles and continue in the same manner as time allows. Invite youngsters to snack on their cereal after completing the activity. Parts of a set

One-third.

Check out the skill-building reproducible on page 146.

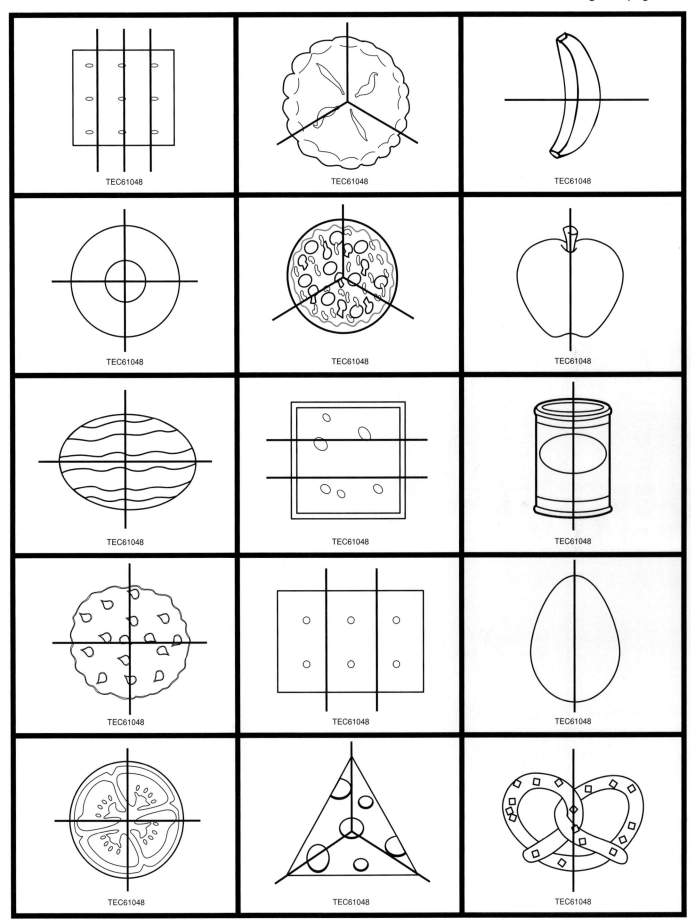

TEC61048

TEC61048

TEC61048

TEC61048

TEC61048

TEC61048

TEC61048

TEC61048

TEC61048

TEC61048

TEC61048

TEC61048

TEC61048

TEC61048

TEC61048

Name

What a Find!

✂ Cut.

Glue to match the fractions.

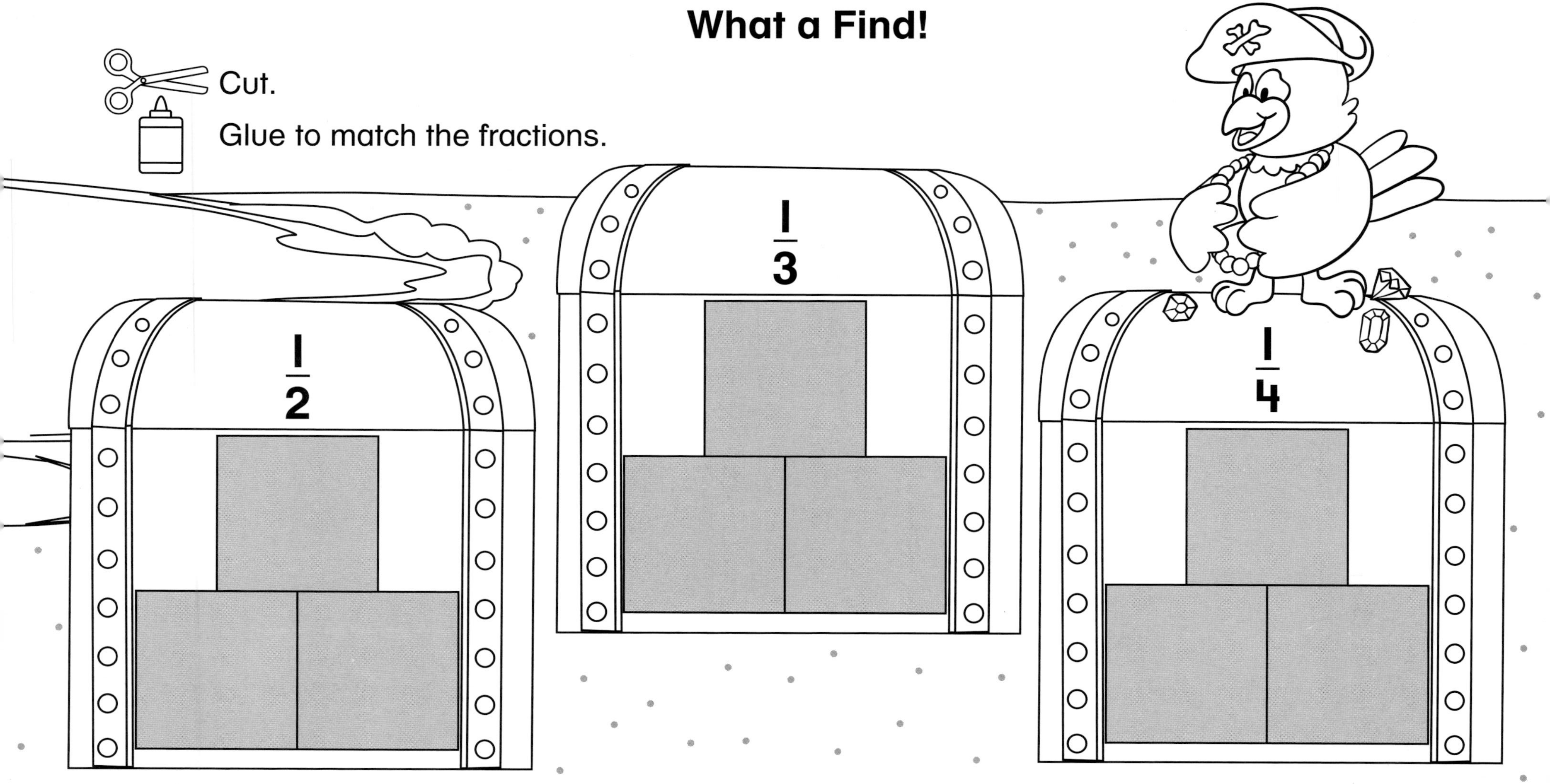

$\dfrac{1}{3}$

$\dfrac{1}{4}$

$\dfrac{1}{2}$

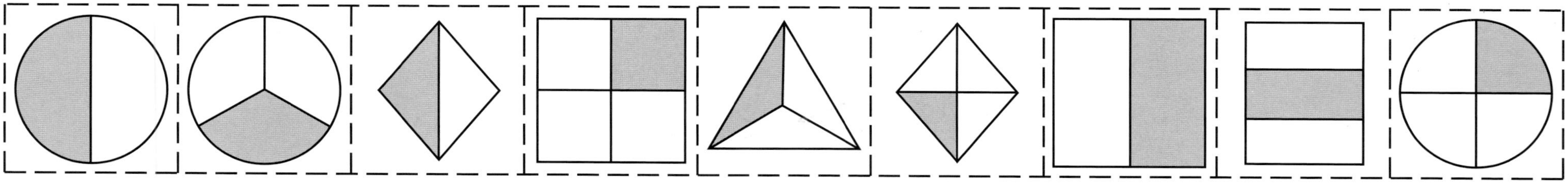

MEASUREMENT, Time, & Money

Handy Measurement

Improve students' nonstandard measurement skills with this handy activity. In advance, create a recording form (similar to the one shown) that lists objects in the room for students to measure. To begin, have each student trace his hands onto construction paper and cut them out. Then show students how to measure using their handprints. Distribute a copy of the recording form to each student and have him use his hand cutouts to measure each object on the form. When students have finished measuring, have student volunteers share their measurements. **Nonstandard measurement**

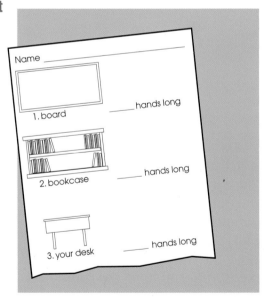

YARN MEASUREMENT

Roll out a ball of yarn for this measurement activity. Provide each child with a length of yarn. Have each student choose a different object in the room. Instruct the student to measure it with the yarn and then cut the yarn the same length as the object. Next, have the student use an inch ruler to measure the length of yarn. Provide each student with a piece of drawing paper. Have the student draw a picture of the object he measured, write the measurement, and then tape the yarn to the bottom of the picture. Display the completed pictures on a classroom wall for students to observe. Standard measurement

trash can

16 in.

Estimating Length

Provide estimating and measurement practice with this easy-to-prepare activity. Create a reproducible with lines of various lengths—all in exact inches. Give a copy of the reproducible and an inch ruler to each student. To begin, have each student record an estimate of the first line's length. Then have her use the ruler to measure the line. Have the student record the actual measurement beside the estimate. Instruct students to continue estimating and measuring the other lines in this same manner. **Standard measurement**

Weigh In

This cooperative learning project carries its own weight! Give each group of four students a balance scale and a collection of objects to be weighed. To begin, have each student list his group's objects on his paper. Then have him write an estimate of each object's weight using a predetermined nonstandard unit of measurement, such as Unifix cubes or clothespins. Next, have each group member, in turn, place an item on the scale and balance the scale by putting the nonstandard units on the other side. Have the student count how many nonstandard units it took to balance the object. Then have each group member record the number on his paper. Continue in this same manner until all of the objects have been weighed.
Weight

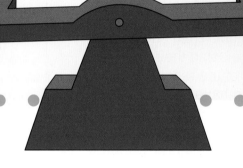

UP OR DOWN?

When students act as a balance scale, they are sure to gain a better understanding of weight. Place two objects of different weights on opposite ends of a balance scale. Lead students to understand that the heavier object goes down on the scale, while the lighter one goes up. Then invite two youngsters to act as a balance scale and stand facing each other. Give each child an object of a different weight, such as a book and a pencil. The child with the heavier object kneels down, while the other child puts her arms above her head and stretches upwards. Continue in the same manner using different objects and different students. **Weight**

Fill 'er Up

This center activity gives students practice with measuring capacity. Place a large container of rice, a measuring cup, and containers of various capacities and shapes (cup, pint, quart, gallon) at a center. Have the student use rice and the measuring cup to fill the containers, counting the cups as they work. Also, have students observe the equal capacities by pouring the contents from one container into another container of the same capacity but of a different shape. *Capacity*

A Timely Ladybug

Use Eric Carle's book *The Grouchy Ladybug* to begin your unit on telling time. Each time the ladybug encounters a different foe, the time of their meeting is depicted on a clock. After sharing this story with your youngsters, use its illustrations to introduce telling time to the hour. Have students carefully examine each hourly clock illustration before having one of them point to the corresponding time written in the text.

As a follow-up activity, provide each child with a copy of the clock pattern on page 154 and a brad. Assist students in attaching the hands to their clocks. Then announce the hourly times used in the book, and have students use their clocks to show the time. **Time to the hour**

DAILY TIMETABLE

With a daily timetable students can easily see how much time they spend on each school activity. Enlist students' help in making a list on the board of their daily school activities. Then record each activity and its time on a 9" x 12" piece of white construction paper. Divide students into as many groups as there are activities. Distribute an activity sheet to each group, and have the members work together to illustrate the activity. Compile the completed activity sheets in chronological order between two construction paper covers. If desired, have students make their own daily timetable booklets that include their before- and after-school activities. *Elapsed time*

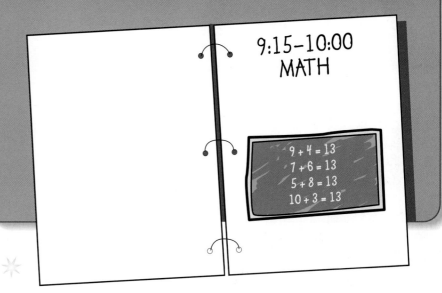

The Magic of a Minute

A minute, is a minute, is a minute—but sometimes it sure doesn't seem like it! Help your students explore the consistency of time with this activity. Obtain a clock that you can set for one minute. First, ask your students to do something that is relatively challenging or tiresome, such as standing on one foot, and time the chosen task for one minute. Then ask students to discuss whether that minute felt long or short. Next, time students doing something they enjoy for a minute, such as talking to a friend. Then discuss how that minute felt. Lead students to conclude that the time elapsed was exactly the same even though it might have felt very different. **Elapsed time**

Race to the Clock

For this class game, label a supply of blank cards each with a different digital time. Place two demonstration clocks on the board ledge. Divide your class into two teams; then have each team line up in front of a different clock. To play, choose a card, read the time aloud, and place it within students' view. The first member of each team quickly approaches his team's clock and displays the corresponding time. After confirming both youngsters' work, have the next pair of students approach the board and repeat the process. Continue in the same way until each child receives a turn. **Modeling time**

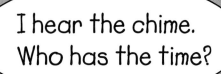

I hear the chime. Who has the time?

IT'S TIME!

This quick idea not only provides real-world practice with telling time, it also doubles as a transition activity! Display a working analog clock in your classroom. Set a timer to ring at a desired time that will not interfere with a lesson. When the timer rings, lead students in chanting, "I hear the chime. Who has the time?" Then call on a youngster to announce the time. Repeat this process several times throughout the day. *Telling time*

Match It!

To prepare for this game, cut out a class supply of the clock cards on page 154. (If there is an odd number of students, include yourself in the activity.) Program each analog clock with a different time and each digital clock to match. Give each youngster a card. On your signal, each student searches for the classmate with the matching clock. Once a pair finds each other, they sit down together. After confirming each match, redistribute the cards for another round of play. *Reading analog and digital times*

How Long?

Help youngsters gain an understanding of different lengths of time with this activity. Place the headers *seconds, minutes,* and *hours* along the top row of a pocket chart. Lead students in naming activities that would take different lengths of time such as writing a name, brushing teeth, or watching a movie. Assign each student a length of time and have her draw and label a blank card with a picture of her participating in a corresponding activity. Collect the cards and invite youngsters to help sort the cards into the pocket chart. **Lengths of time**

THROUGH THE YEAR

This poster will serve as a great visual reminder of the 12 months of the year. To make a poster, have each child fold a large sheet of construction paper in half horizontally and then in half vertically. Next, have him fold it in thirds vertically and crease along all the folds. Ask the child to unfold the paper; then have him draw a line along each fold line to make a 12-block grid. Instruct him to label, in sequence, each block with a month's name and then draw a related picture in each block. **Months of the year**

Calendar Lotto

Here's a fun way to practice using a calendar! Gather a class supply of calendar pages, repeating months as necessary. Give each child a calendar page and a supply of game markers. To begin, announce a date (jot it down for a reference). Each child who has the matching date on his calendar covers it with a marker. Play continues in this manner until a child covers four dates in a row (vertically or diagonally) and announces, "It's a date!" *Calendar*

March						
Sun.	Mon.	Tues.	Wed.	Thurs.	Fri.	Sat.
					1	2
3	4	5	6	7	8	9
10	11	12	13	14	15	16
17	18	19	20	21	22	23
24	25	26	27	28	29	30

Calling All Coins!

Count on this group game to review coins and their values! Give each child a large coin cutout or an imitation coin. Seat youngsters in a circle and ask them to pretend that the center of the circle is a giant piggy bank. After confirming that each student can identify her coin and its value, lead students in the chant shown. At the end of the verse all students holding the named coin stand up and enter the piggy bank. In turn, each standing child names her coin and its value and then returns to the circle. Repeat the chant, substituting a different coin name each time. For an added challenge, have youngsters count the total value of all the coins in the bank. **Coin recognition**

Piggy bank, piggy bank, Empty as can be. Let's fill it with [dimes] for you and me!

Coupon Math

Pair students; then give each child a grocery-store coupon and a supply of coins. Instruct each student to use the coins to show the value the coupon. Have each partner check the student's work. Then, on a given signal, have each student exchange coupons with a classmate. Students continue in this same manner for a predetermined amount of time.
Counting coins

20¢ OFF
Sally's FROZEN YOGURT
ALL VARIETIES
Vanilla Frozen Yogurt
COUPON

MAGNETIC MONEY

Draw several large circles on a magnetic board and label each with a different amount of money. Then, beside the circles, attach sets of magnetic money to the board. For each circle, choose a student and instruct him to place coins in the circle to equal the amount shown. After checking the coins in each circle, have additional students use different coins to make the same amounts. Since there are numerous possibilities, continue in this same manner until each student has had a turn.
Counting coins

$$4 + 3 = 7$$

Heads or Tails?

This center activity gives student pairs practice with counting coins of the same denomination. Place a supply of pennies and a carpet square at a center. To begin, have a child gently pick up a handful of coins and then drop them on the carpet square. Both students sort the coins based on the side that lands faceup (head or tails). One student then counts the coins that landed with heads showing while the other child counts the coins that landed with tails showing. The students then add both amounts together. Have students continue in this same manner for a predetermined amount of time.
Counting coins

A Valuable Menu

Transform your classroom into a restaurant with this small-group idea! Arrange a supply of grocery-store circulars for easy student access. Instruct each child to cut out three different food pictures. Have him glue the cutouts to the left side of a sheet of paper and write a different price less than one dollar to the right of each item. Then invite him to add details to his paper to resemble a menu. When all group members have completed their menus, direct each youngster to trade his menu with another student. Have each child use coins to represent the value of a menu item. After you check his work, direct him to continue with each remaining item. If desired, place the menus and coins at a center for independent practice. **Counting coins**

Kyle's Diner

MILK ....32¢

...............51¢

...............88¢

TO THE BANK!

Reinforce coin-counting skills with this partner game you can bank on! Give each twosome a copy of the gameboard on page 155, a supply of imitation coins (the bank), two game markers, and a die. To begin, a player rolls the die and moves his marker the corresponding number of spaces on the board. Next, he takes the matching amount of money from the bank. Players take turns in this manner until one child reaches the end of the board. Then both players count their coins and, if desired, make any necessary coin exchanges. After students compare their coin amounts to determine who has more money, they return their coins to the bank and play again! Comparing money amounts

The Right Price

Here's a center idea that's right on the money! Trim several construction paper rectangles to resemble price tags. Write a different price on each tag and store the tags in a bag. Place the bag, a supply of blank paper, and crayons at a center. When a child visits the center, she folds a sheet of paper into fourths, draws a square in the center, and traces over the creases as shown. Then she takes a price tag from the bag and writes the price in the center of her sheet. Next, she draws a different combination of coins in each section. After she recounts each group of coins to verify her work, she flips over her paper and repeats the process with a different price tag. **Coin combinations**

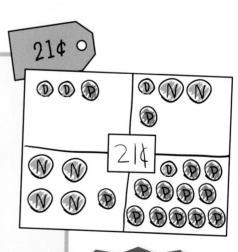

21¢

21¢

Check out the skill-building reproducibles on pages 156–158.

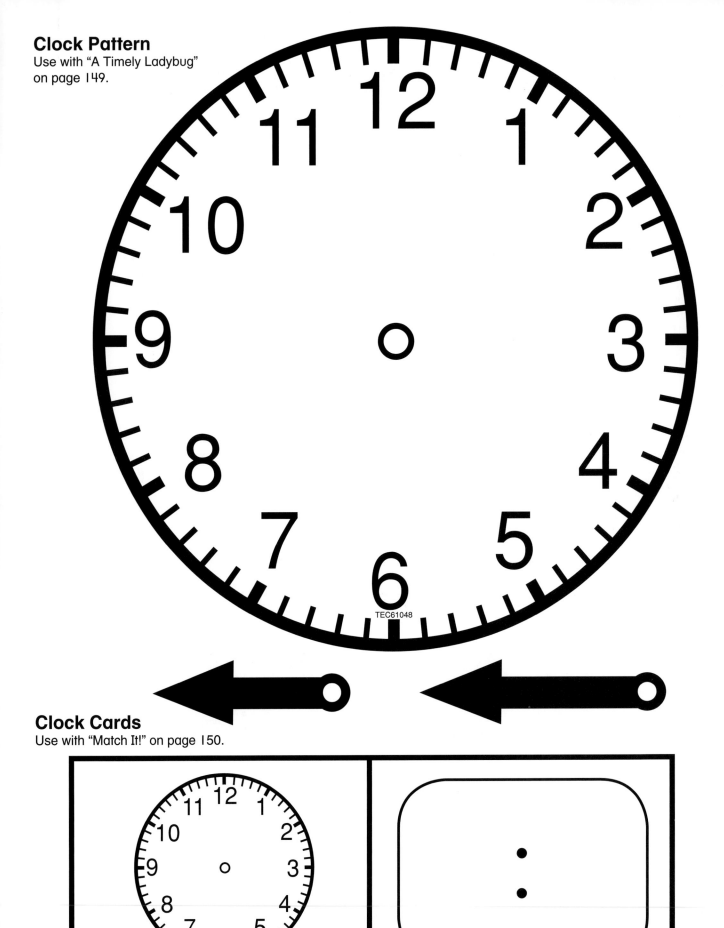

Clock Pattern
Use with "A Timely Ladybug" on page 149.

TEC61048

Clock Cards
Use with "Match It!" on page 150.

TEC61048

TEC61048

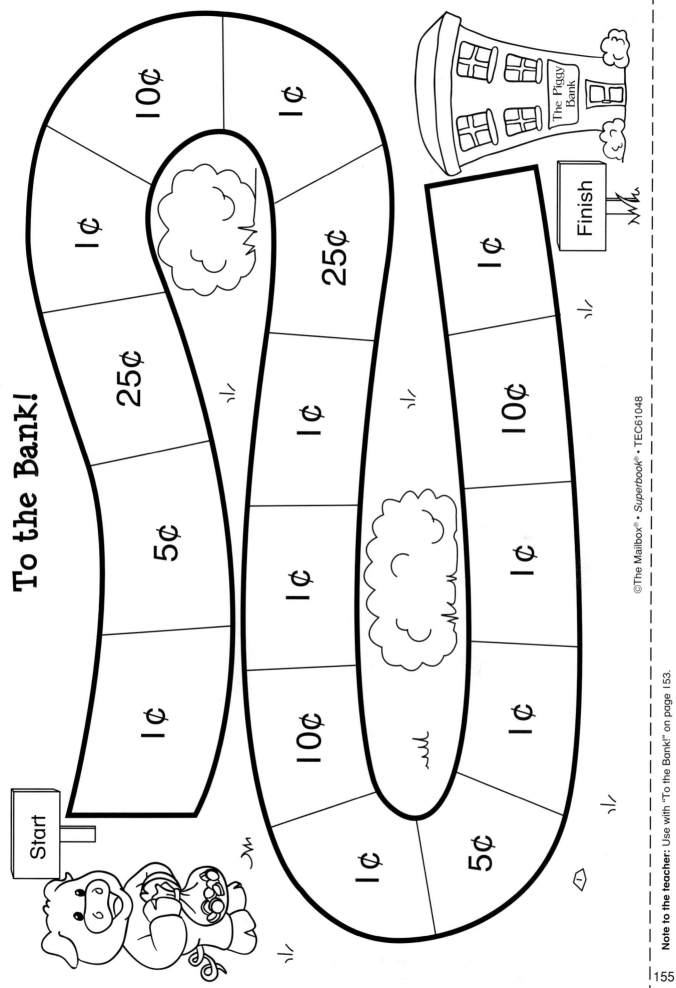

To the Bank!

Start

1¢

5¢

25¢

1¢

25¢

10¢

1¢

1¢

1¢

10¢

1¢

25¢

The Piggy Bank

Finish

1¢

10¢

1¢

1¢

5¢

1¢

Note to the teacher: Use with "To the Bank!" on page 153.

Just My Size

✂ Cut.

Measure each shoe from dot to dot.

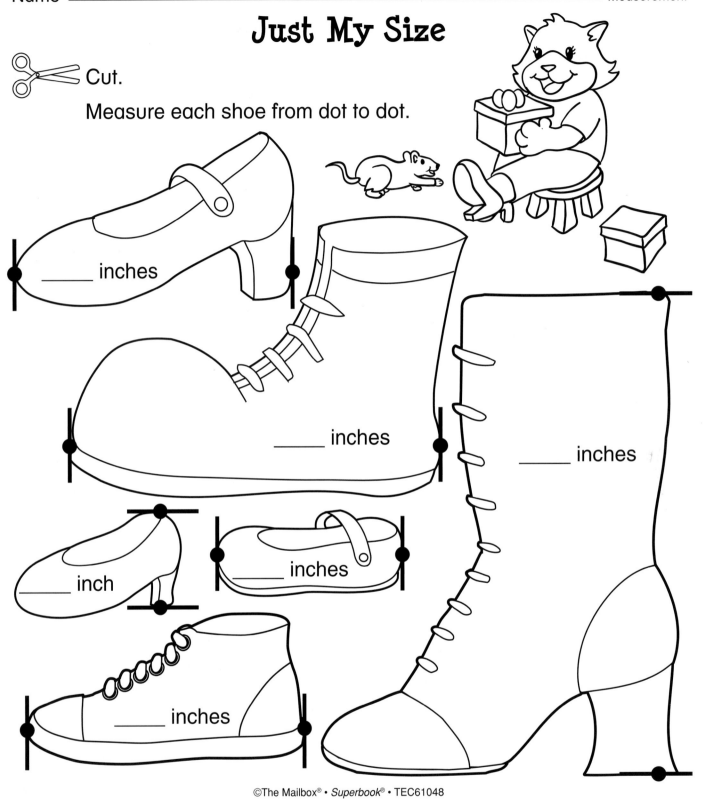

_____ inches

_____ inches

_____ inches

_____ inch

_____ inches

_____ inches

| | 1 | 2 | 3 | 4 | 5 | 6 |

A Proud Moment

Write each time.

Name _____

Munchies Machine

✏ Write the amount of each set of coins.

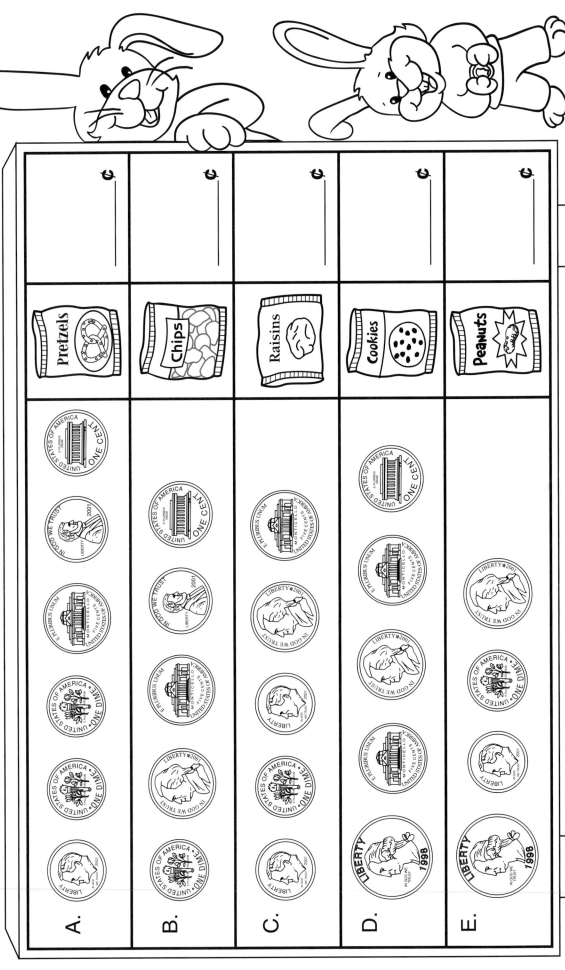

I found a rectangle.

Sam

Shape Search

Provide each child with a maga-zine and a piece of paper. Have each student search for a shape in his maga-zine. When he find one, he cuts it out and glues it to his paper. Then he traces the shape with a black marker and writes a sentence labeling his chosen shape. Bind the completed pages between two construction paper covers and add a title, such as "The First-Grade Shape Search." **Plane shapes**

Pattern-Block Puzzlers

Invite students to explore plane shapes with this small-group activity. To begin, give each child a supply of pattern blocks. Instruct each youngster to use a specific number of blocks to make a designated shape. (For example, ask each child to use four blocks to make a triangle.) After each child has made the featured shape, invite her to share which blocks she used. Then ask her to make the featured shape again, this time challenging her to use a smaller or larger number of blocks or to use different blocks. Have students make additional shapes as desired. **Plane shapes**

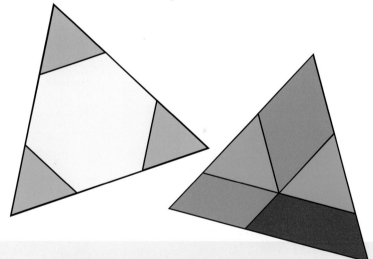

Shape Descriptions

This activity encourages students to observe the attributes of plane shapes. For each small group of students, draw a different plane shape on an index card. Give each group a card and have group members identify and discuss the attributes of their assigned shape. Next, ask a group to describe its shape for the rest of the class. List the group's comments on a sheet of chart paper. When the group is finished sharing, ask the remaining students to guess the shape. After the shape is correctly identified, draw and label a picture of it on the chart paper. Continue in this manner until each group has had a chance to share. Then post the resulting shape posters as a student reference. **Plane shapes**

square
- straight sides
- four sides
- four corners
- all equal sides

Guess the Figure

Increase students' math vocabularies with this game. To prepare, collect a real-world object to represent each geometric solid you wish to review. Display the collection so that each student can see the items. To begin, secretly choose an object and give a clue that corresponds with a characteristic of it, such as "My object rolls." Guide youngsters to eliminate objects from the collection that do not correspond with the clue. Continue to give clues in this manner until a student volunteer correctly guesses the featured item and identifies its shape. Repeat with the remaining shapes as time allows. Solid figures

Geometric Scavenger Hunt

Make a list of solid or plane shapes and copy it to make a class supply. Give each child a copy and instruct her to search the room or another chosen location to find an example of each shape. Have each student record beside each shape's name where she found it. When the hunt is complete, invite students to share the various objects they found for each shape. **Plane shapes or solid figures**

Familiar Faces

Help students see the plane shape faces of solid figures with this hands-on center. In advance, collect a supply of solid figures that have at least one flat face, such as a tissue box or a soup can. (If desired, use a set of solid figure manipulatives.) Label the figures and place them at a center along with a supply of drawing paper and recording sheets like the one shown. A child visits the center and chooses a solid figure. He places the figure on a sheet of drawing paper and traces a flat face. Then he fills in the corresponding blanks on his recording sheet. He repeats this process with the remaining solid figures at the center as time allows. **Solid figures**

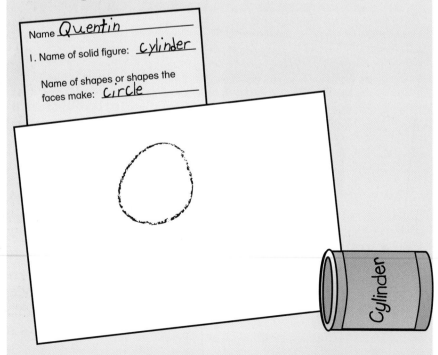

Name Quentin

1. Name of solid figure: cylinder

Name of shapes or shapes the faces make: circle

Cylinder

Munchable Math

Here's a tasty way for students to explore plane shapes and solid figures. Plan a day to have geometric snacks in your classroom. About a week in advance, fill in the appropriate date on a copy of the family letter on page 162. Then copy the page to make a class supply. Complete each letter by naming a snack shape, and send one letter home with each student. Also label a set of blank cards, each with the name of an assigned shape or figure.

On the day of the event, place each labeled card on a table along with a class supply of resealable plastic bags. Have each student place her snack on the table near the corresponding card. Then gather students around the table and give each child a bag. Ask a student volunteer to point to the snack she brought in and announce its corresponding plane shape or solid figure. Challenge students to determine how many sides, corners, and edges (if any) the shapes have. Next, invite each youngster to place a piece of the snack in each bag. Continue in this manner until each child has had a chance to share. Then let the snacking begin!
Plane shapes and solid figures

Creative Creatures

These colorful monsters help review symmetry. To begin, have each child fold a sheet of colorful construction paper in half. To make a monster face, he draws a unique design around the fold and then cuts along the resulting line, keeping the fold intact. He opens the paper and uses a pencil to lightly trace the line of symmetry. He paints details on half of the face, such as an eye and one-half of a mouth. Then he refolds the paper and lightly presses down on it. He reopens the paper to reveal the resulting symmetrical face. When the projects are dry, post them with a title such as "Symmetrical Monsters." If desired, have each student complete a copy of page 163 for additional practice with symmetry.
Symmetry

Funny Fish

To prepare this small-group game, make a fishing pole by attaching a magnet to the end of a length of yarn and tying the other end of the yarn to a ruler. Use construction paper to make a pair of congruent shape cutouts for each group member and place one shape cutout from each pair in a pocket chart. Add details to the other cutouts so they resemble fish and then attach a paper clip to each one. Near the pocket chart, place a length of blue yarn on the floor in a circle to resemble a pond, and place the fish cutouts inside. Set the fishing pole near the pond. Each group member, in turn, uses the pole to catch a fish and then matches it to its congruent shape in the pocket chart.
Congruent shapes

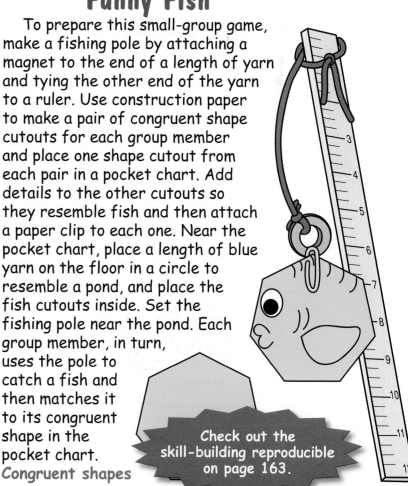

Check out the skill-building reproducible on page 163.

Dear Family,

We have been learning about plane shapes and solid figures. On _____, we

date

will be having geometric snacks at school. Please send in a class supply of a snack in the shape of

_____ on or before that date.

name of figure

Thank you!

Suggestions for Snacks

⬤ Circles
- round cookies
- vanilla wafers

△ Triangles
- tortilla chips
- diagonally cut bread

△ Cones
- Bugles snacks
- candy kisses

◻ Squares
- square crackers
- cheese slices

 Cubes
- cheese cubes
- caramel candies

 Cylinders
- marshmallows
- pretzel sticks

▭ Rectangles
- rectangular crackers
- graham sticks

 Spheres
- Kix cereal
- malted milk balls

Note to the teacher: Use with "Munchable Math" on page 161.

Froggy's Cookies

Draw the line or lines of symmetry on each cookie.

Color by the code.

Color Code
yellow — one line of symmetry
orange — more than one line
of symmetry

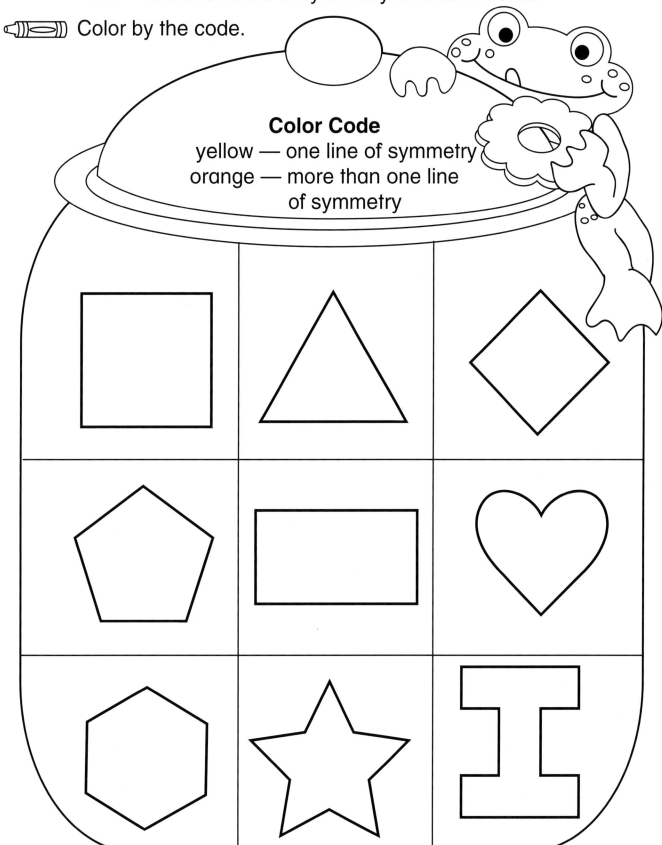

Graphing & Probability

Graphing Topics

Looking for a topic? Check out the following ideas.

- What month is your birthday?
- What is your favorite dessert?
- Are you left-handed or right-handed?
- What is your favorite color?
- How many letters are in your first name?
- How will you leave school today?
- Did you bring your lunch today?
- Are you a boy or a girl?
- What is your favorite sport?
- How many pockets do you have?
- Would you rather have a hot dog or a burger?
- How many teeth have you lost?
- Have you ever slept in a tent?
- Are you wearing sneakers?
- How many pets do you have?
- What is your favorite flavor of ice cream?

Line Up!

Students become part of the graph while choosing a read-aloud selection! Place two book choices on the board ledge. Invite each student to stand in front of his choice. Then have youngsters form parallel lines by holding hands with students in the other group. Lead youngsters to discuss the results of the graph and then read aloud the book with more votes. If desired, use this idea for any question that has two answer choices.
Object graph

Read, Count, and Graph!

Incorporate reading and math with a graphing center that utilizes the side of a file cabinet! Write several sight words on separate blank cards; then attach a magnetic strip to the back of each card. Also, label separate cards with the numerals 2–5. Attach the number cards along the bottom of the file cabinet and the title shown at the top. Place the word cards nearby. When a child visits the center, she reads a word card and counts the number of letters. Then she places the card above the corresponding column label. She continues in the same manner for each remaining card. Encourage her to draw conclusions about the number of letters in her sight words.
Object graph

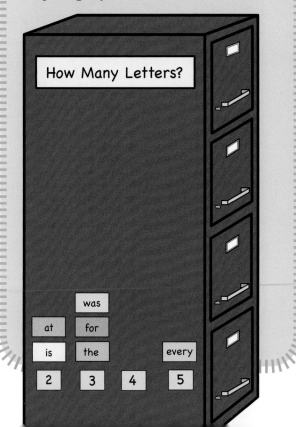

Picture-Perfect Graphs

Begin each day with a graphing activity that uses your students' smiling faces. Laminate a photograph of each child; then attach a magnet to the back of each laminated snapshot. On a magnetic board, prepare a bar-graph outline. Each morning select a subject for the graph and label the columns accordingly. (See the suggestions on page 164.) When a student arrives at school, he attaches his magnet in the appropriate column. Take time each morning to discuss the results of the graph. It won't be long before your students' graphing skills are picture-perfect! **Picture graph**

Tasty Graphing

Reinforce graphing skills with a tasty flair! Give each child a sheet of graph paper and a snack-size bag of M&M's, jelly beans, Skittles, or candy hearts. Have each child sort and graph his candies by color on his graph paper. Then, using a corresponding crayon color, have him color one square for each candy of that color. Encourage each child to write the total number of each color on his graph. Then challenge each child to add the total number of candies. **Bar graph**

CUTIE PIE

Shower Curtain Graphing

Here's an inexpensive way to make a reusable graph! Use a permanent marker to draw a large grid on a plain shower curtain. Place the graph on the floor in an open area of the classroom. Choose a graphing topic (see page 164 for suggestions); then label a card for each answer choice. Place the cards along the bottom of the grid. Have each child draw his choice on a paper square and place it on the graph in the corresponding column. After each student has had a turn, discuss the results. Then simply remove the papers from the graph, fold it up, and store it for another graphing opportunity! If desired, have each student complete a copy of page 170 for additional skill practice. **Picture graph**

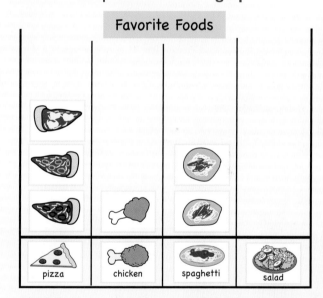

Favorite Foods

| pizza | chicken | spaghetti | salad |

Plenty of Pasta

Colorful pasta provides a great graphing opportunity! Obtain a supply of tricolor pasta. Prepare a blank graph similar to the one shown and make a class supply. Place the graphs, a bowl of pasta, a ladle, and crayons at a center. When a child visits the center, he scoops two ladlefuls of pasta from the bowl. Then he sorts the pasta by color and colors his graph accordingly. Encourage him to study the graph to determine which color has the most, which color has the least, or which colors are the same. **Bar graph**

Name Victor

Pasta Colors

| orange | green | yellow |

Reusable Tally Graph

For a tally graph that can be used over and over again, program a grid on a sheet of poster board; then laminate the graph for durability. During a graphing activity, record student responses on the graph using a dry-erase marker. Afterward simply wipe the markings off with a wet paper towel and the graph is ready to be used again! **Tally chart**

How many pockets are in our class?		
Monday	ⅢⅢ ⅢⅢ ⅢⅢ ⅢⅢ ⅢⅢ ⅢⅢ I	31
Tuesday	ⅢⅢ ⅢⅢ ⅢⅢ ⅢⅢ ⅢⅢ ⅢⅢ III	33
Wednesday	ⅢⅢ ⅢⅢ ⅢⅢ ⅢⅢ ⅢⅢ II	27
Thursday	ⅢⅢ ⅢⅢ ⅢⅢ ⅢⅢ IIII	24
Friday	ⅢⅢ ⅢⅢ ⅢⅢ ⅢⅢ	20

On the Farm

The result of this center is a farmyard full of animals! Copy and cut out a class supply of the animal cards on page 168 and store them in a container. Place the container at a center along with copies of the recording sheet on page 168, construction paper, and glue. A center visitor randomly removes ten cards from the container, sorts the cards, and then completes a copy of the recording sheet. After interpreting his results, he glues his animals to a sheet of paper and incorporates them into a farm scene. If desired, display the completed farms with their corresponding recording sheets. **Tally chart**

Making Choices

To prepare for this class activity, post a graphing question on the board (see page 164 for suggestions). Label each of two containers with a different answer choice and place them near the question. Give each child a Unifix cube. Then, in turn, have each student place her cube in the container of her choice. After all students have made a choice, link each set of cubes together and have youngsters interpret the results. **Symbolic graph**

Do you prefer chocolate or vanilla ice cream?

chocolate

vanilla

Probable Outcomes

These two easy-to-implement activities will get your students thinking! For each activity, have students compile their own information to use in making future predictions. **Probability**

- Have each student roll one die until he rolls a predetermined number, such as five. Have him record the number of turns it took to roll that number. Then have him repeat the activity several times using a different predetermined number each time. Have the student compare the number of rolls needed to reach each number.
- Have each student toss a coin in the air ten times and record which side the coin lands on for each toss.

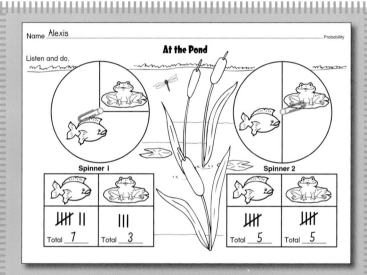

Probability at the Pond

What are the chances of finding a fish or a frog at the pond? Find out with this activity! On a copy of page 169, help each child use a brad to attach a paper clip to each spinner. Direct each student to look at Spinner 1. Ask her to predict which pond animal she is more likely to see. Then have her spin Spinner 1 ten times, recording a tally mark on the chart after each spin. Repeat the same process for Spinner 2. Guide students in discussing the results and concluding that Spinner 2 provides an equal chance for both animals, while Spinner 1 does not. If desired, laminate a copy of page 169 and place it at a center with wipe-off markers for additional practice. Probability

How Likely?

Explore the likeliness of different events with this simple idea! Visually divide a sheet of paper into fourths and label each section with one of the following words: *certain, likely, unlikely, impossible*. Then give each child a copy of the sheet. After discussing the meaning of each term and providing examples, have each child draw and label a corresponding event for each category. Invite students to share their papers to look for similarities and differences between events. Lead them to conclude that the probability of an event occurring may not be the same for every person. **Probability**

Check out the skill-building reproducible on page 170.

Animal Cards

Use with "On the Farm" on page 166.

TEC61048 TEC61048 TEC61048 TEC61048 TEC61048

TEC61048 TEC61048 TEC61048 TEC61048 TEC61048

Name ——————

On the Farm

Tally chart

Animal	Tallies	Total
cow		
horse		
sheep		
pig		
rooster		

Note to the teacher: Use with "On the Farm" on page 166.

Name _____

At the Pond

Listen and do.

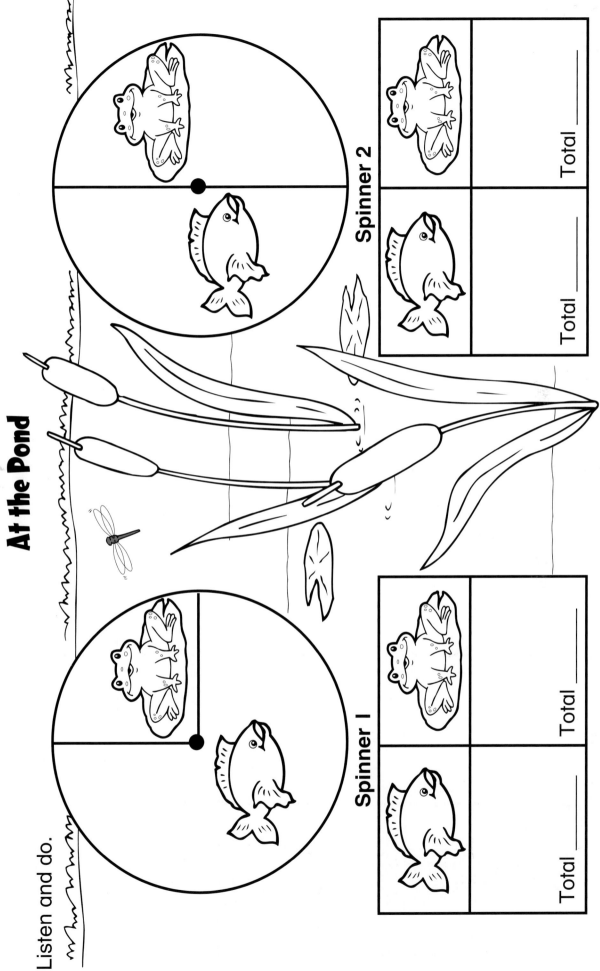

Spinner 1

Spinner 2

Total ____

Total ____

Total ____

Total ____

Note to the teacher: Use with "Probability at the Pond" on page 167.

Name _____

170

Grow, Garden, Grow!

Cut.   Glue to complete the graph.

Garden Insects

bee					
butterfly					
caterpillar					

Look at the graph. ✏️ Write.

A. How many 🦋 ? _____

B. How many 🐝 and 🦋 in all? _____

C. How many more 🐝 than 🐛 ? _____

D. How many fewer 🦋 than 🐝 ? _____

Sorting & Patterning

People Patterns

Patterning will get creative when you use this idea. Each day choose a student to direct several of her classmates to stand in a line according to a pattern of her choice. She may, for example, place her classmates in a boy, boy, girl pattern or in a pattern according to the color of clothing each child is wearing. When the students are in order, have children guess what pattern was created. **Patterning**

Pattern Patrol

Get youngsters on the lookout for patterns with this idea! Each day, assign a different student to be a pattern patrol officer. Have her wear a crepe paper necklace attached to a copy of the badge pattern on page 172. Throughout the day, the officer looks for patterns in the environment, such as on bulletin board border, in floor tile, or on a rug. At a designated time, ask her to share different patterns she found. If desired, write her responses on a chart to keep track of the patterns found. **Patterning**

Ready? Go!

This fast-moving game will get your students in shape with patterns. Gather students together and seat them in a circle. Give each student a red, green, or blue construction paper square. Announce two colors and a pattern sequence, such as AB, ABB, or AAB. Have students holding those color squares meet in a designated spot in the classroom and work together to form themselves into the announced pattern. Enlist the help of the students still sitting to verify that the resulting pattern matches the one stated. Repeat the activity several times using different color combinations. Patterning

Not All the Same!

There are many different ways to sort student-drawn pictures. Announce a simple item for students to draw, such as a flower or a car. Invite each child to draw the item on a blank sheet of paper. After collecting the pictures, seat youngsters in a circle. Place several of the pictures in the middle of the circle for students to view. Then invite a volunteer to determine an attribute by which to sort the pictures. Enlist students' help in sorting by the designated attribute. When students are satisfied with their sort, repeat the process with different pictures and attributes. *Sorting*

These flowers have long stems, and those flowers have short stems!

Sort the crayons by the amount of paper on them.

So Many Ways!

Look no further than your crayon supply for a simple sorting center! Place a supply of crayons in a container. Place the container and several empty crayon boxes at a center. Invite a pair of students to the center. One child announces a sorting attribute. Then the twosome works together to sort the crayons into the crayon boxes. After completing the sort, youngsters return the crayons to the container and switch roles. Challenge the pair to think of several different ways to sort the crayons. *Sorting*

Check out the skill-building reproducible on page 173.

Badge Patterns
Use with "Pattern Patrol" on page 171.

TEC61048

TEC61048

Tropical Treats

Cut.

Glue to extend each pattern.

A.						
B.						
C.						
D.						

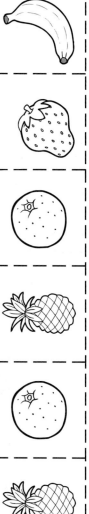

PROBLEM SOLVING

Which Are Chocolate Chip?

Invite students on an imaginary trip to the bakery for some problem-solving practice! Ask students to pretend they want to buy some chocolate chip cookies, which are baked every third batch at the bakery. Explain that they can find a pattern to determine which batches of cookies will be chocolate chip. Write the numbers 1 to 30 on the board. Then ask students which batch of cookies will be the first batch of chocolate chip. After they answer that it will be the third batch, circle the number 3 on the board. Then help students determine that to find the next batch of chocolate chip cookies, they add three to the previous batch number. Lead students in using this strategy to find the next several batches of chocolate chip cookies. **Finding a pattern**

A Shopping Spree

This picture-perfect approach to problem solving involves Goldilocks and the three bears. Present the following problem to students:

Goldilocks went shopping and bought clothes for the three bears. She bought one pair of pants, two shirts, and three hats for each bear. How many total items of clothing did she buy?

To help youngsters solve the problem, draw each of the three bears on the board. Reread the problem and ask student volunteers to draw the corresponding number of clothing items below each bear. Then lead youngsters in counting the drawings to determine the total number of items Goldilocks purchased. For additional reinforcement, present more shopping-themed problems for students to solve. **Drawing a picture**

Lining Up

Your youngsters become amateur detectives when they use clues to solve problems! Using five of your students' names, write clues on the board similar to the ones shown. Also draw five large boxes on the board and label them as shown. To begin, ask the featured students to stand near the board. Then read each clue aloud and have the remaining youngsters help each featured student find the correct box to stand in front of. Change the clues to repeat this activity with a new group of students. **Logical reasoning**

Clues:
Caleb is fourth in line.
Stefan is between Grace and Abby.
Abby is third in line.
Joey is not first in line.

First	Second	Third	Fourth	Fifth

A Library of Word Problems

This small-group activity will provide students with practice in learning what information should be included when writing a story problem. Divide your class into groups and assign each group a number less than ten. Have the group members work together to write story problems that have an answer that equals the group's assigned number. Have students write each story problem on a separate page so there will be room for an illustration. Encourage the students to work through the problems with manipulatives to make sure the necessary information is included. Then compile each group's story problems to make a book. **Story problems**

Story Problems That Equal 3

2 fish were in the pond. 1 more fish came along. How many fish were in the pond?

Family Problem Solving

Each week choose a student to create a word problem with his family's help. Have the student record the word problem along with an illustration on a sheet of drawing paper. Then have the student return the word problem to school and share it with his classmates. Invite the student to call on volunteers to answer the problem. After his classmates respond, ask the student to explain the steps used in solving the problem. Punch holes in each student's paper and store the papers in a three-ring binder labeled "Family Word Problems." **Story problems**

Names	Numbers	Objects
Katelyn	2	
Jake	4	
Jamie	10	
Chanda	6	
Riley	1	
Sean		

Riley had 2 cars. Jake had 1 car. How many cars were there in all?

Word Problems in an Instant

Provide students with problem-solving practice using this word-problem activity. Divide a bulletin board into three sections and label it as follows: "Names," "Numbers," and "Objects." Mount paper strips labeled with students' names on the "Names" section and paper strips labeled with numerals on the "Numbers" section. Mount magazine pictures of a variety of objects on the "Objects" section. To use the board, have a student choose two names, two numerals, and one object. Have the student record the information as a word problem on a piece of paper and then choose either an addition or a subtraction function to solve the problem. Challenge students to use this information to create and solve a variety of word problems. **Story problems**

Check out the skill-building reproducibles on pages 176 and 177.

New Clown Cars

Each clown gets a different-colored car.
Read the clues.
Fill in the chart.

Draw an **X** to show each color a
    clown does not get.
Draw a ✔ to show the color each
    clown does get.

Clues:
Cleo's car is not red.
Clive's car is not blue or green.
Clyde's car is blue.

	red	blue	green
Cleo			
Clive			
Clyde			

1. What color is Cleo's car? _____

2. Whose car is red? _____

3. What color is Clyde's car? _____

A Hungry Team

Turtle's soccer team eats pizza after each game.
Each player eats 2 slices.

Complete the table.
Use it to answer the questions.

Number of Players	1	2	3	4			7	8		10
Number of Slices		4		8	10	12		16	18	

1. How many slices did 6 players eat? _____

2. How many slices did 10 players eat? _____

3. How many players did it take to eat 12 slices? _____

Living and Nonliving Things

Living or Nonliving?

After guiding your youngsters in a discussion about the basic life processes of all living things, take your class on a walk outside to look for living and nonliving things. When you return from the walk, have each student record his observations. To do this, a student folds a sheet of drawing paper in half. Then he unfolds that paper and labels the halves "Living Things" and "Nonliving Things." Next, he draws and labels under the appropriate headings pictures of the things he saw on his walk. To conclude, have students share their drawings with their classmates.

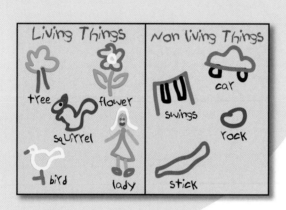

Sorting Living and Nonliving Things

To begin, remind students that living things need food, water, and air to grow and change. Then have students cut pictures of living and nonliving things from magazines. Ask each student to sort her pictures into two groups—*living* and *nonliving* things. Next, challenge each student to sort her pictures of living things into three more groups—*people, animals,* and *plants.* Then, as a class, mount the sorted pictures onto a piece of bulletin board paper divided and labeled as shown. Post the chart and add the title "Living and Nonliving Things."

Checking the List

The handy checklist used in this whole-group activity helps youngsters determine whether something is living. To prepare, make and laminate a large checklist similar to the one shown and post it in your group area. Also cut out a copy of the cards on page 179 and place them in a container. To begin, share the checklist and remind students that a living thing must have all four of the characteristics on the list.

Next, choose a student to draw a card and read the word aloud. Then announce the first characteristic from the checklist. Enlist students' help in deciding whether the item listed on the card has that characteristic. If it does, use a wipe-off marker to check the box. Continue in this manner with the remaining characteristics on the checklist. Then ask students to use the checklist to determine whether the item on the card is living or nonliving. Wipe off the checklist, if necessary, and continue in this manner with the remaining cards.

A living thing...
☐ needs food
☐ needs water
☐ needs air
☐ grows and changes

horse

TEC61048

desk

TEC61048

girl

TEC61048

balloon

TEC61048

tree

TEC61048

candy

TEC61048

baby

TEC61048

lamp

TEC61048

plant

TEC61048

pan

TEC61048

Plants

Plant Needs

Students will sprout a new knowledge for the needs of plants with this banner project. For each student accordion-fold a 6" x 18" piece of construction paper into five equal sections. Instruct each student to vertically unfold her banner and write "Plants need…" and her name on the top section. The student then writes and illustrates a different plant need (air, soil, water, sunlight) in each of the remaining four sections. After completing these sections, the student turns her banner over and draws a picture of a growing plant. Clip these delightful projects to a clothesline suspended in the classroom.

Seeds Up Close

What better way for students to discover seed parts than by seeing them? To prepare, soak a bag of dried lima beans in water overnight. Also draw a picture of the seed diagram (shown) on the board.

Explain to your students that all seeds have three parts in common: the *embryo,* the *food-storage tissue,* and the *seed coat.* Point to the seed coat on the diagram and inform your students that it protects the inside of the seed from injury, loss of water, and insects. Have each student carefully remove the seed coat from her bean. Point to the embryo on the diagram and tell students that it is the baby plant. Have each student open her seed and find the embryo. Next point to the food-storage tissue on the diagram and explain that it contains all the food needed for the baby plant to begin to grow. Instruct each student to find the food-storage tissue in her bean. Now that's a hands-on way to dig into seeds!

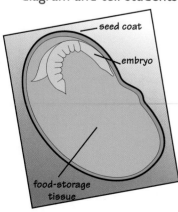

What a View!

Uncovering the different parts of plants is easy with this activity. To begin, explain to students that all plants have roots, stems, and leaves, although these parts may look different on different plants. Also share with students that many plants also have flowers and fruit. Then, to reinforce the different plant parts, have each student make a three-dimensional plant. To do this, a student staples the left edge of a 6" x 12" piece of brown construction paper to the bottom of a 12" x 18" sheet of drawing paper to resemble soil (as shown). Next she tightly rolls a 5" x 7" piece of green construction paper around her pencil and tapes it to prevent it from unrolling. She then carefully removes her pencil and glues the paper roll above the brown paper to create a stem. Next she folds back the brown paper and glues pieces of brown yarn to the bottom of the stem to create roots. Then she glues construction-paper leaves to the stem and uses tissue paper to create a flower as desired. To complete the project, she labels each part of the flower.

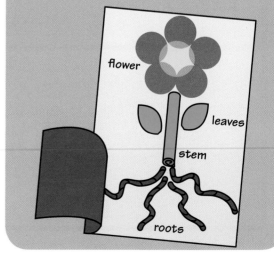

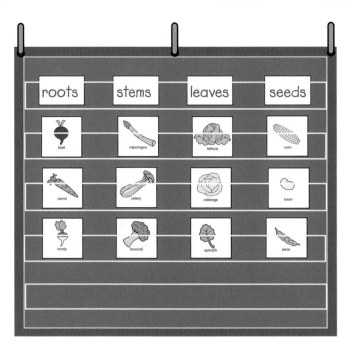

A Feast of Plant Parts

Students are sure to be surprised to learn that some vegetables they may eat are actually roots, stems, seeds, or leaves! Color and cut out a copy of the picture cards on page 182. Label each of four blank cards with a different plant part (roots, stems, leaves, seeds). Place each word card in the top row of a pocket chart. Hold up a picture card and help students determine whether the vegetable is a root, stem, leaf, or seed. Then invite a volunteer to place the card under the corresponding heading. Continue in the same manner for each remaining card. For a follow-up, have students cut out pictures of vegetables from grocery store circulars and sort them in a similar manner.

Watch It Grow!

To prepare for this booklet-making project, write the words *seed, roots, stem,* and *flower* on the board. After reviewing each word, give each child a copy of page 183 and two 4" x 5" construction paper covers. Guide each youngster in reading the booklet pages and completing each sentence with a word from the board. Then have her color, cut out, and sequence the pages.

To complete the booklet, staple the pages between the covers and invite her to title the booklet as desired.

Going Up

Stems support the leaves and flowers of plants. They also carry water and minerals up from the roots to the leaves. To demonstrate this concept, cut one-half inch off the bottom of a leafy celery stalk. Then slice the stalk in half lengthwise from the bottom to about halfway up toward the top. Tie or tape the stem at the halfway point to prevent further splitting. Then place one end of the stalk into a clear plastic cup containing water tinted with red food coloring. Place the other celery end in a similar cup containing regular water. Ask students to predict what will happen to each celery half. Then leave the celery stalks in the water overnight. The next day, check the celery and have your students discuss the changes they observe. (Half of the stalk will be colored red.) Then remove the stalks from the cups, and slice them into several short lengths. Have students use magnifying glasses to view the tiny transport tubes. Explain to students that these tubes carry minerals from the soil to the plant cells. This process provides the flowers and leaves with necessary nutrients. If desired, conclude the activity by serving each student a piece of fresh celery.

Picture Cards

Use with "A Feast of Plant Parts" on page 181.

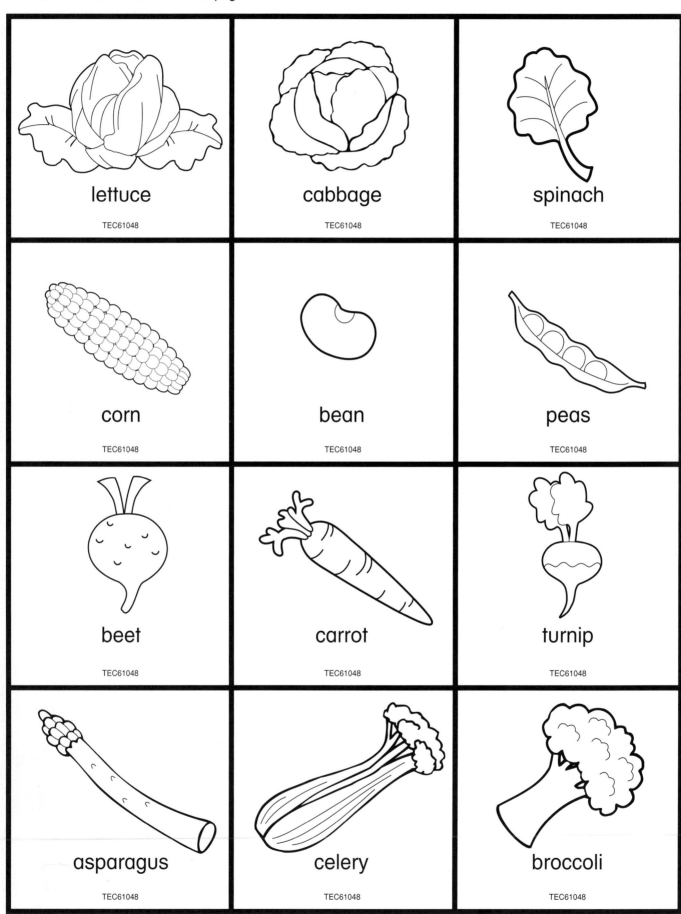

lettuce	cabbage	spinach
TEC61048	TEC61048	TEC61048
corn	bean	peas
TEC61048	TEC61048	TEC61048
beet	carrot	turnip
TEC61048	TEC61048	TEC61048
asparagus	celery	broccoli
TEC61048	TEC61048	TEC61048

Then the _____ grow down,
down, down.

2

blooms for _____

Last, a _____
you to pick!

4

First, a _____ is in the
ground.

1

©The Mailbox® • Superbook® • TEC61048

_____ grows tall

Next, a _____
and thick.

3

✫ Animals ✫

Animal Habitats

Discuss with students that animals need food, water, and cover to survive. Then make a student-generated list on the board of different animals and their habitats. Supply students with an assortment of construction paper, glue, and crayons. Instruct each student to use the materials to create an animal habitat by drawing and gluing animal pictures atop a construction paper habitat background. Collect the completed projects and display them on a wall or bulletin board with the title "Creative Habitats."

Take a Closer Look!

Youngsters' drawings are perfect for camouflaging these animals! To prepare, make several copies of the animal cards on page 186. Cut out the cards and discard the ones that picture animals that do not use camouflage as a defense. After a discussion on camouflaging, encourage each youngster to select an animal card. Have him draw his animal's habitat on a sheet of paper. Be sure to tell him that his animal needs to be able to be camouflaged in the scene. Then have him color, cut out, and glue his animal to his paper. Encourage him to add details as needed to help camouflage his animal. Finally, post students' completed habitats to create an out-of-sight display!

Animal Necessities

Students determine the needs of an animal with this whole-group activity. In advance, program cards with words from the list shown and stack the cards by your pocket chart. Label the pocket chart as shown to create two columns.

To begin, announce the name of an animal. (If desired, choose an animal from page 186 and display the card for youngsters to see.) Invite a youngster to take a word card, read the word aloud, and place the card in the correct column. Continue in this manner with other students until each card is in the chart. For additional practice, simply remove the cards, change the animal, and begin again.

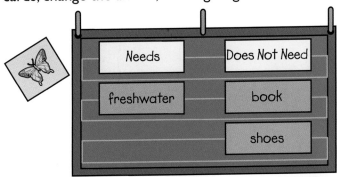

Needs	Does Not Need
freshwater	book
	shoes

food	clothes	Mom
freshwater	toys	shoes
saltwater	book	dirt
shelter	bath	nest
warmth	bed	cage

A Sorting Hoopla!

Challenge youngsters to sort animals by their characteristics. Color and cut out a copy of the animal cards on page 186. Then ask students to brainstorm animal characteristics. Write students' responses on 3" x 5" cards. (Some good characteristics to include are size, what they eat, where they live, number of legs, color, and body coverings.) Next, gather students in a circle. Arrange two plastic hoops on the floor to resemble a Venn diagram; then place a characteristic card at the top of each hoop. Have students take turns placing an animal card in the correct section on the diagram. If a card does not belong, it should be placed outside the circles. Continue the hoopla by changing the characteristics for a new round.

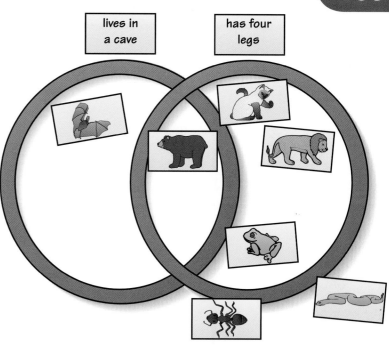

Guess What I Am

Have students demonstrate their knowledge about animals with this unique activity. Each child will need a large sheet of construction paper folded lengthwise into thirds, and a piece of writing paper one-third the size of the construction paper. Have each student choose a different animal and then write three clues about the animal on her writing paper. Each youngster then glues the clues to the bottom third of her construction paper and illustrates a picture of the animal in the middle. Next, she folds down the top third of her paper and adds the title "What Am I?" Provide time for students to share the clues with their classmates, revealing the picture when it is guessed correctly.

What Am I?

Chelsey

I am an insect.
I am red with black spots.
I have 2 pairs of wings.
What am I?

What a Change!

Students explore the life cycles of four different animals with this game! Color and cut out a copy of the life cycle cards on page 187. Mix up the cards and store them in a bag by your pocket chart. Label each of four rows on your chart with a different animal name: *butterfly, frog, bird,* and *spider*. Also number four columns to correspond to the different life cycle stages. To begin, invite a youngster to remove a card from the bag and place it in its corresponding location on the chart. Continue with more volunteers until each card is matched to the correct animal and is in sequential order!

Animal Cards

Use with "Take a Closer Look!" on page 184 and "A Sorting Hoopla!" on page 185.

TEC61048

TEC61048

TEC61048

TEC61048

TEC61048

TEC61048

TEC61048

TEC61048

TEC61048

TEC61048

TEC61048

TEC61048

TEC61048

TEC61048

TEC61048

TEC61048

TEC61048

TEC61048

TEC61048

TEC61048

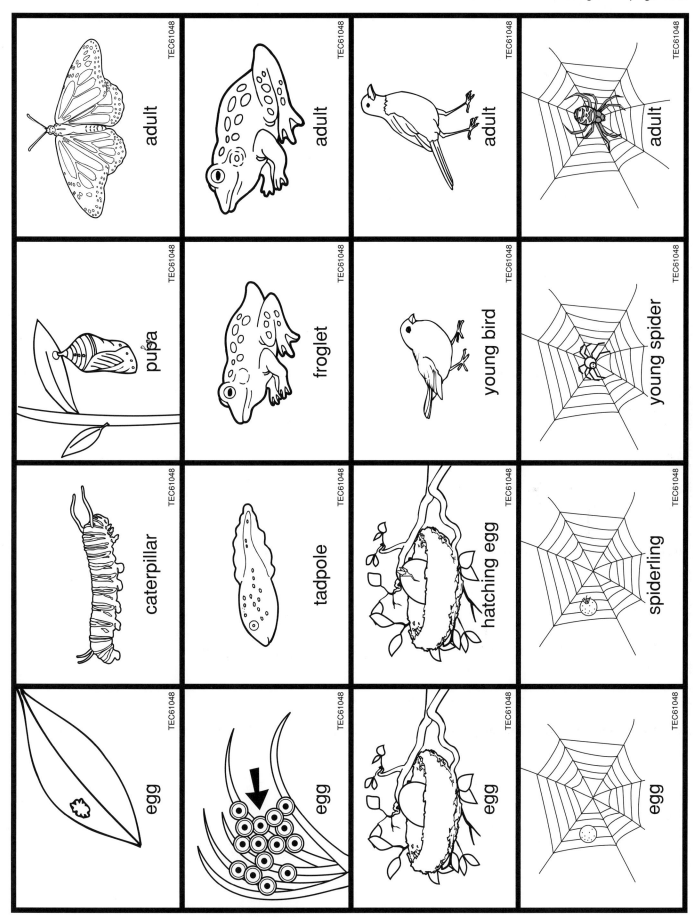

Seasons and Weather

A Booklet of All Seasons

These creative booklets are a fun review of the four seasons. Make four copies of one wallet-size photograph of every child. To make a booklet, a student trims his duplicated photos and glues each one to a separate sheet of paper. On each sheet, he draws a picture to represent a season, incorporating himself into the drawing. Next, he writes about each season. He staples the completed pages between two construction paper covers and adds a title, such as "[Student's name] Through the Seasons." If desired display the seasonal booklets at a reading center for all to enjoy.

I like to throw snowballs in winter.
It is cold.
My mom makes me hot chocolate.

bathing suit

Summer

Which Season?

Review the four seasons by involving youngsters in this hands-on game. Have each student color and cut apart a copy of the season cards on page 190. To play the game, announce a seasonal item or holiday, such as a rake, a snowman, or Mother's Day, and ask each student to hold up the corresponding season card(s). When necessary, involve students in a discussion of why more than one card may be held up for some of the items. For another variation, have a student volunteer announce the items for his classmates.

What's the Temperature?

To prepare this sorting center, cut out a copy of the thermometers on page 191 and glue each one to a separate sheet of tagboard. Then cut pictures from magazines or catalogs of appropriate clothing for each of the given temperatures. Store the pictures at a center along with the thermometers. A student visits the center and reads the temperature on each thermometer. Then she sorts each picture onto the corresponding thermometer. After each child has visited the center, enlist students' help to post the pictures with their thermometers.

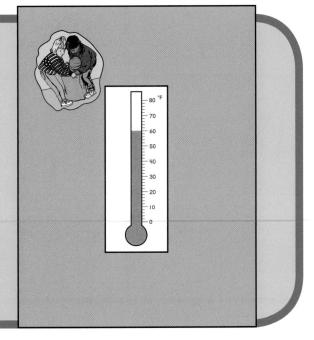

Hot, Hot, Hot!

This simple experiment shows students the effects of the sun's heat. Put several chocolate chips in each of two small pans. Find a shaded spot outside to place one pan and a spot in direct sunlight to place the other. After returning to the classroom, have students predict what will happen to the chocolate chips in each pan and record their responses on a chart as shown. After about 30 minutes, ask students to help you check the chips and share their observations. (Wait time may vary based on the day's temperature.) Lead youngsters to realize that the chips in the direct sunlight melted because of the heat from the sun. The chips in the shade had some of the sun's heat blocked; therefore, they were less likely to melt.

Predictions	
In Shade	In Sunshine
I think they will stay the same. Taryn	I think they will turn into blobs. Marsha

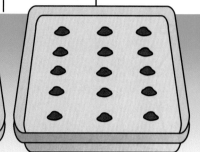

Wind Direction

Students will see from which direction the wind is blowing by using windsocks. Explain to students that the wind is named the direction from which it blows. For example, an east wind blows from east to west. To make a windsock, a student decorates a 6" x 18" strip of construction paper and then rolls it into a cylinder. Next he staples or glues the overlapping ends together. Then he glues colorful crepe paper strips inside the lower rim of the project. To prepare the project for hanging, punch two holes opposite one another near the top of the cylinder. Thread a length of yarn through the holes and tie it securely. To use the windsock, the student takes it outside and observes which way the streamers are blowing. If desired post cardinal directions outside so students can determine from which direction the wind is blowing.

Weather Watchers

Reinforce your youngsters' weather observation skills with this daily weather-watching activity. For each student, make five copies of the recording sheet on page 190; then stack the pages and staple them between two construction paper covers. Give a booklet to each student, and have him personalize the front cover with weather words and pictures. Each morning have students observe and discuss the weather and then record their observations on their recording sheets. For a fun follow-up, fill a box with articles of clothing for all possible types of weather conditions. Then have a student volunteer hold up examples of appropriate clothing for the day's weather.

Season Cards

Use with "Which Season?" on page 188.

 **Winter** TEC61048	**Spring** TEC61048
Summer TEC61048	**Fall** TEC61048

Name _____   Day _____

Time _____

1. The ☀ is ⃝ shining
   ⃝ not shining

2. I see 🌥 in the sky. ⃝ yes ⃝ no

3. The 🌡 reads _____°.

4. The temperature is
   ⃝ cold ⃝ cool ⃝ warm ⃝ hot

5. Today I will see 💧. ⃝ yes ⃝ no

6. Today I will see ❄. ⃝ yes ⃝ no

What's today's weather?

©The Mailbox® • Superbook® • TEC61048

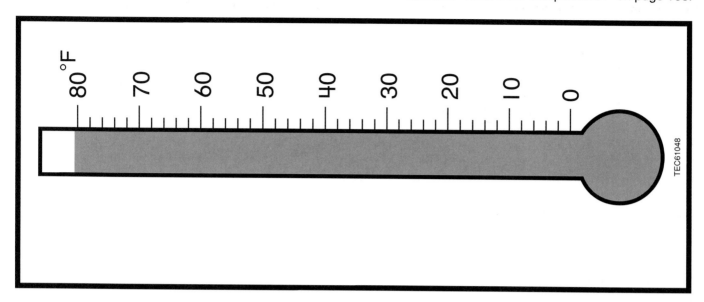

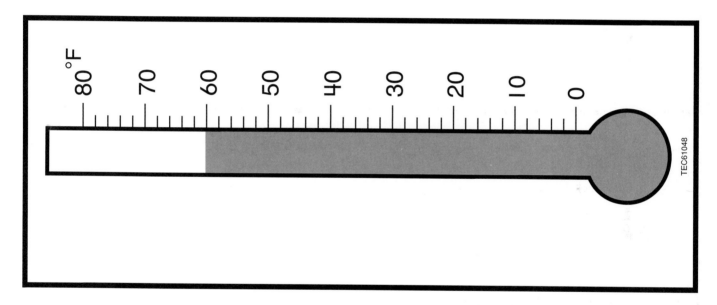

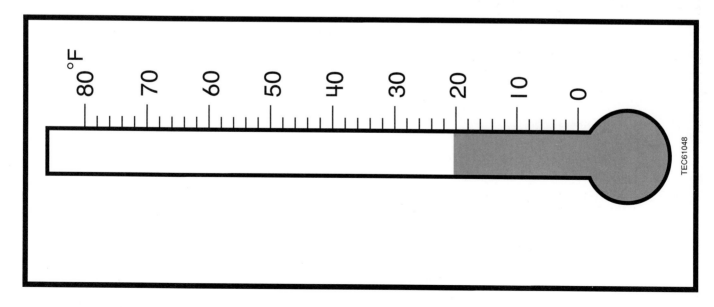

Rocks

A Rock Hunt

Introduce your first graders to the topic of rocks with a rock hunt. Provide each student with a plastic grocery bag (or shoebox) and a craft stick. Then, for homework, ask each student to use his materials to dig and collect seven to ten rocks. Set guidelines for the size of the rocks, such as smaller than the student's fist.

When the rocks have been brought to school, make sure each student's rock collection is labeled with his name. Next, divide a sheet of poster board into four columns. Title the columns *shape, color, texture,* and *luster;* then explain each property as it relates to rocks. Have students examine their rock collections and brainstorm descriptive rock words. List students' responses under the correct headings. Then mount the word collection on a classroom wall for students to refer to throughout your rock unit.

shape	color
flat round oval	brown black white

texture	luster
smooth bumpy jagged	shiny dull sparkly

Comparing Rocks

Now that your rock hounds have rounded up some rock vocabulary, it's time to put it to use! In advance, copy words from the poster created in "A Rock Hunt" onto sentence strips. Then use two plastic hoops to form a Venn diagram in an open area of your classroom. To begin the activity, have each student choose a rock from her rock collection and place a personalized piece of masking tape on it. Then gather students in a circle around the Venn diagram. Place a labeled sentence strip in each of the outer sections of the diagram. Have each student examine her rock and, in turn, place her rock in the correct category. Rocks that fall in both categories should be placed in the overlapping section of the two circles. Rocks that do not fall in either category should be placed outside of the circles. After each student has had a turn, return students' rocks and repeat the activity using different categories.

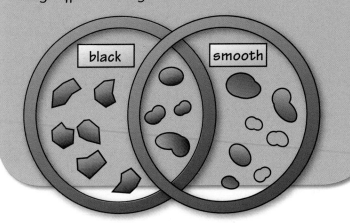

A Changed Rock

Help students discover how a metamorphic rock is formed with this hands-on activity. Give each child two balls of play dough in one color and one ball in another color. Working atop a waxed paper square, have each child gently press down on each of the three balls with the palm of his hand. Then instruct him to stack the play dough, alternating the colors. Explain that this model represents layers of a sedimentary rock. Next, have each child apply heavy pressure to the "rock" by repeatedly pressing down hard on all three layers. Then ask volunteers to describe how their "rocks" changed. Lead students to conclude that the pressure applied to the "rock" changed it into a metamorphic rock.

Check out the skill-building reproducible on page 193.

Rock Observations

✏️ Write.

I can draw my rocks.	What color are they? 🖍	Are they flat or round?	Are they rough or smooth?	Are they dull or shiny?
Sample	gray	flat	smooth	dull
Rock 1				
Rock 2				
Rock 3				

©The Mailbox® • Superbook® • TEC61048

Note to the teacher: Have each student or small group use three rocks to complete a copy of this page.

Matter

What Is Matter?

Help students better understand matter with this simple activity. Tell students that matter is anything that takes up space and has weight. Then have each student find three items in the classroom that are matter and illustrate them on a sheet of drawing paper. After students complete their drawings, invite each student to share his illustrations with the class. Lead students to the discovery that almost everything that can be seen and touched is matter.

book   pencil   desk

Matter Takes Up Space

This small-group activity shows students that two things can't be in the same space at the same time. Divide students into small groups; then provide each group with a permanent marker, a rock, and a plastic cup half-filled with water. Ask a student from each group to draw a line on his group's cup to mark the water level. (Be sure to remind students to take the readings from eye level.) Then have each group carefully place a rock in the cup (without letting any water splash out). Next, have another student in each group mark the new water level. Have the students in each group compare their two water levels. Conclude the activity by explaining to students that the water level increased because the rock is matter.

MARKO

Three States of Matter

Solid: Send students on a scavenger hunt for solids. Give each student a copy of page 195 and read the clues aloud. Challenge each student to find solids in the classroom with the given properties. Have her write the name of each solid or draw a picture of it in the space provided.

Liquid: Show students that a liquid has no shape of its own with this easy demonstration. Pour water into several different-sized containers. For each container, have a student volunteer draw on the board the shape of the water in the container. Guide students to understand that a liquid takes the shape of the container it is put in. Then, for a follow-up, write a student-generated list of different kinds of liquids on the board. Have students use the properties of matter to describe each liquid on the list.

Gas: This whole-group demonstration will help students understand that gases are matter, they cannot be seen, and they spread out to fill containers. To begin, gather a small paper lunch bag near the top and hold it so that there is only a small opening. Then blow into the bag to fill it with air. Use your hand to hold the opening of the bag shut as you lead students to understand that there is air in the bag and that it takes up space.

Solid Scavenger Hunt

Find a solid to match each clue.
Draw or write.

1. a solid that is heavy	2. a solid that is soft
3. a solid that is nonliving	4. a solid that is very small
5. a solid that can tear	6. a solid that can bend

SOUND

Sounds All Around

Here's a fun way to tune up students' observation skills. Invite each student to bring in a small household item with which he can make sounds, such as a set of measuring spoons or a piece of sandpaper. Ask students to sit in a circle with their items. Have each student, in turn, demonstrate his noisemaker and invite his classmates to describe the sound.

Next, instruct each youngster to place his item in the center of the circle. Ask students to cover their eyes. Make a sound with a chosen item and challenge students to identify it. Have students uncover their eyes; then reveal the item. To continue, ask students to cover their eyes again and make a different sound for them to identify.

Hear! Hear!

To prepare for this small-group activity, collect four empty plastic bottles with caps, such as shampoo bottles. If the bottles are not opaque, cover them with paper. Place each of the following groups of items in a different bottle: buttons, rice, pom-poms, and marbles. Cap the bottles and number them from 1 to 4. Give each student a copy of the recording sheet on page 197 and explain that each bottle contains one group of pictured items. Instruct each student to shake the first bottle, silently guess its contents, and then write her guess in the appropriate box on her paper. Instruct the youngsters to repeat the shaking and predicting process with the remaining bottles. Then have them open the bottles and record the actual contents.

Copycat Challenge

For this matching game, collect two identical sets of the school supplies listed to the right. Display one set of supplies. Then stand with the second set behind an easel or in a similar location so that students cannot see the supplies. To begin, make a sound with a concealed item as described. Invite a volunteer to imitate the sound with an item on display. After you reveal how you made the sound, ask the volunteer to take your role for more guessing fun.

School Supplies and Actions
construction paper (rip)
dice (toss)
crayons (roll)
scissors and paper (cut)
pencil (tap)
writing paper (rattle)

Sensational Sounds

Follow your teacher's directions.

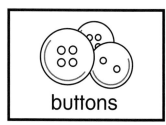

buttons

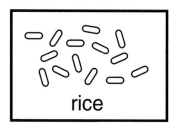

rice

pom-poms

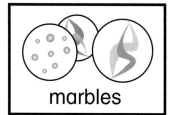

marbles

Bottles	Guesses	Answers
1		
2		
3		
4		

Dental Health

Inside a Tooth

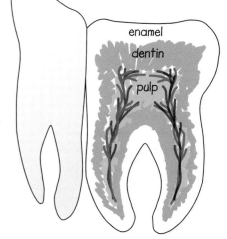

This activity gives students a look inside a tooth. To make a tooth-shaped project, each child folds a 12" x 18" sheet of white construction paper in half. Using the pattern on page 199 as a template, he places one side of the tooth pattern flush with the fold and traces around three sides of the shape. After cutting on the resulting outline, he opens his tooth shape and uses a pink crayon to color pulp in the center of the tooth. Next, he uses an orange crayon to color dentin around the pulp. Then he uses blue and red crayons to draw nerves and blood vessels in the pulp section of the tooth. Finally, he labels the enamel, the dentin, and the pulp sections.

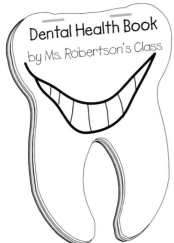

Dental Health Book
by Ms. Robertson's Class

Dental Health Class Book

This class book project gives students the opportunity to write about good dental health practices. Make a class supply plus one extra of the pattern on page 199. Invite students to help brainstorm a list of things involved in maintaining good dental health. Encourage each youngster to choose a different idea from the list to write and illustrate on her tooth pattern. After she is finished writing, have her cut out her pattern. Once all of the pages are complete, prepare a cover similar to the one shown. Stack the pages behind the cover and staple them to finish the class book.

Brush, Brush!

Guide students to understand the importance of brushing to help keep sugar from making cavities with this nifty demonstration. In advance, hard-boil two eggs. To begin the demonstration, place one egg in a container of water and one egg in a container of cola. Set the eggs aside. The next day, remove the eggs and compare them. Students will observe that the egg from the container of cola is stained but the other egg has retained its appearance. To extend the activity, use a toothbrush and toothpaste to remove the stain from the tainted egg. Conclude the activity by reminding students that proper toothbrushing helps to keep stains from forming on teeth.

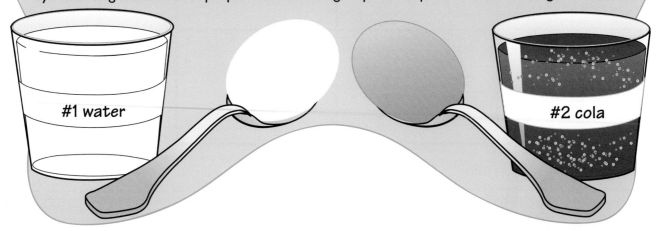

#1 water

#2 cola

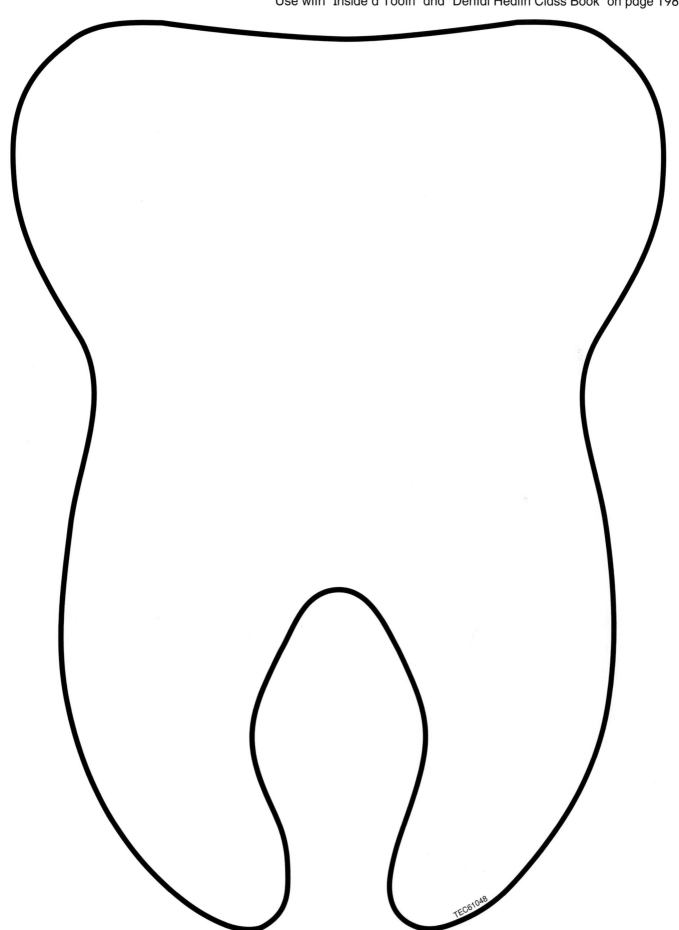

TEC61048

NUTRITION

Great Groups

This pocket chart activity is a perfect introduction to the five food groups. To prepare, cut out a copy of the food group cards on page 201. Cut out several pictures of foods from grocery store sales circulars, being sure to include foods from each food group. Glue the pictures and cards on tagboard for durability. Then place each food group card in a different row of a pocket chart and set the pictures nearby.

To begin, read each displayed card, in turn, and identify the examples pictured on the card. Next, have a volunteer take a picture and name the food. Then have him point to each displayed card, in turn, pausing for his classmates to give a thumbs-up if they think the food is in the corresponding group or a thumbs-down if they do not think it is in that group. Confirm the correct group and have the volunteer place the picture in the corresponding row. Continue as described until all of the pictures are displayed.

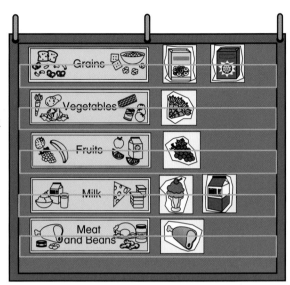

SNACK SORTING

Reinforce your youngsters' knowledge of healthful snacks with this sorting activity. Remind students of the importance of choosing snacks that are low in sugar and fat, such as fruits and vegetables. Place a large grocery bag labeled "Healthful Snacks" and another bag labeled "Low-Nutrition Snacks" in a prominent location. Ask students to bring to school empty snack packages or pictures of snack-food items. Have students place their packages or pictures in the appropriate grocery bags. Then check the contents of each bag with students and discuss the nutritional value of each healthful snack.

Magnificent Meals

Let your future restaurateurs plan nutritionally sound meals! In advance, create a chart showing the recommended servings for each food group. To begin, divide students into groups of three. Provide each group with three paper plates and a supply of old magazines or grocery store sale's circulars. Challenge each group of students to cut out pictures of food and glue them to the paper plates to create three well-balanced meals—breakfast, lunch, and dinner. Remind each group to refer to the chart in planning its meals. After the groups have created their meals, invite one group at a time to share its work.

 # Grains

TEC61048

 # Vegetables

TEC61048

 # Fruits

TEC61048

 # Milk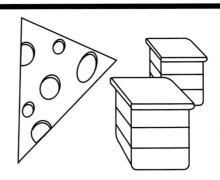

TEC61048

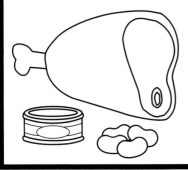 # Meat and Beans

TEC61048

My Family and Me!

Here We Are!

Here's a unique art project that helps kids get to know one another. Provide each student with a small paper plate on which she draws her face. The student then introduces herself by drawing her hobbies, family, interests, and other favorites on a sheet of paper. To complete the project, she uses art materials to add arms, legs, and hair. Mount these "students" on your classroom walls for everyone to meet!

What's Your Favorite?

Help students discover that because of their similarities they have plenty in common and because of their differences they have a lot to offer each other. Make a class supply of page 204. Ask each child to complete the "My Favorite" column independently; then compare the results classwide for an overall view of your students' interests. Have students record the class similarities on their papers. If something is found to be a favorite of many, celebrate by featuring it in your classroom.

Jason

ME TREE

These handy creations will help students learn about and appreciate their special traits and abilities. Have each child trace his hand and forearm on a sheet of brown construction paper; then have him cut out the shape and glue it onto a sheet of light-colored construction paper to resemble a tree. Next, have students cut pictures from old magazines that depict their likes and interests. These cuttings become the leaves for each child's tree as they are glued in place. Display these special sprouts on a classroom wall and encourage students to compare their favorite things.

Pops — August 30, 1945

Daddy — May 10, 1972

Mommy — February 9, 1973

Brittany — January 2, 1999

Me — May 28, 2001

All in Line!

Youngsters showcase the birth order of their family members with this timely idea. In advance, send home a note asking parents to write down the names, birthdays, and birth years of each family member. After receiving the information, have each student draw a picture of each family member on a separate blank card. Then have her label each card with the name and birthday of the family member. Next, help each child sequence her cards from oldest to youngest and glue them to a long tagboard strip. Invite students to share their resulting timelines with the class.

Family Flags

These family flags serve as symbols of your youngsters' families. Have each student draw on a sheet of paper a picture of her family and then write a sentence explaining what makes her family great. Mount each resulting flag on a slightly larger sheet of colorful construction paper. Then add a poster board pole. Display the flags for all to see before sending them home with your students.

Dad Mom

Owen Me

The Lassiter Family helps each other.

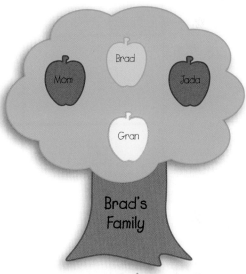

Brad

Mom Jada

Gran

Brad's Family

Branching Out

Who are the people in your students' families? Find out with this family tree project! Give each child a small apple cutout for each member of his immediate family and one for himself. Ask him to write the name of a different family member on each apple. Then direct each student to glue the apples onto a sheet of green construction paper and trim a treetop shape around them. Next, have him personalize a brown construction paper tree trunk and glue it to his treetop. Display the completed trees together with the title "Our Family Orchard."

Check out the skill-building reproducible on page 205.

What's Your Favorite?

Write your favorites.
Compare with your classmates.
Tally how many like the same.

	My Favorite	How Many Others Like It?
Animal		
Book		
Color		
Number		
Food		
Song		
Sport		
Subject		

©The Mailbox® • Superbook® • TEC61048

All About _____

I am _____ years old.

My birthday is _____.

My favorite foods are…

My favorite color is

_____.

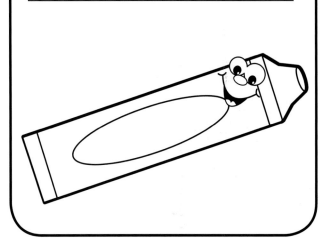

This is my family and me!

- -

Note to the teacher: Give each child a copy. Have her write her name at the top of the page and complete each sentence. Display the completed papers with the title "Read All About Us!"

Economics & Community

Needs and Wants

Here's an activity that will really hit home with your students and will open a discussion about needs and wants. Give each child a sheet of paper and ask him to fold it in half. Instruct him to place the fold on the left side and draw two lines as shown. Then have him cut on the lines (through both layers) to form a house shape. After each child decorates the front of his house with crayons, ask him to unfold his paper and draw pictures of items that he actually has in his home. Encourage him to include items from different rooms in his home. After each child has drawn several items, discuss the difference between a want and a need. Ask students to circle their needs with a red crayon; then have them circle all their wants with a blue crayon. Have several volunteers share items from each of the categories to complete your discussion.

A Dynamic Display

The results of this activity will help students see the difference between wants and needs. In advance, divide a large sheet of bulletin board paper into two halves. Label one half "Wants" and the other half "Needs." Then mount the chart on a classroom wall. To begin, have each child cut out from unneeded magazines five pictures that interest her. Next, ask student volunteers, one at a time, to glue each cutout onto the chart in its appropriate category. Leave the display in your classroom throughout your study of wants and needs for a quick visual reminder.

Wants | Needs

Mystery Community Member

This fun guessing game helps students learn who's who in their community. Have each child draw and color a picture of a community helper on a 9" x 12" sheet of construction paper. On a large index card, have the student write three clues about the helper he drew. Instruct each child to fold the construction paper in half. With the fold at the top, ask him to glue his clue card to the larger folded sheet as shown. In turn, ask each student to share his clues while the remaining students try to determine the helper's identity. If desired, display each drawing on a wall outside your classroom so other students can have fun guessing too.

This person uses water.

This person wears a special uniform.

This person saves lives.

Firefighter

Good or Service?

To prepare for this whole-group activity, gather a supply of advertisements that include a variety of goods and services. Consider using the classified ads from your local newspaper. After reviewing the definitions of *good* and *service* with your students, read aloud one of the advertisements. Have students decide whether the advertisement is for a good or a service and discuss the reasons why. Repeat with several ads, making sure to include a few examples of both goods and services. If desired, have each student complete a copy of page 208 for additional skill practice.

Everyone's Important

Emphasize to your class that the key to a *community,* a group of neighborhoods, is people who live there working together. To help students appreciate all the components of a community, have them imagine a community with something (or someone) missing. For example, ask students what it would be like if there weren't a grocery store in their community. How would it change their daily routines? Repeat the question several times—taking away a different entity each time. What would it be like without any police officers? How would life change without a gas station? Students will soon see the importance of every part of a community through this valuable discussion.

Check out the skill-building reproducibles on pages 208 and 209.

A BUSY DAY

Monkey will pay for some goods and services.
Read the list.

Color each box by the code.

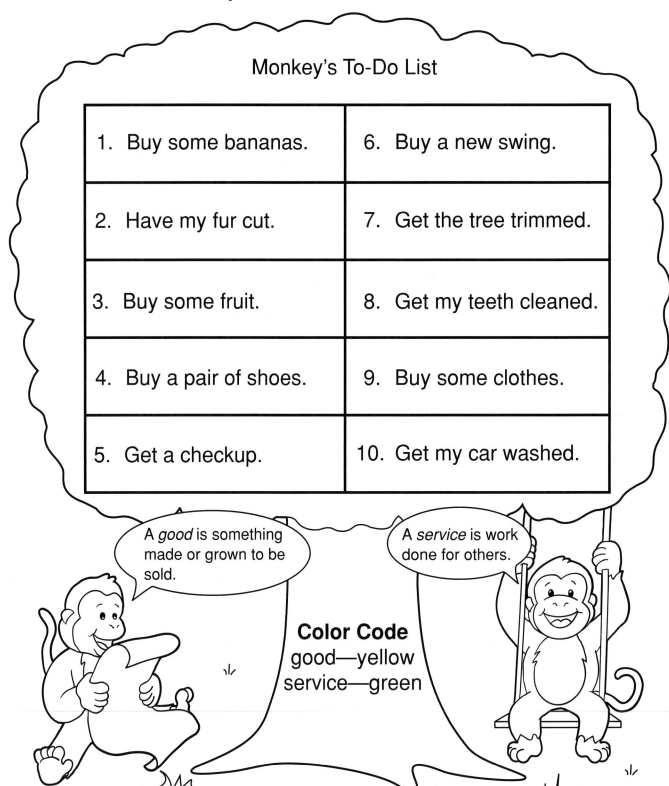

Monkey's To-Do List

1. Buy some bananas.	6. Buy a new swing.
2. Have my fur cut.	7. Get the tree trimmed.
3. Buy some fruit.	8. Get my teeth cleaned.
4. Buy a pair of shoes.	9. Buy some clothes.
5. Get a checkup.	10. Get my car washed.

A *good* is something made or grown to be sold.

A *service* is work done for others.

Color Code
good—yellow
service—green

Cheese, Please!

✏️ Draw pictures to show a producer and a consumer.

✏️ Write to tell about each picture.

A producer makes goods or does a service.

A consumer buys goods and services.

Producer	**Consumer**

_____

_____

_____

_____

Map Skills

Cardinal Clues

Help students remember the order of the cardinal directions on a compass rose with this clever phrase. Beginning at north and moving clockwise, point to each direction as you say, "**N**ever **E**at **S**oggy **W**affles." To practice this memory aid, have students make several sets of intersecting lines on a sheet of paper, and then have them fill in the cardinal directions on each to create a compass rose. Have them repeat the sentence aloud as they fill in the directional symbols. Before long students will have no trouble remembering where each direction belongs. If desired, have students complete a copy of page 213 for additional skill practice.

Map Maneuvering

Students will enjoy creating their own maps to use with this nifty activity. Provide each child with a sheet of graph paper that has two-inch squares. Ask him to create a map by adding symbols as desired. When the maps are complete, pair students for some map maneuvering. Have students in each pair exchange maps and ask each other questions about finding their way on the maps. For example, one child might ask how to get to the grocery store from the gas station. The person reading the map might respond, "Go two blocks north and three blocks east." No doubt your youngsters will have fun maneuvering their way around these maps!

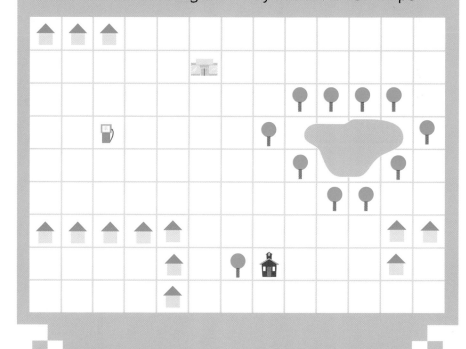

Bird's-Eye View

To explain how a map is viewed, try this discovery activity. In advance, arrange several objects from your desk on a serving tray. Give each student two sheets of white paper. Place the tray on a table where students can view it and ask each student to draw one of the items. Now place the tray on the floor next to the table. Ask students if they think their objects will look different from this view. Then display several maps to show that they are viewed as if you were a bird looking down. Next, have students, in turn, stand next to the tray and look down onto it. While each student is viewing the tray from above, have him draw his object again on the other sheet of paper. When all the drawings are complete, post each child's pair of drawings on a bulletin board titled "Which Ones Are From a Bird's-Eye View?"

That's the Key!

Try this fun activity to teach your students how to make a map key. Explain that a *map key* is a list that explains the symbols on a map, and a *symbol* is a simple drawing that represents an actual object. With notebooks and pencils in hand, take your youngsters on a tour of your school and school grounds. Ask each student to create symbols of particular objects you point out, such as a chair, a computer, a sidewalk, or a slide. When you return to your classroom, create a map key on a sheet of poster board using your students' suggestions. Have students use the key for future mapmaking activities.

Map Key

chair = ⊢

desk = ▭

slide =

tree = △

computer =

Key Cards

Reinforce the use of map symbols with this easy-to-make matching game. Take photographs of several things in your neighborhood, such as a road, bridge, tree, and fire station. Glue each photo onto a colored 5" × 7" card. Show each photo to your class and ask them to help you design a simple symbol for that landmark. Draw each symbol on a white 5" × 7" card. When each photographed place or object has a matching symbol card, place the cards at a center. Then have pairs of students play a game of Memory using the cards. With all the cards facedown, a child draws one colored card and one white card in search of a match. If the cards match, she keeps them. If the cards do not match, she turns them back over. The game continues until all the cards are matched.

Student Room Arrangements

Students will jump at this chance to rearrange the classroom. In advance, make several copies of the classroom symbols on page 212. Then cut them apart, sort them, and place them in a central location. Next, divide your class into four or five small groups and give each group a sheet of paper. Tell students in each group that they are to work together to decide on a new arrangement for the classroom. (Remind students of the things that can't be moved from their current locations.) Using the classroom symbol cards, have each group glue the cards onto the paper to achieve the desired room arrangement. If desired, help each group arrange the room according to its design for one day.

Check out the skill-building reproducible on page 213.

Classroom Symbols
Use with "Student Room Arrangements" on page 211.

desk	desk	desk	desk	desk	desk	desk	desk	desk	desk
desk	desk	desk	desk	desk	desk	desk	desk	desk	desk
							desk	desk	desk
							desk	desk	desk

table

bookshelf

window

window

board

ABC

teacher's desk

TEC61048

table

door

door

bookshelf

window

window

board

ABC

Name _____

Getting Around the Campground

Look at the map.
Answer the questions.

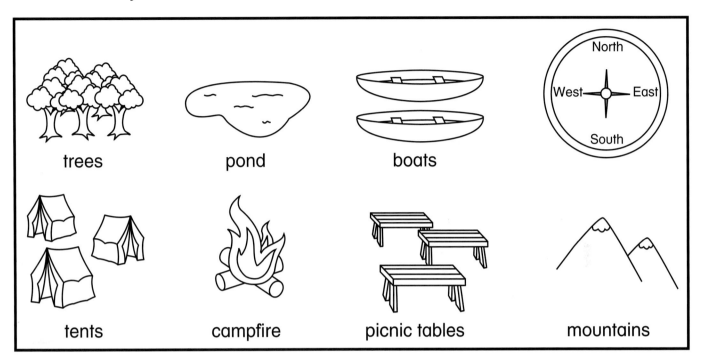

trees   pond   boats

tents   campfire   picnic tables   mountains

1. What is **south** of the pond? _____

2. What is **east** of the pond? _____

3. What is **south** of the boats? _____

4. What is **north** of the tents? _____

5. What is **north** of the campfire? _____

6. What is **west** of the campfire? _____

7. What is **south** of the trees? _____

8. What is **east** of the picnic tables? _____

United States Symbols

A NATIONAL SYMBOL

When the bald eagle was chosen as a symbol of America long ago, it did not make everyone happy. Other suggestions for our national symbol included the turkey and the rattlesnake. After sharing this information with your students, have each youngster draw her suggestion for a national symbol on a sheet of drawing paper. On the back of the paper, have her write a sentence explaining why she chose this symbol. Then compile and bind the completed projects into a class book titled "Other Ideas for Our National Symbol."

Patriotic Display

This proud replica of our nation's flag will beat all others—hands down! Ask each child to trace his hand onto red, white, and blue construction paper several times. After your students cut out their handprints, have them sort them into piles by color. On a large sheet of white bulletin board paper, draw a rectangle in the top left corner to represent the flag field. Assist students in gluing the blue hand shapes onto the rectangle. Then have students glue the red and white hand shapes in rows to create the flag's stripes. Complete the design by adding 50 white star cutouts or star stickers to the blue section. Display the resulting flag in the hallway or school lobby for all to see.

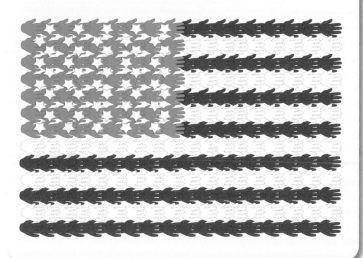

Life-Size Lady Liberty

Give your students a firsthand look at the Statue of Liberty's size with this small-group activity. In advance, write each feature and its corresponding measurement from the list shown on a separate index card. To begin, explain that the Statue of Liberty is one of the largest statues ever built and stands 151 feet 1 inch tall at the entrance to New York Harbor. Then give each group one of the index cards, a roll of masking tape, and a yardstick. Take students outside or to an open indoor area. Then help each group use the yardstick to measure the length, width, or height of the feature listed on its card and mark the dimension on the floor with pieces of masking tape. Next, direct each group to tape its index card to its feature. Once the activity is complete, lead the class in a viewing of all of the enormous features!

Approximate Measurements	
Width of an eye:	2 feet 6 inches
Length of nose:	4 feet 6 inches
Width of mouth:	3 feet
Length of forefinger:	8 feet
Length of hand:	16 feet 5 inches
Height of torch:	21 feet

Check out the skill-building reproducible on page 215.

United States Symbols

Read.

Cut out the symbols.

Glue to match.

Our country has many symbols. Our  has

stars and stripes on it. We say the  each day

at school. The  is where our president lives.

Our national bird is the  . The

stands for freedom.

©The Mailbox® • Superbook® • TEC61048

Pledge of Allegiance

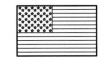

White House

flag

bald eagle

Statue of Liberty

Constitution Day

Constitution Day, celebrated annually on September 17, marks the anniversary of the day in 1787 when delegates completed and signed the United States Constitution.

A Class of Citizens

Under the Constitution, United States citizens have many rights and responsibilities. Explain to youngsters that a right is a freedom that you have and a responsibility is something you should do. Then ask students to name different rights and responsibilities that they have as citizens of a classroom. Write their responses on a chart similar to the one shown. Next, invite each student to draw a self-portrait on a sheet of paper and use red, white, and blue paper squares to create a frame. Display the completed portraits with the chart and add the title "We Are First-Grade Citizens!"

Rights	Responsibilities
We can choose our lunch from the cafeteria.	We should keep the room clean.
We can read a lot of different books.	We should do our best work.

We the Students

Ask students what the classroom would be like without rules. Then explain that the U.S. Constitution is like a list of guidelines for the leaders and citizens of the United States. On a sheet of bulletin board paper, write a student-generated list of classroom rules for the students and the teacher. Next, ball up the paper and flatten it out to resemble a tattered scroll. Invite each child to use a pen with a feather attached to it to sign her name on the bottom of the paper. When all youngsters have signed, explain how this classroom document is similar to the Constitution. *(They both provide guidelines to follow and have signatures of the members who created the document.)*

We will raise our hands when we have questions.
We will always listen when others talk.
We will do our best work.
We will not hit other people.
The teacher will give everyone a turn.
The teacher will treat everyone equally.
Lisa Gerri Joanna Sammy Kurt Tyrone Ms. Jones

Right On!

Celebrate the freedoms that U.S. citizens are guaranteed under the Constitution with this idea! After discussing the many rights and privileges American citizens have, give each child a sheet of construction paper. Have him write about a privilege that he feels is important; then have him add a corresponding illustration. Display students' completed papers with the title "We Have Rights!"

Check out the skill-building reproducible on page 217.

Celebrating Citizens

 Cut. Read each sentence.

Glue to match each sentence to a picture.

| She is voting. | He is making a speech. |
| They are holding flags. | They are going to church. |

CENTERS

Where Is Everybody?

Try these easy ideas to keep tabs on which students have visited a center.

- Each week create a simple chart, similar to the one shown, for students to refer to daily. Reprogram the chart each week or at the beginning of the center rotation cycle.

Center Schedule	Mary, Sue Paul, Mike	Amy, Jane, Harry, John	Gina, Rachel, Bob, David	Wendy, Joe, Rose, Roger
Monday	math	writing	spelling	language
Tuesday	writing	language	art	spelling
Wednesday	language	art	math	writing
Thursday	art	spelling	writing	math
Friday	spelling	math	language	art

- To allow students independence in choosing their centers, use a pocket chart and personalized cards to create a chart similar to the one shown. When it is time for centers, have each student place his card in the column of the center he would like to attend. Be sure to set a limit on the number of students allowed at each center.

Centers, Centers, Everywhere!

Need more room for your classroom centers? Then try these ideas for making the most of unused space.

- Place a chart stand between two desks as shown. On each side of the chart stand, suspend a poster labeled with directions. Students can sit on either side of the chart stand and complete a center activity. Changing the centers is as simple as changing the posters.

- Place a strip of magnetic tape on the back of a learning center; then stick the center onto the side of your file cabinet and place the necessary materials nearby.

- Convert a paint easel to divide a room. Suspend a center task on the easel.

- Cut off the top, the bottom, and one side of a large box to create a center area. Desks can also be placed around the outside of the box for additional centers.

Picture-Perfect Writing

If you enjoy taking photographs, here's an easy way to provide your budding authors with loads of writing inspiration! Mount several snapshots on individual pieces of construction paper; then exhibit five or six photos at a center. (Save the rest of the mounted photos for later use.) Have each student write a story about her favorite snapshot or create a dialogue between the members of the picture. Encourage students to share their writings with the class. When desired, just replace the existing photos at the center and you have a brand-new writing center! **Writing**

Open-Ended Gameboard

Make your own board games for students with this nifty idea. Copy the gameboard pattern on page 222 onto tagboard. Add a clever title to the front of the gameboard and the directions with a skill to practice on the back. Program the spaces with vocabulary words, sight words, or curriculum-focused questions; then laminate the board for durability. Place the gameboard, a die, and game markers at a center for student use. Skill review

Alphabet Soup

Warm up to beginning letters with a bowl of alphabet soup. To prepare, cut 26 elbow noodle shapes from tan construction paper. Program each cutout with a different letter of the alphabet; then laminate them if desired. Attach an adhesive-backed magnet strip to the back of each noodle; then store the noodles in a bowl. Place the bowl, a metal spoon, and a class supply of recording sheets, like the one shown, at a center.

To use this center, a child places a spoon in the bowl to attract a magnetized noodle. He reads the letter on the noodle and then writes four words on his recording sheet that begin with the letter. The student continues in this manner to complete his sheet. Initial consonants

Matthew

Write the letters you chose in each soup bowl.
Write four words that start with each letter.

s	sit	so
	see	sock
d	dog	dig
	dish	Dan
h	he	hat
	hide	hammer
c		
f		

Book Jackets

Just as a book's jacket gives a reader information about the story, these student-made book jackets showcase youngsters' favorite parts of stories! To make one, a child folds the two ends of a horizontally positioned 9" x 12" sheet of paper so they meet in the middle, making two flaps. Then he folds down the top corners of the flaps to resemble a jacket collar as shown. Next, he writes the book's title and author on the outside of the jacket and writes or illustrates a favorite part of the story on the inside. If desired, clip the completed jackets on a clothesline near the reading center and encourage youngsters to refer to the display before choosing a book to read.
Responding to literature

First-Class Contractions

To prepare, write a different contraction on each of several envelopes. If desired, add a decorative sticker to resemble a stamp on each envelope. Write each contraction's two words on separate blank cards. Also prepare an answer key. Place the cards, the envelopes, and the answer key at a center. A child sorts the cards into the corresponding envelopes. Then she opens each envelope and checks her work with the answer key. **Contractions**

Grade-A Words

Serve up some decoding practice at this "eggs-cellent" center! To prepare, cut out a supply of yellow construction paper circles (yolks) and label each one with a different onset. Also cut out three white paper egg whites and label each one with a different rime. Place the egg cutouts, copies of the recording sheet on page 223, and a highlighter at a center. A child chooses an egg white and copies the rime onto the first column of a recording sheet. Then she places a yolk on the egg white to form a word. She reads the word and writes it on her recording sheet. Once the column is complete, she reads each word again and highlights the real words. She continues in the same way for each remaining rime. **Onsets and rimes**

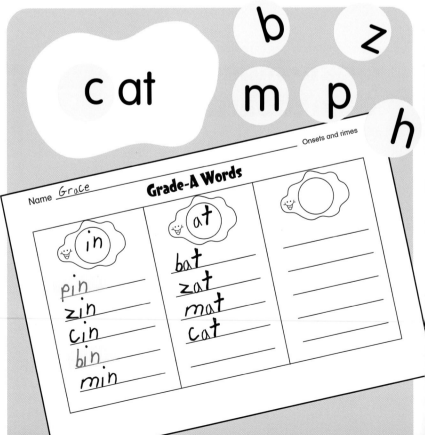

Three in a Row

This versatile center allows for up to four students to practice identifying beginning sounds or vowels! After choosing the desired skill, cut out a copy of the picture cards on page 223 and label the back of each card for self-checking. Visually divide each of four tagboard strips into ten sections. Then program each strip with a different arrangement of letters to correspond with the picture cards.

Place the cards picture-side up at a center along with the game strips and a supply of game markers. A player chooses a card and names the picture. After the other players identify the appropriate sound, she flips the card over to check their responses. Then each child covers the corresponding space on her game strip. Play continues in the same way until one child covers three letters in a row. **Beginning sounds or vowels**

Hands Down!

Youngsters get their hands on punctuation practice with this small-group center! To prepare, program each of four 12" tagboard strips with ending punctuation marks as shown. Cut out a copy of the sentence cards on page 224 and program the back of each card for self-checking. Place the cards and strips at a center. Arrange for two to four students to visit the center. To play, one player reads a sentence card aloud. Then each child places his hand on the corresponding punctuation mark on his strip. Next, the reader flips the card over and announces the answer. After players check their answers, a different child becomes the reader for the next round of play. *Ending punctuation*

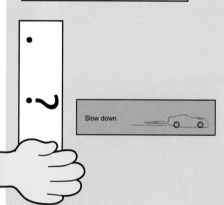

Slow down

Super Sleuths

Invite your young private eyes to visit this center to unravel the mystery of capitalization rules! On each of several paper strips, write a different sentence, omitting capitalization. Then prepare an answer key with the correct capitalization. Place the answer key, strips, and an ink pad at a center stocked with writing paper and pencils. A youngster chooses a strip, reads the sentence, and copies it on her paper using proper capitalization. Then she makes a fingerprint over each mistake she corrected and checks her work using the answer key. She continues in the same manner as time allows. **Capitalization**

tim walked home on monday.

jan went to new york city.

Felicia

Tim walked home on Monday.

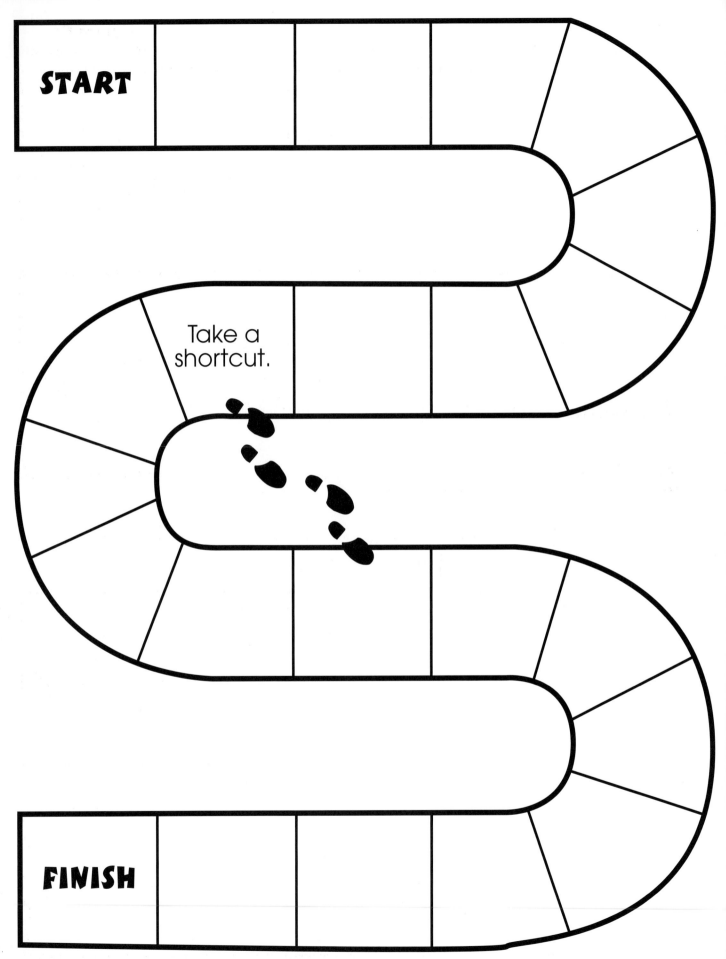

START

Take a
shortcut.

FINISH

Note to the teacher: Use with "Open-Ended Gameboard" on page 219.

Name _____ Onsets and rimes

Grade-A Words

Sentence Cards

Use with "Hands Down!" on page 221.

He wears a big hat	The dog has a bone
Two mice eat cheese	The sun is hot
Where is the bike	Do you see the bird
May I have a cookie	Is the girl sad
Look out for the ball	Boy, this is fun
Pizza is the best food	Slow down

TEC61048

MATH Centers

Racing Order

Youngsters start their engines and practice ordering numbers at this center! Add details to a long strip of black bulletin board paper to resemble a racetrack. Label each of several colorful racecar cutouts (patterns on page 228) with different numbers. Place the cars, racetrack, and a hundred chart at a center. A child randomly chooses five cars and places them in numerical order on the racetrack. After verifying his placement by referring to the hundred chart, he removes the cars and chooses five more to play again. **Number order**

Dozens of Doughnuts

Invite your young bakers to help make and pattern doughnuts. In advance, cut out a class supply of brown construction paper circles to resemble doughnuts. Divide your class into three groups and direct each group to decorate its doughnuts using a different art material. Consider materials such as glitter (sugar), puffy paint (frosting), and confetti (sprinkles). When the doughnuts are dry, place them at a center along with a plastic spatula. When a pair of youngsters visits the center, one child uses the spatula to make a doughnut pattern; then the other child extends it. After the pair reads the pattern, they switch roles to create a different pattern. Patterns

Collecting Spots

Pairs of youngsters give ladybugs their spots when they visit this center! Cut out two construction paper copies of the ladybug pattern on page 228. Place the cutouts at a center along with two dice and a supply of black pom-poms (or black paper circles). When a pair of students visits the center, one player rolls the dice and places the matching number of pom-poms on her ladybug. The other child takes a turn in the same manner. Next, each child announces the amount of spots on her ladybug; then they decide which bug has more or fewer spots. To play another round, youngsters remove the spots and roll the dice again. **Comparing numbers**

I have more!

A Shopping Spree

Cut pictures of kid-pleasing items from old magazines. Glue the pictures to the inside of a file folder. Label the pictures with prices; then decorate the front of the folder. Place the folder at a center with a supply of imitation coins. A student counts out and places a matching amount of coins on each item. Check student work or provide an answer key listing possible coin combinations for each item. **Counting coins**

A Handful of Estimation

Reinforce estimating and counting skills at this hands-on center. To begin, fill or partially fill several disposable bowls each with a different item that is suitable for estimating and counting. Label each bowl; then place the bowls at a center along with a supply of recording sheets like the one shown. A student chooses a bowl; then he estimates the number of items he could pick up in a handful and records his estimate. Next he takes a handful of the items and counts them. After recording his count, he places the items back in the bowl. The student repeats this procedure for each of the remaining bowls. When all students have completed the center, simply empty the bowls; then refill the bowls as desired and relabel them accordingly. **Estimating**

Name Alex

Item	Estimate	Count
links	20	25
bears	13	7

Fish Measurement

This colorful center can easily be tailored to meet your youngsters' measurement needs. Cut out an assortment of colorful construction paper fish in various lengths. Number each fish; then make an answer key by programming an index card with each fish's length. Place the fish, measuring tools, and the answer key at a center. A student measures each of the fish and records his answers on a sheet of paper. Then he checks his work using the answer key. **Measurement**

Shapes in a Row

To prepare, cut out ten different shapes from colorful construction paper. Program ten blank cards each with a different ordinal number from *first* through *tenth.* Place the cards, cutouts, and ten game markers at a center. A child arranges the cutouts in a horizontal line. Then he chooses a card, places a marker on the corresponding cutout, and announces the shape. He continues in the same manner for each remaining card. Then he removes the markers and rearranges the shapes to play again. **Ordinal numbers**

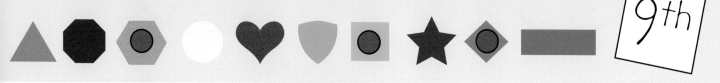

Scoop and Graph

How many cubes are there in all?

Which color has the most?

Which color has the fewest?

How many red and yellow cubes are there in all?

Scoop and Graph

Unifix cubes make this center a snap to prepare! Place at a center a supply of Unifix cubes in a tub and a large scoop. Also post a list of questions, similar to the ones shown, nearby. A student uses the scoop to remove several cubes. Then he sorts the cubes by color and connects each set. To complete the activity, he places the resulting towers side by side and answers the questions. **Graphing**

Shower-Curtain Gameboards

Plastic shower-curtain liners paired with beanbags make great manipulative centers! Use a permanent marker to visually divide a liner into equal-size sections; then program each section with a math fact. Place the resulting gameboard and a bean bag at a center. Students take turns tossing a beanbag onto the gameboard and determining the answer. If desired, program the liner to review other math skills. Math facts

$1 + 2 =$	$5 - 3 =$	$2 + 4 =$	$1 + 3 =$	$4 - 1 =$
$3 + 3 =$	$2 - 1 =$	$6 + 1 =$	$3 + 4 =$	$5 - 2 =$

Racecar Patterns

Use with "Racing Order" on page 225 and "Ready, Set, Read!" on page 230.

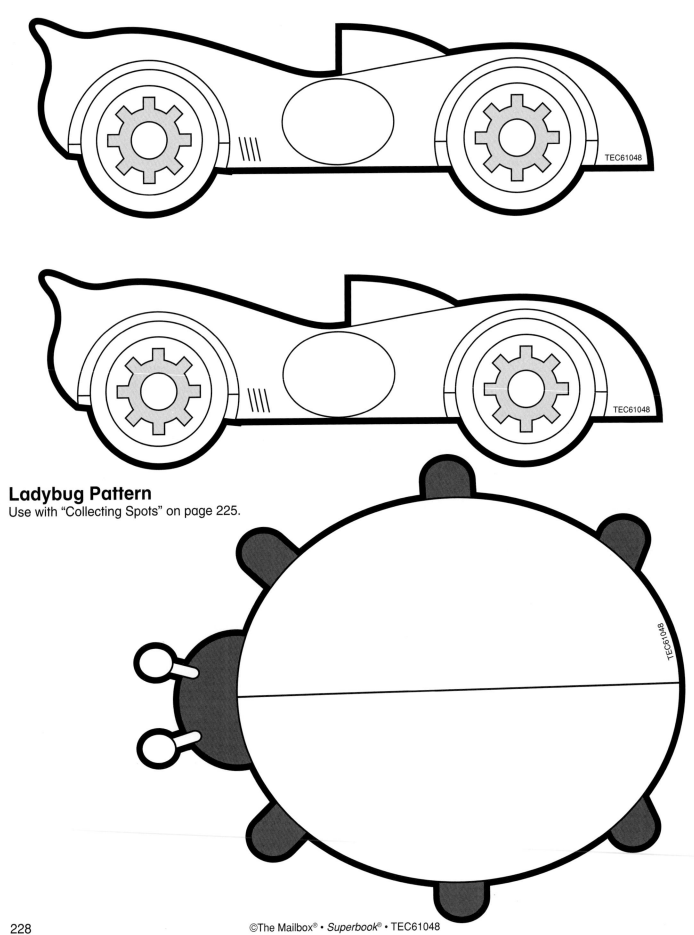

TEC61048

TEC61048

Ladybug Pattern

Use with "Collecting Spots" on page 225.

TEC61048

GAMES

Rhyme Lines

Everyone moves and everyone learns with this rhyming activity. Divide your students into two teams and have them line up in two lines. Choose one team to begin; then announce a word. The student at the front of Team One states a rhyming word and then moves to the end of the line. The first player on Team Two repeats this process with a different rhyming word. Alternating from Team One to Team Two, repeatedly ask each student to say a different rhyming word until one team is unable to think of another one. Award the last team to say a rhyming word a point. To continue the game, announce a new word and begin where play left off. The team with more points at the end of the designated game time wins! **Rhyming**

What's Missing?

Sharpen students' visual memories while reviewing content-area words. Write the words you want students to review on separate cards; then tape the cards to the board. Have students study the words. Then ask students to cover their eyes while you remove a card. When a student identifies the missing word, challenge him to spell it and/or give the definition. Continue the game by removing a different card each time. *Vocabulary*

dog	cat
bird	pet
food	water
fish	puppy

Switcheroo

This quick and easy class game is a perfect way to review familiar words! Label blank cards with different words, repeating words as necessary to make a class supply. To play, seat youngsters in a circle and give each child a card. Then announce a word. Each youngster with the word quickly stands up, repeats the word, and sits down. After announcing a few words in this manner, say, "Switcheroo," signaling each student to pass his card to the student on his left. Continue announcing words and switching cards as time allows. *Word recognition*

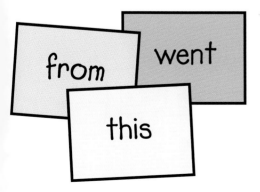

from

went

this

Word Watchers

Students use teamwork to form words with this lively game! Label separate large cards with different letters, using different colors for the consonants and vowels. Invite three students to stand in front of the class. Give one child a vowel and each of the others a consonant; then direct them to stand side by side. Have volunteers direct the standing students to form a word. If a real word cannot be formed, encourage youngsters to suggest which letters to replace. For example, if the letters spell "tid," a child may suggest replacing *i* with *e* to form the word *Ted.* Continue in the same manner, inviting different students to hold the letter cards.
Making words

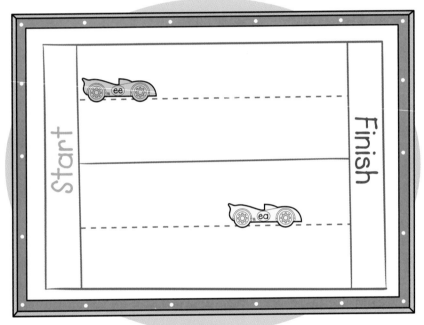

Ready, Set, Read!

Here's a winning way for youngsters to practice spelling patterns! Draw a section of a racetrack on a magnetic board. Program two racecar cutouts (patterns on page 228) with different spelling patterns. Adhere a strip of magnetic tape to the back of each car; then place them on the board. Also, label a supply of blank cards with different words for each spelling pattern.

To begin, a child chooses a card, reads the word, and identifies the spelling pattern. Then she moves the corresponding car ahead one car length. Play continues in the same manner until one car reaches the finish line. Spelling patterns

Sneaky Snake

To prepare, use page 233 to make a class supply of snake gameboards and one set of picture cards. Place the cards in a bag. Randomly program each board with five of the following blends: *fl, fr, sn, gl, st, sk, cl.* Then give each child a gameboard and five game markers.

To begin play, remove a card from the bag and name the picture. A youngster identifies the initial blend; if he has the blend on his board, he covers it with a marker. When the "Sneaky Snake" card is drawn, each student removes one marker from his board. When all the cards have been drawn, return them to the bag and continue play until a student covers each blend on his board and announces, "I caught the snake!"
Initial-consonant blends

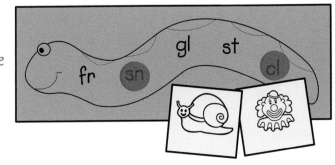

Team Challenge

Review addition and subtraction facts with a quick game of Team Challenge. Divide the class into two teams. Have a student from each team come to the board. Write an addition or a subtraction problem on the board for each student. Set a time limit during which the two players try to solve their problems. If a player solves his problem correctly, his team scores one point. If solved incorrectly, his opponent can try to correct the problem. If he does, that player scores an extra point for his team. Continue in this same manner until each student has had a turn. Addition and subtraction

ADDITION TIC-TAC-TOE

Tic-tac-toe your way to reinforcing addition skills. Draw a large tic-tac-toe grid on the board. Divide the class into an X team and an O team; then give each team a pair of dice. To play, have a player from each team, in turn, roll both dice and add the numbers together. The team with the highest sum gets to place its X or O on the tic-tac-toe grid. The first team to complete a row vertically, horizontally, or diagonally wins! **Addition**

Anywhere Scavenger Hunt

1. flag
2. fruit
3. funnel
4. faucet
5. fan

If you find yourself with a few extra minutes, engage your students in a scavenger hunt. Divide your class into groups; then assign each group a search category. For example, you might ask a group to find items that begin with *f* or things that are cube-shaped. Set a timer, and let students begin searching. As each item is found, have a team member write it in a list or draw a picture of it. When time is up, count the number of items each group found. *Skill review*

Preparing Pizza

Trim a large piece of bulletin board paper to resemble a pizza; then add desired details. Cut out a supply of red paper circles (pepperoni) and place them in a bag. Seat youngsters in a circle and place the pizza and bag in the center. Set a timer for a desired amount of time, up to five minutes.

To play, invite a child to roll two large dice and announce the total amount of dots. Have another student place the corresponding number of pepperoni pieces on the pizza. Have students continue in this manner until the timer rings. At that signal, lead students in counting the pepperoni pieces on the pizza. Then remove the pepperoni and reset the timer to prepare another pizza! For an added challenge, have students count by twos, fives, or tens. **Counting**

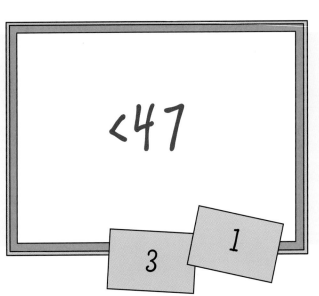

Quick Numbers

For this game, give each child ten blank cards. Have her label each card with a different number 0–9. On the board, write a two-digit number along with a greater than or less than sign. Challenge students to use their cards to make a number that completes the math sentence. Invite youngsters to share their numbers to verify their answers. Comparing numbers

Piggy Banks

Saving pennies is the object of this partner game! Program a copy of a piggy bank pattern from page 234 with a money amount. Then copy and cut out a bank for each pair of students. Give each twosome a bank, a die, and a supply of imitation coins. To play, designate one child the player and the other the banker. The player rolls the die and places the corresponding amount of pennies on the bank. After each roll, the banker studies the coins to determine whether any exchanges are necessary (for example, exchanging five pennies for a nickel or two nickels for a dime). Play continues in this manner until the amount in the bank matches or exceeds the programmed amount. Then youngsters switch roles and play again! *Money*

Sneaky Snake!

GLUE

TEC61048

TEC61048

TEC61048

TEC61048

TEC61048

TEC61048

TEC61048

TEC61048

©The Mailbox® • *Superbook*® • TEC61048

Piggy Bank Patterns

Use with "Piggy Banks" on page 232.

TEC61048

TEC61048

Differentiating Learning

Practice in a Box

Here's a simple way to provide each student with just-right skill practice! To prepare, write each child's name on a separate blank card. Obtain a supply of shoeboxes or small tubs. In each box, place materials and directions for students to practice a desired skill. Consider items such as file folder games, word cards, math fact cards, or magnetic letters. Attach the hook side of a Velcro fastener to one side of each box; then attach the loop side of a Velcro fastener to the back of each child's name card. Each week, attach name cards to the appropriate boxes to provide each student with the practice she needs. Change the materials in the boxes as needed.

1. Choose a picture card.
2. Find the beginning letter.
3. Check.
4. Repeat.

Cheri

Color-Coded Centers

To make sure students choose center activities that are at their individual levels, try this idea! Write each student's name on a blank card; then laminate the cards. Establish a color-coding system for the varying levels of your center activities. Place a color dot sticker on each center activity to identify its level. Use a wipe-off marker to draw on each name card a color dot that corresponds with the level of center you would like each student to visit. Store the cards in an easily accessible location. During center time, direct youngsters to take their cards with them to choose activities that match their cards. To adjust a student's level, simply wipe off the color dot and replace it with a different color.

Brianna

Chet

Chart It!

Do your small instructional groups have different skill-based needs? If so, use this versatile chart to help you monitor the progress of the students in each group! For each group, program a copy of the chart on page 237 with the group's name, the date, and its students' names. Then write a different skill or goal at the top of each column. Keep this chart handy when working with small groups. Make notes on it as needed to track the varying levels of your students.

Name	Skill	Rereads after self-correcting	Uses visual cues	Uses meaning cues			
Daniel		most of the time	✓	✓			
Gillian		✓	needs prompts	often			
Alec		rarely needs prompts	✓	✓			
Latoya		read the text without any errors	✓	✓			
Veronica		text seemed too hard	needed a lot of support	✓			

Guided-Reading Group 2 **Checklist** Date February 20–24

Note to the teacher: Use with "Chart It!" on page 235.

Solve and Stick

This idea is just perfect for students whose fine-motor difficulties interfere with them completing math skill sheets. To prepare for one child, program a supply of sticky dots with the answers to a skill sheet, making sure to include some incorrect responses as well. When completing a skill sheet, a child solves a problem, identifies the sticker with the corresponding answer, and then adheres the sticker to the answer space.

Individual Reading Collections

Provide students with independent-reading books at their individual levels with these book boxes! Obtain a class supply of empty cereal boxes. Remove the tops and then trim the boxes as shown. After each student decorates his box, label it with his name. Store the boxes in an easily accessible area. In each child's box, place books that are at his independent-reading level. Periodically rotate the books to keep interest high. If desired, invite each student to help you select appropriate books for his box.

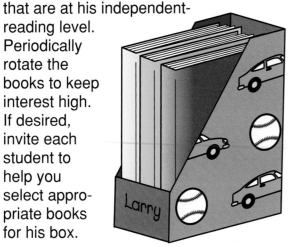

Ready Record

Try this tip to help organize each student's word lists, reading level, math level, and more! Program a copy of page 238 with the date and then copy a class supply. (If several students have the same word lists, write them on a copy of the page; then copy the desired amount.) Write any relevant information—such as reading levels, titles of guided-reading books, or math fact levels—where indicated. Hole-punch the papers and store them in a three-ring binder for easy access. If desired, send home a copy of each child's chart for parents to view. Repeat the same process each week or as needed.

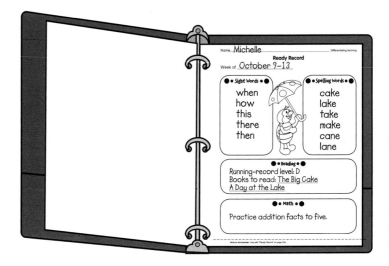

Highlighting Hints

If some of your students need extra help when completing skill sheets, the following bright ideas are for you!

• Have students highlight key words or icons in the directions.
• Instruct students to highlight operational signs on math problems before they begin work.
• Ask youngsters to highlight the initial letters of words for initial-sound identification or ABC-order practice.
• Have youngsters highlight the words in the word bank.

Checklist

Date _____

Name	Skill					

Note to the teacher: Use with "Chart It!" on page 235.

Ready Record

Week of _____

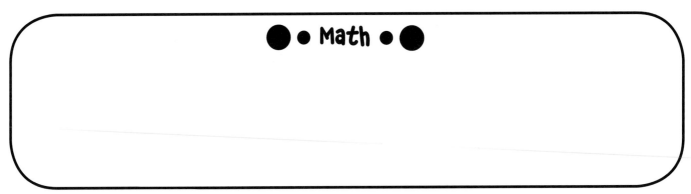

Note to the teacher: Use with "Ready Record" on page 236.

Tracking Progress

Record each student's progress in your classroom with this easy record-keeping system. Set up a notebook with a divider tab for each child. Place several sheets of notebook paper behind each tab. Each day circulate with a clipboard and sticky notes. Write your anecdotal notes and stick them to the clipboard. At the end of the day, simply transfer the notes for each child onto one of her pages in the notebook.

Portfolio Folders

Encourage your students to take an active role in maintaining their portfolios with these nifty tips. To begin, provide a variety of arts-and-crafts supplies, including glue, markers, crayons, cutouts for tracing, and scraps of construction paper. Have each student personalize the cover of her portfolio and then decorate it to reflect her likes and interests.

Once the folders have been decorated, give each student a sheet of smiley-face stickers. When a student wants a paper filed in her portfolio, she attaches a sticker to it; then she returns it to a designated basket. If desired, change the color of the stickers to reflect the start of a new grading period. Students will enjoy earmarking their papers. And later, during teacher-student portfolio reviews, it will be easy to tell which papers were student-selected.

Picture the Progress

Here's a simple idea to help keep track of your students' individual progress. Purchase a flip-top photo album like the one shown. Personalize a card for each student and insert each card into a different plastic sleeve. When you wish to make a note about or check on a student's progress, his card is readily available.

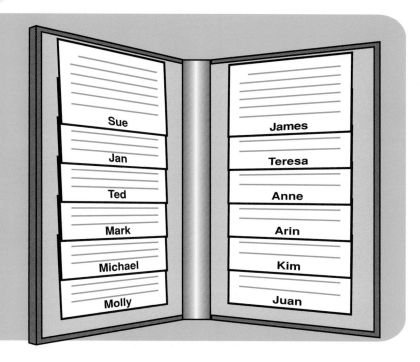

Write Through the Year

Monitor youngsters' writing, spelling, and handwriting progress with this ongoing record. Program the writing assessment on page 241 with a desired fall date and copy the page to make a class supply. On the designated day, announce a simple sentence for students to write on the prepared paper. Repeat it several times until each child is satisfied with her writing. After collecting and evaluating the writing samples, file the papers until the next season. Then date the papers and repeat the dictation process in the winter and spring. By the year's end, students will be delighted to see the improvements in their writing!

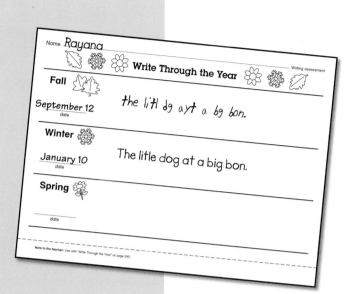

Assessment Call

Instead of simply calling a student over to you to complete his individual assessments, sing him this merry melody! You are sure to gain his attention and make him feel at ease.

(sung to the tune of "Pawpaw Patch")

Where, oh where, is dear little [Andrew]?
Where, oh where, is dear little [Andrew]?
Where, oh where, is dear little [Andrew]?
Please come over here to visit me!

Timesaver Tubs

Here's a simple way to assess students on a variety of skills! For each skill you would like to assess, obtain a plastic tub or storage container. Label each tub with a different skill and place the necessary supplies, recording sheets, and pencils in each. For example, to assess letter knowledge you may include letter cards, a set of magnetic letters, and a letter checklist. After completing and evaluating a child's assessment, file the recording sheet or notes for future reference.

Letter Knowledge

Name _____

Write Through the Year

Fall

date _____

Winter

date _____

Spring

date _____

Note to the teacher: Use with "Write Through the Year" on page 240.

Name _____

Wise Work

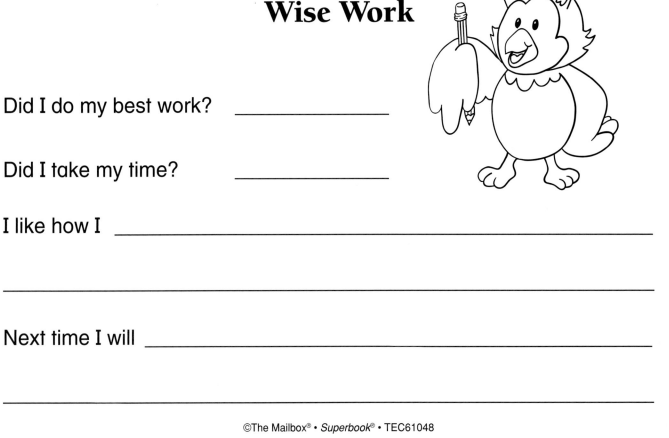

Did I do my best work? _____

Did I take my time? _____

I like how I _____

_____

Next time I will _____

_____

- -

Name _____ Self-assessment

So Proud!

I am proud of this work because

_____

_____

_____

Note to the teacher: Have a student assess a piece of work and complete one of the forms above. Staple the form to his paper and file it for future reference.

English Language Learners

8:30   Calendar

8:45   Reading

Picture-Perfect Routine

Instead of just telling students what activity is next, show them! To prepare for this schedule idea, take photos of students during routine activities and during each special subject, such as art and music. Or enlarge the schedule cards on page 246 for easy viewing in a group and then color and cut out the cards. Each morning, post the day's schedule as desired. Then display selected photos or schedule cards beside the corresponding times. Since students will know what to expect, they're sure to feel comfortable in your classroom!

From A to Z

Make it easier for students to remember letter-sound relationships with this kid-pleasing approach. When you introduce a letter-sound relationship, show students the letter and say the corresponding sound. Then model a relevant action and have the youngsters imitate it. For example, you might pantomime biting into an apple when you say the short /a/ sound and point up for the short /u/ sound.

That Bears Repeating!

This tip works well for English language learners who need reading help or extra time to process oral information. When you assign students independent work, such as solving story problems or responding to a journal prompt, make a recording of yourself presenting the task. For example, record yourself reading the problems or announcing the prompt to students. Arrange for each youngster who needs support to listen to the recording with headphones. Encourage him to replay the recording as many times as needed to gain understanding. He'll be able to work at his own pace, and you'll be free to monitor students.

School Tools

Clarify classroom instructions with this simple strategy. Color a copy of the school supply cards on page 247. Cut out the cards and then back them with tagboard for durability. Store the cards near the board or a pocket chart. As you give students instructions for an activity, pause when you mention a featured supply and display the appropriate card. After all of the supplies are displayed in the order that they are needed, repeat the instructions, pointing to each card in turn. The pictures will help youngsters understand the instructions. Plus, they'll be a reminder of what students need to do!

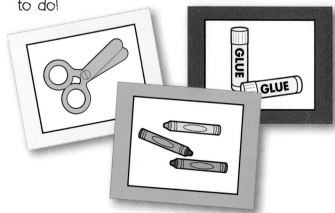

Valuable Storytimes

When it comes to developing vocabulary and language skills, read-alouds are some of the best teaching tools. Use these storytime suggestions and the recommended titles to reinforce a variety of skills.

- **Alphabet Books:** Use grade-appropriate selections to introduce chosen words. Then guide youngsters to use the words in sentences.
- **Predictable Books:** Promote oral expression by inviting youngsters to join in the reading. Then encourage students to revisit the books on their own.
- **Wordless Books:** Introduce key words as you discuss the pictures with students. Then write student-generated phrases or sentences that tell about the pictures.

Alphabet Books

Eating the Alphabet: Fruits and Vegetables From A to Z by Lois Ehlert

26 Letters and 99 Cents by Tana Hoban

Predictable Books

It Looked Like Spilt Milk by Charles G. Shaw

I Was Walking Down the Road by Sarah E. Barchas

Wordless Books

Frog Goes to Dinner by Mercer Mayer

Pancakes for Breakfast by Tomie dePaola

Super Sentences

Here's a simple activity that sharpens both speaking and reading skills. To begin, gather three or four animal pictures. After you label the pictures with the names of the animals, display them near a sheet of chart paper. To begin, show students which animal you like the most. Then think aloud as you write, "I like the [animal name]." Write your name after the sentence as shown. Next, invite a student to show which animal he likes the most. Have him say a sentence modeled on your sentence. Then write the sentence and his name. Continue as described with the remaining students. Over the next few days, lead students in reading the sentences several times. For additional practice, modify the activity for different topics.

cat

dog

I like the cat. (Ms. Johnson)
I like the dog. (Shamir)
I like the cat. (Hakib)
I like the rabbit. (Sari)
I like the fish. (Ahmed)

Draw First!

Since drawings represent a child's thinking, they make a perfect bridge to writing. To respond to a prompt, have each English language learner draw a picture. Guide her to tell about her completed picture; use sticky notes to add labels. Then instruct the youngster to refer to the labels as she completes the writing assignment.

To break down the task of completing a graphic organizer, ask each student to represent the information she wants to include by drawing pictures on sticky notes and placing them on her paper. Then help her move the drawings one at a time and replace them with the corresponding words.

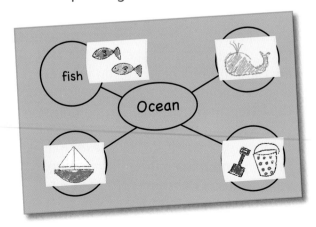

Songs and Chants

What better way to promote oral language than with repetitive songs and chants? After all, they provide plenty of opportunities for modeling, and every student can successfully participate. Incorporate actions or props to enhance students' understanding.

Good Morning!

Start each day with this song to establish a classroom community. No doubt youngsters will be eager to use facial expressions and actions to convey the featured feelings.

(sung to the tune of "Mary Had a Little Lamb")

Hello, hello, how are you?
How are you? How are you?
Hello, hello, how are you?
How do you feel today?

Are you sleepy or very glad?
Are you scared? Are you sad?
Are you surprised or very mad?
How do you feel today?

Ready to Work

This catchy chant not only sets an upbeat tone for the day but it also reinforces school-related vocabulary.

Teacher:	We're at our desks. *(Students echo.)*
Teacher:	We're ready for the day. *(Students echo.)*
Teacher:	We have pencils.
Students:	Pencils.
Teacher:	Crayons. *(Students echo.)*
Teacher:	Scissors. *(Students echo.)*
Teacher:	Glue. *(Students echo.)*
All:	We're ready for the day. Are you?

Time to Eat

Just before lunchtime, establish a steady clapping rhythm and lead students in this chant. It's a fun way to review food-related vocabulary and prepare your class for lunch!

Teacher and students:	Munch, munch, it's time for lunch.
Teacher and students:	What will we eat today?
Teacher:	Vegetables? *(Students echo.)*
Teacher:	Meat? *(Students echo.)*
Teacher:	Fruit? *(Students echo.)*
Teacher:	Or something sweet? *(Students echo.)*
Teacher and students:	What will we eat today?

Schedule Cards

Use with "Picture-Perfect Routine" on page 243.

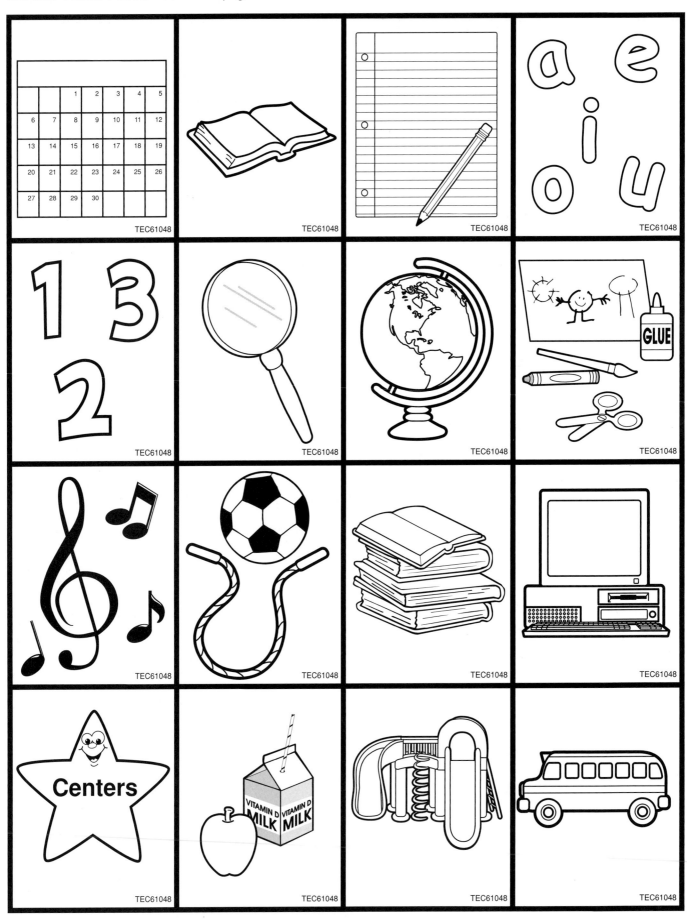

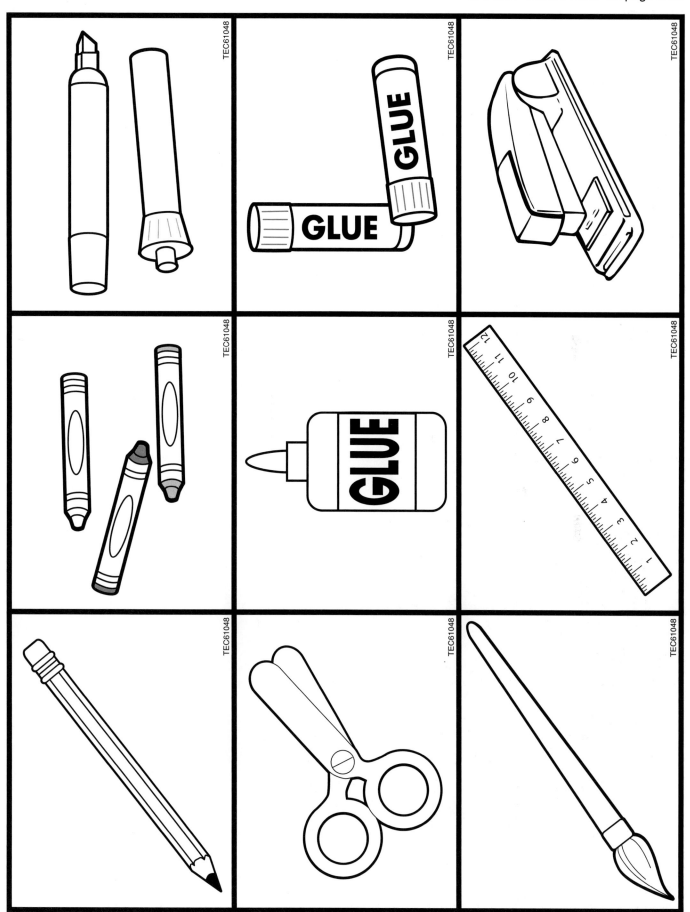

Bulletin Boards & Displays

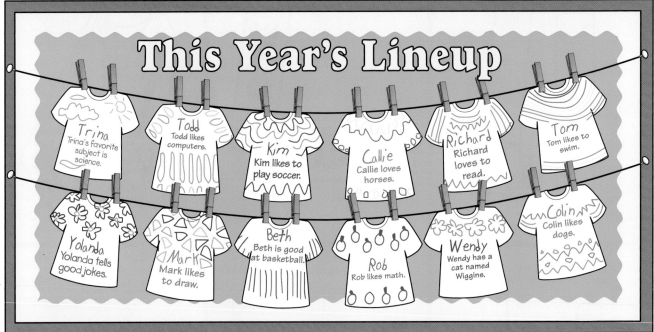

Spotlight your new student lineup with this eye-catching display. Have each student cut out, personalize, and decorate a construction paper T-shirt cutout. Add the title and then display the T-shirts using clothespins and lengths of heavy string. Each day ask a few students to tell something special about themselves. Record each child's response on his T-shirt.

This back-to-school bulletin board is sure to put a polish on a great school year! Cut an apple shape from construction paper for each student. Instruct students to use art supplies to decorate their apple patterns to resemble themselves. Display the completed cutouts on a bulletin board decorated with construction paper branches.

Student writing and fall colors add seasonal style to this fall bulletin board idea! Mount the title and brown construction paper tree branches. Make a class supply of the leaf-shaped writing paper on page 258. A student writes about the season and then draws a related picture in the blank space provided. Glue the writing paper atop a slightly larger leaf cut from fall-colored construction paper. If desired, have each child glue tissue-paper squares around her leaf. Mount the completed leaves on the branches.

Ask students to cut pumpkin shapes from orange bulletin board paper. Then have students cut out, personalize, and attach green paper stems to the resulting cutouts. Display a pumpkin for students to observe. Then have them brainstorm words that describe the pumpkin as you record their responses on the board. Have each child write a different description of the pumpkin on his pumpkin cutout; then mount each pumpkin on the bulletin board.

Celebrate National Children's Book Week with a display that is sure to get youngsters revved up for reading! After a child reads a favorite book, invite him to write the title on a copy of the car pattern on page 259. Then have him write or draw a picture about the book and sign his name. Post the completed cars on a board decorated like the one shown. If desired, periodically update the cars to showcase different books.

THINKING THANKFUL THOUGHTS

Students can show their thankful thoughts when they create this fine-feathered friend. Enlarge, color, and cut out the turkey on page 260. Give each student a light-colored construction paper turkey feather. Have each child write her thankful thought on the feather. Mount the turkey, the feathers, and the title as shown.

Set the mood for wintertime writing with this motivational display. Mount a large igloo cutout and the title. Have each student write a story about winter on writing paper; then attach each story to a white circle cutout. Mount the resulting snowballs around the igloo. Scatter snowflake cutouts around the board to complete the frosty display.

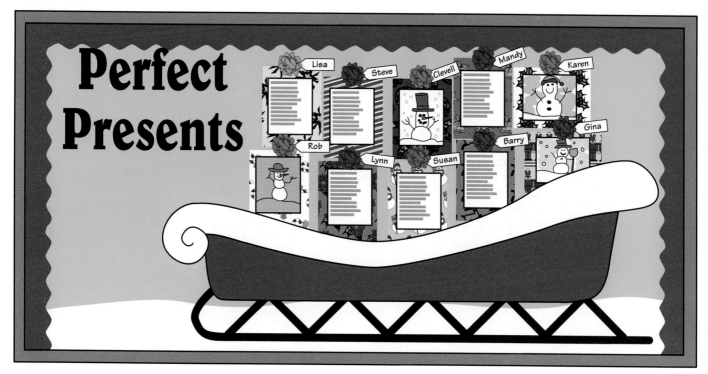

Mount a large sleigh cutout, the title, and one 9" x 12" sheet of wrapping paper per student. Have each student personalize a gift tag; then attach the tags and self-adhesive bows above the sheets of wrapping paper. Have each student select a sample of his best work. Attach the work samples to the presents as shown. Replace students' work samples as desired.

Ring in the New Year with this festive, three-dimensional display. Using a variety of arts-and-crafts materials, have students decorate face-shaped cutouts to resemble themselves. Next, have each child write a self-improvement goal on a light-colored triangle, add desired details, and glue it to the top of his face cutout. Assist each student in making a cut by the mouth and inserting a party blower through the hole. (Use tape as needed.) Mount the completed projects and title as shown.

Celebrate Dr. Martin Luther King Jr.'s birthday with this inspiring bulletin board. With students, discuss Dr. King's life and his work for equality and peace. To follow up the discussion, have each child use a variety of art supplies to create a picture of himself. Each child then writes his own dream on a cloud-shaped piece of white paper and glues cotton balls around its edges. Mount the student replicas with their cloud cutouts on the board for a dreamy display!

Spread the message of friendship with this simple, heartwarming bulletin board. Mount the title and a large red construction paper heart. Have each student draw a picture of herself being a good friend. Trim the drawings and glue them to the heart in a collage-fashion. Add a border of smaller hearts if desired.

Salute our country's possible future presidents with this patriotic bulletin board! To begin, discuss the qualities of a good president. Then assist each student in creating a silhouette cutout of himself. Next, on a piece of writing paper, have each child write why he would make a good president. Mount students' writing assignments on construction paper and display them next to students' silhouettes.

Make a class supply of the shamrock pattern on page 261 on green construction paper. After a brainstorming session of green items, have each student cut out his pattern and write a riddle about a green item. Then have each child trace and cut out a matching shamrock shape from lined paper and write the answer. Display completed shamrocks and answers (one atop the other) as shown. If desired, have students sponge-paint a shamrock border.

Guess who's hatching. Your students, that's who! Copy the egg pattern from page 262 onto light-colored construction paper for each student. Have each student write a description of himself on the lines and then decorate the top of his egg. Then have each child cut his egg pattern on the bold line. Glue a photograph of each child to the top edge of the egg's bottom half; then use a brad to attach the two halves on the left edge. Mount the completed projects and the title shown.

What do your youngsters like to do on a rainy day? Find out with this display idea! Give each child a light blue construction paper raindrop. Have her write and illustrate something she likes to do on a rainy day. Post students' completed raindrops along with a character and the title shown.

Write the title shown on a large sun cutout. Mount the sun and add student hand cutouts to resemble sun rays. Invite students to discuss some of their favorite memories from the school year. Then have each child write about a memory on a sheet of writing paper. Post students' writing samples on the display.

Showcase your students' greatest work in this class gallery. Cut gold or silver poster board into various-size picture frames with standard 8½" x 11" openings. Laminate each frame; then staple each frame to the board, leaving an opening at the top. When a student's work merits extra recognition, simply slip her paper into a mounted frame.

Extra! Extra! Read all about this appealing idea to spotlight students' work. Mount 10½" x 13" pieces of newspaper on the board. Mount the newspaper pieces, the title, and a newspaper border on the board as shown. Help each student attach his work atop a newspaper. Encourage students to keep their displays current.

This tail-waggin' job-assignment display will have your youngsters eager to perform classroom duties. Enlarge several copies of the doghouse pattern on page 263 and program each with a classroom job title. Color, cut out, and laminate each pattern. Cut a slit in each dog bowl; then mount the patterns on the board. Duplicate and cut out a class supply of bone patterns from page 263. Personalize one end of a bone for each child and then laminate it. Assign a classroom duty by placing a bone cutout in each dog bowl, and you'll be ready for some hardworking hounds.

Showcase youngsters' birthdays with this simple display. Help each child label a balloon cutout with his name and birthday. Then invite him to add decorations. Attach a length of yarn to each balloon; then mount the balloons and title as shown.

Leaf Pattern
Use with "We Love Fall!" on page 249.

by _____

TEC61048

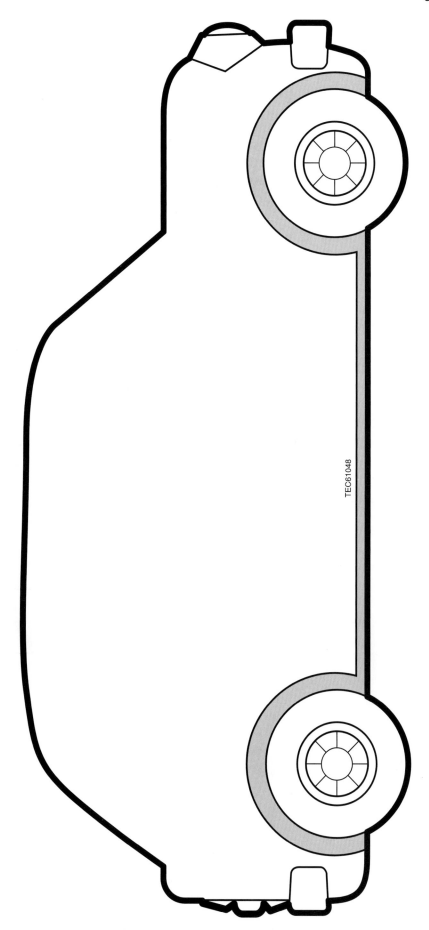

TEC61048

Turkey Pattern

Use with "Thinking Thankful Thoughts" on page 250.

TEC61048

TEC61048

Egg Pattern

Use with "Look Who's Hatching!" on page 254 and "Spring Greetings" on page 294.

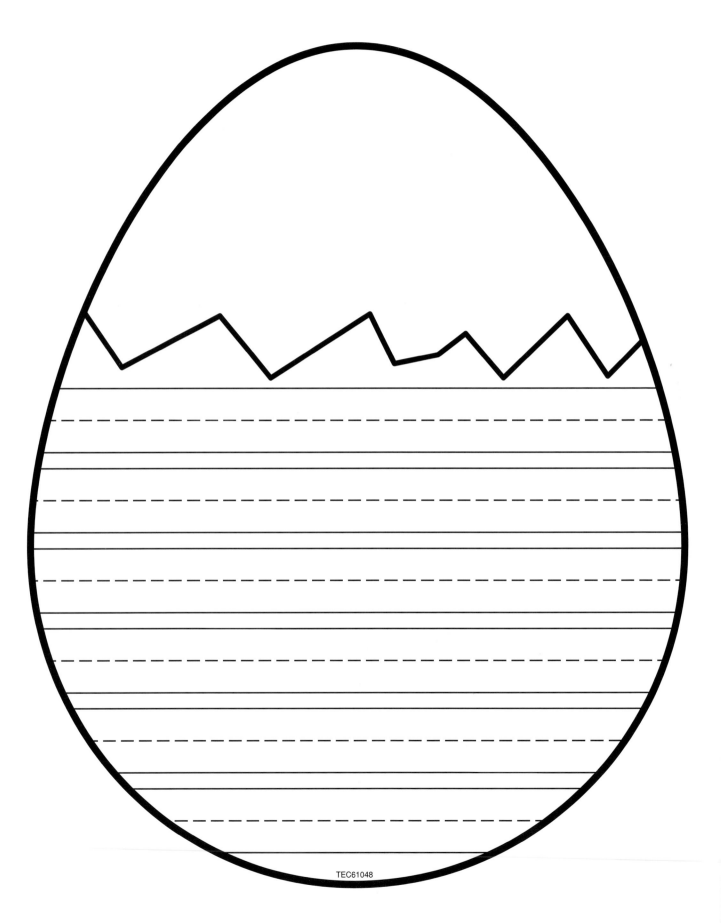

TEC61048

TEC61048

TEC61048

CLASSROOM MANAGEMENT

Checking In

Here's an idea for combining daily attendance and lunch count. Program a copy of the class list on page 272 as shown. Write each student's name on the list; then make several copies and place one copy on a table near the door each morning. As students arrive, have them check the "I'm here" column and the appropriate lunch column. You'll know at a glance which students are at school and what their plans are for lunch.

Class List	I'm here	Brought a lunch	Buying a lunch	Milk only	Buying a snack
1. Beth					
2. Hannah	✓	✓			
3. David					
4. Mike	✓		✓		
5. Zach	✓		✓		
6. Kim					
7. Rob					
8. Mary		✓			
9. Pam	✓		✓		
10. Sheila	✓	✓			
11. Becky	✓				
12. Barry					
13. Donna	✓		✓		
14. Cathy	✓				
15. Jennifer	✓	✓			
16. Clevell	✓	✓			✓
17. Susan	✓		✓		
18. Lisa	✓				
19. Karen	✓	✓			✓
20.	✓		✓		
21.					
22.					
23.					
24.					
25.					

Take a Number

During times you're busy, use this orderly technique to handle students' requests for help. Sequentially number a supply of construction paper squares. Laminate each card; then punch a hole at the top of each card. Suspend the cards in numerical order from a prominently located hook. When a student needs your help, he simply takes a card and waits for you to call his number when you are available.

Colorful Table Teams

Use color-coded student desks to help manage your classroom. Arrange your students' desks in groups of four; then attach a different-colored construction paper circle or self-adhesive dot to each desk in a group. Determine four jobs, such as paper collector, roll taker, table manager, and materials distributor. Then, during cooperative-learning activities, assign jobs by making a color choice. This teamwork will help keep the room more organized, and it will help students feel more responsible for their tasks.

Fantastic Folders

Personalized homework folders help ensure that homework and other important papers reach home safely. Personalize a two-pocket folder for each student. Label one pocket "Homework" and one pocket "Other Important Papers." Near the end of each day, have students tuck their homework papers and any other important notes into the appropriate pockets of their homework folders. Request that parents check the contents of their children's folders each day and ensure that the homework assignments are returned in the folders the next day. These handy folders will become a regular part of your students' daily routines in no time at all!

HOMEWORK

OTHER IMPORTANT PAPERS

Attention, Please

What do students do when they hear a rhythm of clap, snap, clap? Join in, of course! To help quiet students down between activities or to gain their attention, establish a simple pattern of claps, snaps, and/or slaps. Pause; then repeat the pattern again. Continue in this manner, challenging students to repeat the rhythmic pattern during each pause. It won't take long before you have their undivided attention.

Help to the Rescue!

This easy-to-make chart will make assigning helpers a cinch! Make a copy of the helper cards on page 273. Cut out the cards and glue each one to the front of a library card pocket. Display the pockets on a chart. Then label 3" x 5" index cards with the names of students who will be responsible for the jobs, and insert a card into each pocket.

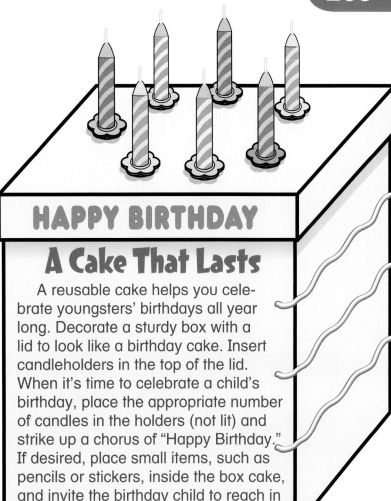

HAPPY BIRTHDAY

A Cake That Lasts

A reusable cake helps you celebrate youngsters' birthdays all year long. Decorate a sturdy box with a lid to look like a birthday cake. Insert candleholders in the top of the lid. When it's time to celebrate a child's birthday, place the appropriate number of candles in the holders (not lit) and strike up a chorus of "Happy Birthday." If desired, place small items, such as pencils or stickers, inside the box cake, and invite the birthday child to reach in and choose one.

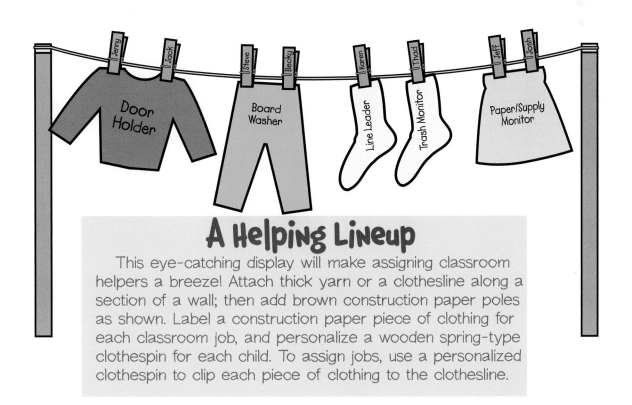

A Helping Lineup

This eye-catching display will make assigning classroom helpers a breeze! Attach thick yarn or a clothesline along a section of a wall; then add brown construction paper poles as shown. Label a construction paper piece of clothing for each classroom job, and personalize a wooden spring-type clothespin for each child. To assign jobs, use a personalized clothespin to clip each piece of clothing to the clothesline.

Easy-to-Find Reproducibles

Try organizing your favorite reproducibles with this helpful tip. Label a divider page for each month of the school year or for each subject area. Hole-punch your favorite reproducibles and place them into the binder according to the subject area or when they will be used. Your reproducibles will be right at your fingertips when you need them.

Theme Storage

Organize theme-related books, art ideas, and center activities in theme storage boxes. Label a large, clear storage box (or plastic sweater container) for each theme used during the school year; then sort your teaching materials into the boxes. Store the stackable containers in a cabinet. This system makes retrieving your materials a snap!

Pumpkins

File It!

Help students keep track of their ongoing work with this organizational tip. Using students' first names, label a tab on an accordion folder for each child. Have each student place any unfinished work in his file at the end of the day. Then, the following morning, have him retrieve his work to complete. Say good-bye to crumpled, incomplete papers in the back of your students' desks.

Tom
Bonita

Literature Folders

This method is sure to help organize your literature-based units. To organize your literature units, store a book in one side of a pocket folder and tuck ideas for related activities and sample art projects into the other pocket. Now, when you're looking for teaching ideas related to a specific book, they'll be a cinch to find!

Storage Tips

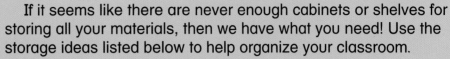

If it seems like there are never enough cabinets or shelves for storing all your materials, then we have what you need! Use the storage ideas listed below to help organize your classroom.

- Funnels—Place a ball of yarn in each of several funnels and pull the yarn end out of each spout.

- Bandage Boxes—These handy boxes can be used to store cards for different games. For easy identification, attach labels to the front of the boxes.

- Hardware Storage Boxes—These boxes are great for organizing and holding stickers, as well as other small office supplies.

- Hanging Shoe Bags—Shoe bags with pockets work great for storing materials such as scissors, rulers, markers, and glue.

- 35mm Film Containers—Students can use old film containers to store their lunch money, lost teeth, or small manipulatives.

- Ice-Cube Trays—These convenient trays work well for holding small amounts of colorful paints as well as an assortment of minisupplies.

- Tennis-Ball Containers—Students can use these containers instead of pencil boxes to store their pencils and crayons.

- Margarine Tubs—Another nifty container for storing small manipulatives.

- Silverware Trays—These trays work well for holding paintbrushes, rulers, markers, and colored pencils.

Early Finishers

Looking for a way to eliminate the phrase "What do I do now?" from your students' vocabularies? Try this tip! At the beginning of the school year, have students brainstorm an "I'm All Finished" list. Tell students to imagine that everyone else in class is working quietly and they have finished early. What could they do without disturbing others? Record their responses, along with the suggestions below, on a piece of poster board, and display it in a prominent location.

Read a book.	Practice math facts.	Read a magazine.	Read a class-written story.	Write the numbers 0–100.
Write a story.	Count the months to your birthday.	Design a school T-shirt.	Visit the school or classroom library.	Play a quiet game.
Make an art project.	Work on a puzzle.	Draw a map of the classroom.	Design a book cover for a favorite book.	Write a letter to the principal.
Clean and organize your desk.	Write in your journal.	Go to a center.	Write a poem.	Make a puppet.
Use a calculator to solve math problems.	Work on the computer.	Write a letter to a friend.	Make a card for parents or a friend.	Study spelling words with a friend.
Practice handwriting.	Check the extra-work box .	Make a gameboard.	Write a recipe for a favorite food.	Write word problems for a friend to solve.
Draw a picture.	Clean an area of the classroom.	Work on a class newspaper.	Create an ad for a new kind of candy.	Draw a family portrait.

Students in the Spotlight

Add a twist to parent-teacher conferences by inviting your students to provide their thoughts about their strengths and weaknesses. In advance, brainstorm a list of questions to ask students concerning their academic and social progress. Use the questions to help create a reproducible similar in format to the one shown; then make a copy of the form for each student. A few days prior to the conferences, meet with each student to discuss the questions on the form and record her responses. At the parent-teacher conference, review with parents their youngsters' responses. Parents will be amazed at their children's awareness of academic strengths and weaknesses.

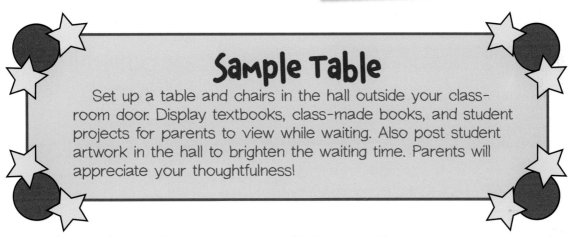

Name: Mikayla Shenkel   **Date:** Oct. 14, 2007

1. **What do you think is your best subject at school? Why?**
   Reading. I like to read fun stories.
2. **What subject do you think you need to work harder in?**
   Math.
3. **What can you do to improve in this subject?**
   I can pay attention better and practice with flash cards.
4. **Do you think you do your neatest work?**
   I try to. Some days I'm not as neat.
5. **Do you get your assignments turned in on time?**
   Most of the time. Sometimes I forget to do all my work.
6. **How do you get along with your classmates?**
   They are my friends. We have fun playing tag at recess.

Sample Table

Set up a table and chairs in the hall outside your classroom door. Display textbooks, class-made books, and student projects for parents to view while waiting. Also post student artwork in the hall to brighten the waiting time. Parents will appreciate your thoughtfulness!

Planning for Successful Conferences

Try these teacher-tested tips to establish a friendly atmosphere and positive attitudes at your next parent-teacher conference:

 Place paper and pens at the table for parents to use to take notes if needed.

 Reduce the chance of intimidating parents by making sure your seat and the parents' seats are at an equal height.

 Cover the table with bulletin board paper that has been decorated by your students.

 Provide reproducibles in boxes labeled according to subjects. Parents can choose from these for their children to use as reinforcement at home.

 Place photographs of students taken during special events in a photo album for parents to view.

 Have all student work samples in a folder for parents to view.

Field Trip Treasure Hunt

Make any field trip a day to remember by making a treasure guide. In advance, contact your tour guide to find out what points of interest will be discussed and toured. On a sheet of paper, draw some of the things that the youngsters are likely to see. Make a copy of this treasure guide for each child. Prior to the trip, show the guide to students. After returning from the trip, have each child mark each item he encountered on the trip. When students take their guides home, they will easily remember the highlights of the trip and be eager to share them with their families.

Easy Identification

Make it easy for you and your chaperones to keep track of your class on field trips. The day before the field trip, send home a note with each child asking that he wear a specific color shirt. Now that's an easy solution to an often-difficult problem.

Chaperone Nametags

Here's a handy idea that will help chaperones remember the students in their groups. Make a nametag similar to the one shown for each chaperone. Then write the names of the students in his group on the back of his nametag. If a student is missing, the chaperone simply checks the back of his nametag for a quick reference.

Mr. Noon

John	Brent
Carol	Sophia
Sam	Charida

Welcome Banner

Have students work in small groups to make welcome banners for upcoming substitutes. Provide each group with markers and a piece of bulletin board paper. Then have each group draw pictures on its banner. Next, ask each student in the class to sign his name on each group's banner. Store the banners in a handy spot. Assign two students to be in charge of choosing a banner and displaying it whenever there is a substitute teacher. What a great way to welcome the substitute teacher!

Good-News Report

Here's a management tip that's sure to help substitutes. At the beginning of the day, have the substitute post on the board a large sheet of paper labeled "Good-News Report." Then, throughout the day, have her record students' positive behaviors and good deeds. Ask her to leave the report on your desk. Since students will be eager to be added to the list, they'll be on their best behavior!

Putting Names With Faces

Make your substitute's day easier by adding this timely addition to your substitute folder. Simply obtain a photo of each of your students and tape the pictures to a sheet of construction paper. If desired, photographs can be arranged to resemble a pictorial seating chart. Then write the name of each student under his photo. Copy this page and include the copy with the substitute's other materials. Using this aid, your substitute can begin immediately to develop positive rapport by calling each child by name.

Substitute-Teacher Folder

A substitute-teacher folder is just what your substitute needs to carry out the day. Complete a copy of the class list on page 272 and the substitute information sheet on page 274. Place the completed reproducibles in a folder labeled "Substitute Lifesavers." Then, whenever you're going to be absent, simply place your lesson plans in the folder and leave it on your desk. Your substitute is sure to agree that this packet is a lifesaver!

Check out the management reproducibles on pages 275–278.

Class List

1.											
2.											
3.											
4.											
5.											
6.											
7.											
8.											
9.											
10.											
11.											
12.											
13.											
14.											
15.											
16.											
17.											
18.											
19.											
20.											
21.											
22.											
23.											
24.											
25.											

Note to the teacher: Use with "Checking In" on page 264, "Substitute-Teacher Folder" on page 271, and with everyday classroom management.

Line Leader	Door Holder	Pencil Monitor
Paper/Supply Monitor	Board Washer	P.E. Equipment Monitor
Attendance Clerk	Light Monitor	Trash Monitor
Library Monitor	Girls' Rest Room Monitor	Boys' Rest Room Monitor

Substitute Lifesavers
Substitute-Teacher Information

Faculty Information

Principal: _____

Assistant
Principal: _____

Secretary: _____

Helpful Teachers: _____

_____

Aide(s): _____

_____

Procedures

Start of the Day: _____

_____

Attendance: _____

Fire Drill: _____

Recess: _____

Lunch: _____

Behavior Policy: _____

Children With Special Needs

Health: _____

Supervision: _____

Learning: _____

Student Pullouts for Special Programs

Name   Class   Day/Time

_____

_____

_____

_____

Classroom News

Teacher: _____   Date: _____

Monday _____
_____
_____
_____
_____

Tuesday _____
_____
_____
_____
_____

Wednesday _____
_____
_____
_____
_____

Thursday _____
_____
_____
_____
_____

Friday _____
_____
_____
_____
_____

Looking Ahead

Help Wanted

Superstars

Reminders

Note to the teacher: Use to keep parents informed of classroom happenings.

Name: _____

Goal: _____

Aim high!

©The Mailbox® • *Superbook*® • TEC61048

Happy Birthday,

_____!

From: _____

Date: _____

©The Mailbox® • *Superbook*® • TEC61048

Note to the teacher: Use copies of the incentive chart to have students track their progress as they work toward their goals. Use the birthday certificate as desired.

276

Weekly Update

Name: _____

| = Outstanding | | = Needs Practice |
| = Satisfactory | | |

Week of:										
Listens Carefully										
Stays On Task										
Follows Directions										
Treats Others With Respect										
Follows Class Rules										
Does His/Her Best Work										
Parent's Initials										

Conference Reminder

Student: _____

Teacher: _____

Room: _____

Date: _____

Time: _____ to _____

See you then!

Conference Reminder

Student: _____

Teacher: _____

Room: _____

Date: _____

Time: _____ to _____

See you then!

Note to the teacher: To use "Weekly Update," fill in the grading codes with your own symbols and fill in each week's dates where indicated. At the end of each week, complete the checklist and send home a copy with each student. Have her return it with a parent's initials the following school day. To use "Conference Reminder," complete a copy and send it home prior to the date of the conference.

Extra Help Needed

_____
date

Dear Parent,

_____ needs extra help with _____

_____.

Here are some suggestions for how
you can help your child at home:

_____

_____

_____

_____

Thank you.

Sincerely,

_____
teacher's signature

SCHOOL NOTE

To:

From:

Note to the teacher: Make a supply of "Extra Help Needed" and send one copy home with students as needed. Make a supply of the messages on the bottom half of this page to use as needed.

Motivation & Positive Discipline

WANTED:
Responsible First Graders

Round up responsible buckaroos with this unique bulletin board activity. Decorate a bulletin board (similar to the one below) that lists responsible behaviors. Discuss the behaviors with your youngsters; then explain that you will be looking each week for students who exhibit these responsible behaviors. At the end of the week, reward each deserving child with a roundup award from page 285.

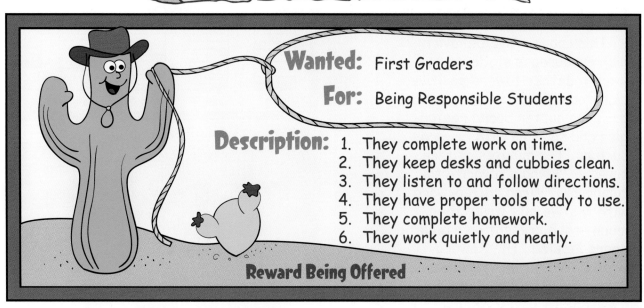

Wanted: First Graders

For: Being Responsible Students

Description:
1. They complete work on time.
2. They keep desks and cubbies clean.
3. They listen to and follow directions.
4. They have proper tools ready to use.
5. They complete homework.
6. They work quietly and neatly.

Reward Being Offered

Auction Tickets

What first grader doesn't love treats? With that in mind, motivate your youngsters by holding an auction each month. To begin, copy and cut out a supply of the tickets on page 284. Each afternoon (or each Friday), give a ticket to each student who has exhibited good effort and behavior during the day (or week). Have students color and store their tickets in personalized envelopes. Then, at the end of each month, hold an auction during which students can "spend" their tickets on inexpensive items.

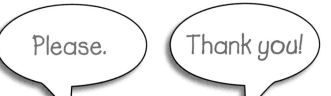

Please.

Thank you!

Marvelous Manners

Encourage good manners in your classroom with weekly marvelous manners certificates. Each Monday briefly review classroom rules and polite phrases, such as "Thank you" and "Excuse me." Then, during the week, look for students who demonstrate marvelous manners. Every Friday, present each deserving student with a personalized manners certificate from page 284. What a polite and peaceful classroom you'll have!

We Earned It!

This cooperative behavior plan encourages students to work together toward positive classroom behavior. In advance, program poster board rectangles and squares with rewards such as "Ten minutes of free time" or "Bring a favorite toy tomorrow." Wrap each reward with festive gift wrap; then mount each present on a bulletin board labeled "The Reward Board." When the class reaches a predetermined goal, such as everyone turning in their homework, reward the class by having a student unwrap a present.

Ten minutes of free time

Cooperation Graph

Reinforce group efforts using a cooperation graph. Decorate and label a bulletin board similar to the one below. To begin, have the students generate ideas about good teamwork. Then divide students into small groups and assign a team number to each group. During the next several cooperative-group activities, reward each team that shows good teamwork by coloring a bar on the graph for that team. When all the teams reach each predetermined mark on the graph, celebrate with a class reward. Consider homework passes or free-time privileges for the first two prizes, and a pizza or ice-cream party for the grand prize. It won't be long before students realize that teamwork really pays off!

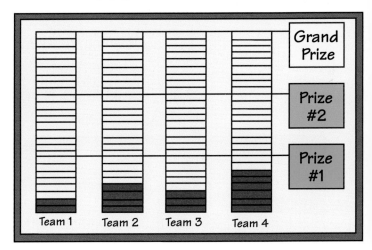

Grand Prize

Prize #2

Prize #1

Team 1   Team 2   Team 3   Team 4

The Royal Corner

The opportunity to be the king or queen of the royal corner can entice students to complete their very best work. Place a beanbag chair, a pillow, several stuffed animals, a crown to wear, and a variety of books in a classroom corner. Reward students who complete satisfactory work with visits to the comfy, royal corner. Students will surely feel as if they are getting the royal treatment!

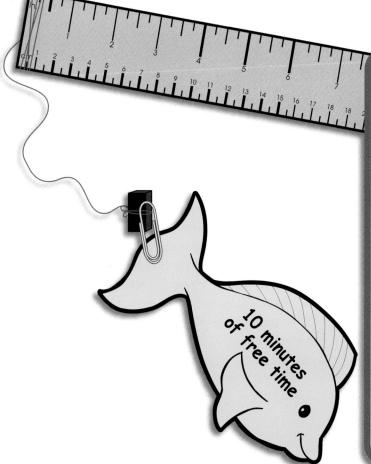

10 minutes of free time

Fishing for Rewards

Inspire your first graders to excel with a fishing program. Cut out several fish-shaped patterns (page 285) and program each pattern with a different reward. Attach a large paper clip to the tail of each fish and place the fish in a bucket. To make a fishing pole, attach a magnet to one end of a string length; then tie the length of string to a ruler. When a student completes a predetermined number of assignments neatly and accurately, she gets to "go fishing" for a reward. To keep motivation high, periodically place new fish with different awards in the bucket.

Homework Motivator

Encourage all students to complete their homework with this cooperative plan. Decide on a reward treat, such as popcorn or ice cream, and draw a line on the board for each letter in the treat. For each day all students turn in their homework, randomly fill in a letter on the board for the treat. When all the letters are filled in, reward students with the designated treat. For a variation, use this idea to encourage perfect attendance!

Work Champs

To maintain high-quality work, use the pencil-shaped punch card on page 285. First, give each student a pencil-shaped card and have him personalize it. Each time a student demonstrates high-quality work on his assignments, he earns a punch on his card. When his card is completely punched, he redeems it for a small treat or a special privilege.

_ _ _ c _ r n

Positive People

Get your students drawing for this self-esteem booster. Have each student draw a picture of himself dressed in his favorite clothes and then write his name on the drawing. When completed, each self-portrait is passed around the classroom. Everyone takes turns writing positive comments or words on each classmate's drawing. When all portraits have been circulated around the classroom, they are returned to their owners and read. Students will be thrilled to read what their classmates wrote!

Me or You

Students will appreciate themselves and others after playing this motivating game. Write the word "YOU" on five small index cards. Write the word "ME" on five additional index cards. Place the cards in a container. To play, arrange students in a circle. Pass the container to the first student and ask him to draw a card. If he draws a "ME" card, have him say something nice about himself. If he draws a "YOU" card, have him say something nice about the person to his left. Have the student place his card back in the container; then continue playing until each child has had a turn.

Secret Pals

Enhance positive feelings among students by assigning a classmate to each student in the class. Tell students to keep the identities of their pals secret. Then have each student write her secret pal a letter telling her how special she is. Encourage students to include compliments about their secret pals' unique qualities and talents. Have each student sign her letter anonymously. At the end of the day, collect the letters and read them aloud to the class. After reading each letter, reveal the identity of the secret pal so that everyone has a chance to thank her special friend for the compliments.

> Dear Cathy,
> You are a great friend. Thank you for helping me with my math. You are so good with place value. You are also a great artist.
>
> Your secret pal

Hidden Notes

Help build students' self-esteem by hiding special notes in unexpected spots. Each day write a quick note of praise, thanks, or encouragement to three students. After students have left for the day, tuck the notes in students' desks, in their daily journals, or in their pockets on a class pocket chart. Imagine your students' faces when they find these special notes!

Artist of the Week
Chad

Good work, Chad!

You are a good drawer.

I like your picture.

Cool drawing!

Art Appreciation

Honor your youngsters' creativity by having an "Artist of the Week." Each week display a piece of artwork from a different student. If desired, decorate a poster board frame with glitter and place the artwork in the center. Post a blank piece of paper beside the display. Encourage students to write comments on the paper praising their classmate's artwork. At the end of the week, let the artist take his artwork and his comments home.

Achievement Album

Commemorate your students' milestones and achievements by keeping a class scrapbook. Purchase a ready-to-use scrapbook or a photo album. Then, throughout the year, add to the album pictures and announcements of your students' special achievements. Encourage students to decorate index cards on which they write about personal achievements. Students will enjoy looking through the album throughout the year.

Name _____ Student self-evaluation sheet

Work Watchdog

How did you do on _____?
Color a face to answer each question.

1. Did I listen?

2. Did I work quietly?

3. Did I do my best?

4. Am I proud of my work?

5. Did I enjoy my work?

Note to the teacher: Use to encourage student self-evaluation and reflection on assignments.

Auction Tickets

Use with "Auction Tickets" on page 279.

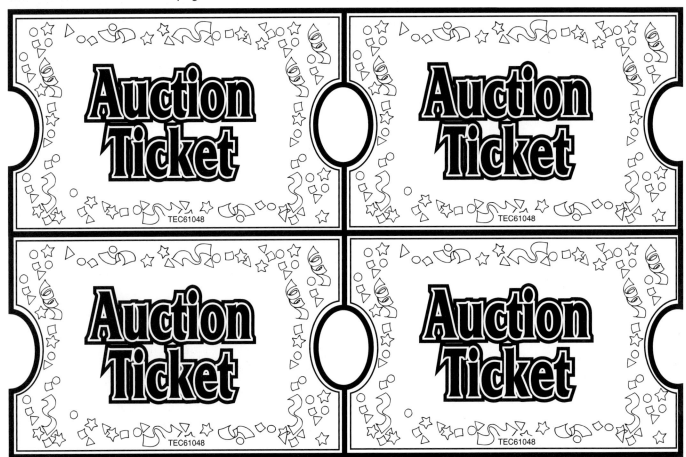

Manners Certificate

Use with "Marvelous Manners" on page 280.

Award

Use with "Wanted: Responsible First Graders" on page 279.

Put 'er here, Pardner!

You have been a responsible wrangler this week!

To: _____

From: _____

Date: _____

TEC61048

Fish Pattern

Use with "Fishing for Fair Shares" on page 143 and "Fishing for Rewards" on page 281.

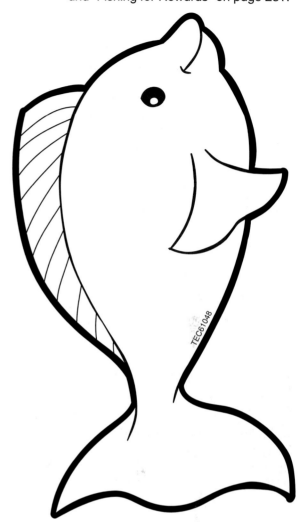

TEC61048

Pencil Pattern

Use with "Work Champs" on page 281.

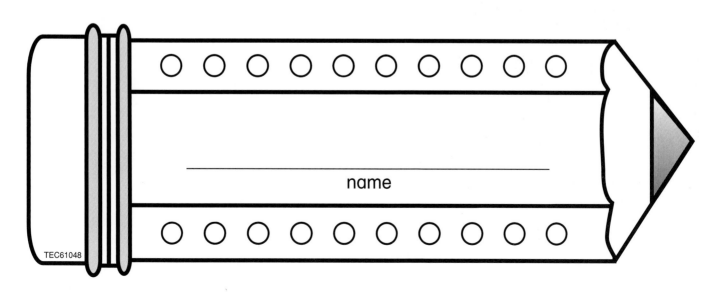

name

TEC61048

Five-Minute Fillers

Good News!

Put a smile on everyone's face with a few minutes of good news each day! Write each child's name on a craft stick; then place the sticks in a decorated container. Whenever you have a few extra minutes, randomly pull a stick from the container, read the child's name, and ask her for some good news. The student may choose to announce something that has happened to her, her family, or a friend. Place the child's stick aside and continue removing sticks from the container, one at a time, as time permits. Be sure to continue the activity the next day, beginning with the students whose sticks are still in the container.

Stacie

Animal Challenge

Have a few minutes to spare? No sweat! Play a quick game of Animal Challenge. Begin by deciding on an animal. Once you've decided, call on students, in turn, to guess the animal by asking questions that can be answered with yes or no. If desired, invite the student who guesses the correct animal to whisper an animal for the next game. Students quickly realize the importance of listening to their classmates' responses, as well as which questions are the most effective.

Does the animal have fur?

Does the animal live in a cold place?

5 10 15 20 25 30 35 40 45 50

Sound Off!

Whenever you have a bit of extra time, you can use it to improve your youngsters' skip-counting skills. Begin by announcing a counting pattern, such as tens, fives, or twos; then point to a student to start the counting. After the child announces the starting number, quickly point to another student to say the next number in the pattern. Continue in this same manner until students reach a predetermined number.

A Shopping Spree

Take your students on an imaginary shopping spree for lots of productive learning fun! First, decide with the help of your students what kind of store you'll be shopping in today. Will it be a pet store, a grocery store, or a toy store? Then, beginning with the letter *A*, have youngsters work their way through the alphabet, naming things you can buy in the selected store that begin with the appropriate letter. It's an instant activity that hones students' phonetic skills!

At the grocery store, you can buy a <u>carrot</u>.

What's the Rule?

Sharpen your youngsters' observation skills with a game called What's the Rule? One by one, physically sort students into groups. Challenge students to determine the rule that you are using to sort them. For example, your rule for sorting might be as simple as students who have shoes that tie and those who don't. The first student to guess the rule makes up the rule for the next sorting game.

Categories

Sharpen students' listening skills with the game Categories. Ask each child to stand beside his desk. Announce a category, such as food or things to do outside, and set a time limit of five seconds for students to contribute a word to the stated category. If a student gives a wrong answer or can't think of an answer, he must sit down. Play continues until one student remains standing.

What's in Your Name?

In turn, call each child to the board and write her name in large capital letters. Ask her classmates to find hidden words in the child's name. Record students' responses on the board. Students will be eager to tell parents just how special their names are.

<u>ELIZABETH</u>

bet

lit

hit

bat

at

Spot the Mistakes

When your lesson takes less time than you had planned, fill the extra minutes with this simple activity. Write a sentence on the board, deliberately including spelling, capitalization, and punctuation errors. Have each student correct the sentence and write it on a piece of paper. Then ask a student volunteer to correct the sentence on the board. Students will be thrilled at the chance to correct your work!

We're going on a field trip today?

The Picture Box

If some of your youngsters find themselves with time to spare, suggest they go to the picture box. Keep a box filled with a variety of laminated magazine pictures. When a youngster has some time on his hands, he may select a picture from the box and write something about it. Children who want to share their writing can be given an opportunity to do so during a daily sharing time.

"What If...?"

This five-minute filler enhances your students' thinking skills. Present a what-if situation to your students and challenge them to brainstorm the pros and cons of the situation. Consider situations such as "What if we went to school only on the weekends?" or "What if Christmas were in July?" Be sure to allow each child a chance to add his thoughts about the topic.

Problem Solvers

Students can be great problem solvers when given the chance. Choose a problem in the school, such as trash on the playground or a noisy cafeteria. Ask students to brainstorm solutions to the problem, and record their responses on chart paper. Next discuss the advantages and disadvantages of each solution; then challenge students to determine the best solution from the list. Write the chosen solution on a piece of paper and present it to the principal. Surprisingly enough, your youngsters may think of more creative solutions than you or your coworkers.

I do not think hamburgers are the best fast food. I like pizza because...

In My Opinion

This partner activity improves communication skills and requires no planning. To play, pair students; then announce a statement such as "Hamburgers are the best fast food" or "Soccer is a hard sport to play." Each partner then has one minute to express a personal opinion about the statement. Be sure to remind students that there is no wrong opinion. Ready? Start talking!

ARTS & CRAFTS

Grandparents' Wall Hangings

Here's a great gift for students to give to their grandparents on National Grandparents Day. Begin by providing each student with an 8" x 10" piece of colorful tagboard and a 6½" x 8½" piece of drawing paper. Help each student hole-punch a hole on each side at the top of the tagboard. Next, have the student draw a picture on the drawing paper of her grandparent(s) and herself and then glue it to the center of the tagboard. The student then glues craft foam shapes around the illustration to create a frame. Assist each student in threading a length of yarn through the two holes and tying the ends to create a hanger.

Fall Foliage Drawings

Enlist your students' help in collecting colorful autumn leaves for this project (or prepare a supply of fall-colored leaf cutouts). To make a fall drawing, have each student glue his leaves in any position onto a sheet of construction paper. Then have students use crayons or markers to draw a picture incorporating the leaves in a unique way. What a great way to stretch your students' imaginations!

Candy Corn Mosaics

Let the popular fall candy turn your art lesson into a special treat! Have youngsters tear orange, yellow, and white construction paper into approximately nickel-size pieces. Next, give each student a piece of candy corn and ask him to observe the arrangement of the three colors on the candy. Then give each student a piece of black construction paper with a chalk-drawn outline of a piece of candy corn. Have the student spread glue to fill the shape and then arrange the paper pieces on the glue to resemble a candy corn piece. Adapt this idea to create other fall mosaics, such as jack-o'-lanterns, spiders, or leaves.

A Grand Gobbler

In advance, tint several containers of water each with a different of color of food coloring. To make a turkey, a child uses eyedroppers to drip colored water over a flattened coffee filter. While the filter is drying, he glues craft feathers or feather cutouts along the upper rim of another coffee filter. Next, he colors and cuts out a copy of the turkey patterns on page 297. To complete the turkey, he glues the two filters together and glues on the patterns as shown.

Indian Corn

Harvest a bumper crop of colorful Indian corn with this tissue-paper activity. Have each student wad brown, orange, yellow, and black squares of tissue paper and then glue them onto a tagboard corncob cutout (pattern on page 297) to resemble Indian corn. Then have each student trace his cob cutout onto a brown paper lunch sack and cut on the outline (through both layers). Next, have him trim one end of the two resulting cornhusk shapes into a point; then slightly crumple the shapes.

To assemble the project, place the ear of corn between the two cornhusks and fan the tops slightly. Then staple the lower edges in place. If desired, fashion a bow from raffia, and glue it to the project as shown.

Hanukkah Star

Hanukkah greetings abound from this festive project. Have each child place a white five-inch construction paper square between two blue five-inch construction paper squares. Have him place a tagboard star cutout (patterns on page 298) on the stack and trace the pattern. Then direct him to cut it out, fold the star in half, unfold it, and staple on the crease. Separate the star layers and attach a yarn handle.

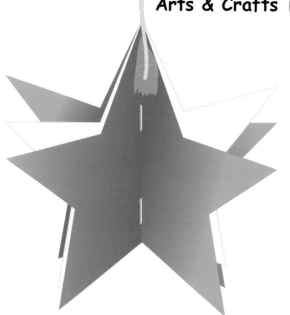

Peppermint Ornament

Commemorate the winter holidays with this sweet project! To make a peppermint ornament, a child uses a craft stick to paint red lines around the edges of two three-inch tagboard circles. When the paint is dry, she writes her name and the current year on the center of one circle and glues a small photo of herself on the other circle. Then she tapes a ribbon hanger to the back of one circle and glues the undecorated sides of both circles together. To complete the project, help her wrap the peppermint in a 9" x 10" piece of plastic wrap, seal the plastic with glue, and tie the sides closed with ribbon as shown.

Sparkling Snowflake

To make a snowflake, a student glues cotton swabs to a three-inch tagboard circle as shown. Next, he spreads glue on the tagboard circle and sprinkles glitter on the glue. When the glue is dry, attach these glistening snowflakes to winter bulletin boards or to your classroom walls to create an indoor blizzard.

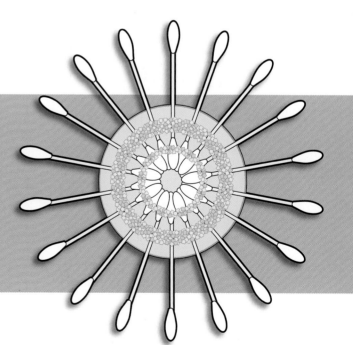

KWANZAA KINARAS

Enlighten your students as to the traditions of Kwanzaa with this festive kinara (candleholder) and the mishumaa saba (seven candles) that are traditionally lit during the seven-day Kwanzaa celebration.

Materials for each student:
7 clothespins
red, green, and black paints
paintbrush
9" x 12" sheet of brown
   construction paper

seven 1" x 2" pieces of yellow
   construction paper
scissors
glue

Steps:
1. Fold the sheet of brown construction paper into thirds lengthwise to form three narrow columns.
2. Open up the paper and make a one-inch fold on each of the long edges.
3. Glue these two folds together to make a triangular base for the kinara.
4. Paint three clothespins red, three clothespins green, and one clothespin black. Set them aside to dry.
5. Cut a flame shape from each of the seven pieces of yellow construction paper.
6. Glue each flame cutout to the handheld end of a painted clothespin.
7. Clip each clothespin to the kinara base as shown.

A Star-Studded New Year

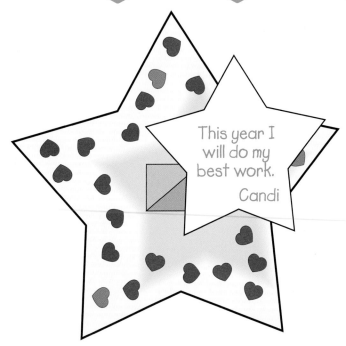

This year I will do my best work.
Candi

Ring in the new year with this star-studded display. Make a white construction paper copy of one of the star patterns on page 297 for each student. Then enlarge a copy of one of the star patterns and make a class supply on yellow construction paper. To begin, give each student one white and one yellow star. The student cuts out both stars and then writes a personal goal for the new year on the white star. She accordion-folds a 1" x 3" strip of yellow construction paper and then glues one end of the strip to the center of the yellow star and the other end to the back of the white star. To complete the project, she adds glitter or sequins around the border of the larger star.

Valentine Bags

These adorable heart creatures double as Valentine's Day mailboxes. Each student will need one white paper lunch bag, a four-inch red construction paper square, two 1" x 5" strips of red construction paper, two 1" x 8" strips of red construction paper, and colorful paper scraps. To begin, a student cuts out one heart from the construction paper square, decorates it to resemble a head, and glues it to the top of the bag as shown. Next, he accordion-folds the four construction-paper strips. He then glues the two shorter strips to the side of the bag for arms, and the two longer strips to the bottom of the bag for legs. Encourage students to use the paper scraps to cut out smaller construction paper hearts as hands and feet; then invite youngsters to use crayons to decorate and personalize their bags.

Cherry Tree Pencil Holders

Celebrate George Washington's birthday with these eye-catching pencil holders. In advance, gather a class supply of small cardboard tubes and cut six ½-inch slits on each end of each tube. To make a pencil holder, a student paints the outside of a tube brown, then sets it aside to dry. As the tube dries, he cuts a treetop shape from each of three 3" x 4" pieces of green construction paper. Next, the student hole-punches several cherries from a small piece of red construction paper and glues them onto the treetop cutouts. After the tube has dried, the student folds the tabs out on one end of the tube to create roots. On the other end of the tube, the student slides each treetop cutout between two slits as shown. Tape each student's tree to his desk by its roots. There's sure to be no chopping down of these cherry trees!

Rainbow Flyer

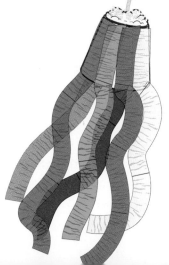

Colorful strips fly through the air with this golden craft! To make one, a child glues tissue paper or crepe paper strips in rainbow colors to an upside down foam cup as shown. Next, he tapes a yarn hanger to the top of the cup and glues on cotton-ball clouds. To complete the project, he drizzles glue over the clouds and sprinkles on gold glitter.

A "Hand-some" Bouquet

Your classroom will bloom with these spring flowers. Have each child place the palms of her hands in green paint and then on a piece of construction paper as shown. (Be sure to add a squirt of dishwashing liquid to the paint to make cleanup easier.) When the paint is dry, have the student cut out ten construction paper flowers and glue one flower to each finger. Then have her personalize her paper as desired. Voilà, a floral masterpiece!

Spring Greetings

Hatch an Easter bunny with this card-making project.

Materials for each student:
2 egg cutouts (use the egg pattern on page 262 as a template)
two 4" construction paper circles
scrap construction paper in various colors
glue
scissors

Steps to make the egg:
1. Cut one egg in half using a zigzag line to create a cracked egg.
2. Glue the edges of the cracked egg's lower half to the uncut egg pattern to create a pocket.
3. Glue the top edge of the cracked egg's top half to the uncut egg pattern to create a flap.

Steps to make the bunny:
1. Cut one construction paper circle in half to create ears.
2. Glue the resulting ear cutouts to the top of the other circle.
3. Add construction paper features to the bunny's face.

Steps to assemble the card:
1. Lift the top flap and slip the bunny into the pocket of the egg.
2. Personalize the front of the egg as desired.
3. Write an Easter message on the back of the egg; then deliver the egg to someone special!

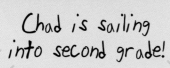

Sail Into Second Grade

Making this year-end art project is a breeze! To make a hull of a sailboat, a student paints the bottom side of a paper plate. When the paint is dry, he folds the plate in half (with the painted side out) and uses a hole puncher to punch a hole in the center of the folded edge. To create a mast, the student places a pencil through this hole and tapes it to the inside of the plate. Next, he decorates a diagonally cut piece of paper for a sail; then he punches two holes in it and inserts the pencil through the holes as shown. To complete the project, the student staples along the open edge of the paper plate and personalizes it as shown.

Chad is sailing into second grade!

Initial Art

This simple and fun art project is sure to stretch your students' imaginations! Provide each student with a bulletin board letter of his first initial. Have him trace the letter on construction paper, cut it out, and then glue it in any position onto a sheet of construction paper. Challenge each student to use crayons to draw a picture incorporating the letter in some distinctive way.

Pet Parade

No scissors are required to make an amazing animal! To make one, a child folds a 12" x 18" sheet of construction paper in half. Next, she tears sections from the open sides to make the shape of a chosen animal's body. She creates body parts—such as a head, tail, or ears—from the torn pieces of paper and glues them to the animal. Then she uses crayons and paper scraps to add desired details.

Art Recipes

Puffy Paint

⅓ c. white glue
2 tbsp. paint
2 c. nonmenthol shaving cream

Mix the paint and the glue together. Then fold in the shaving cream until the color is well blended. Use the paint mixture shortly after making it.

Sparkling Dough

1 c. flour
½ c. salt
1 c. water
2 tbsp. vegetable oil
1 tbsp. cream of tarter
⅓ c. glitter
¼ c. powdered tempera paint

Combine the ingredients in a saucepan. Cook over medium heat, stirring until a ball is formed. Knead the dough until cool. Store the dough in an airtight container.

Magic Putty

2 parts regular white Elmer's Glue
(not Elmer's School Glue)
1 part liquid starch

Mix ingredients. Let dry in air. Have students experiment with it and write down their observations: it bounces, it stretches, it lifts pictures from newspapers. Store the putty in an airtight container.

No-Cook Modeling Dough

2 c. flour
1 c. salt
water
food coloring or tempera paint
2 tbsp. vegetable oil (optional)

Mix the ingredients using enough water to create the desired consistency. If desired, add oil to keep the dough from hardening; then store it in an airtight container after each use.

Turkey Patterns
Use with "A Grand Gobbler" on page 290.

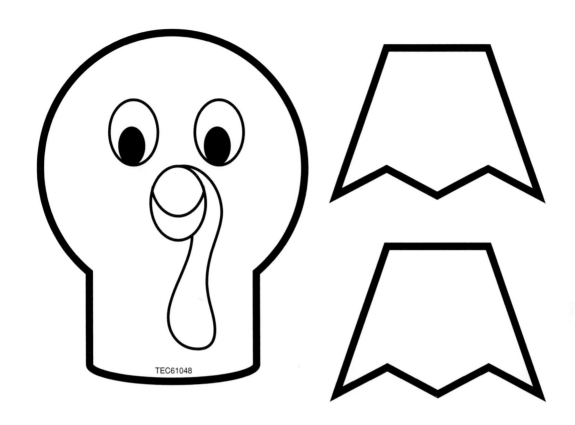

TEC61048

Corncob Pattern
Use with "Indian Corn" on page 290.

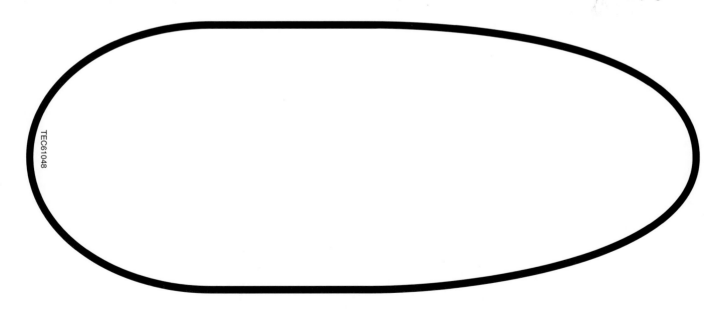

TEC61048

Star Patterns

Use with "Hanukkah Star" on page 291 and "A Star-Studded New Year" on page 292.

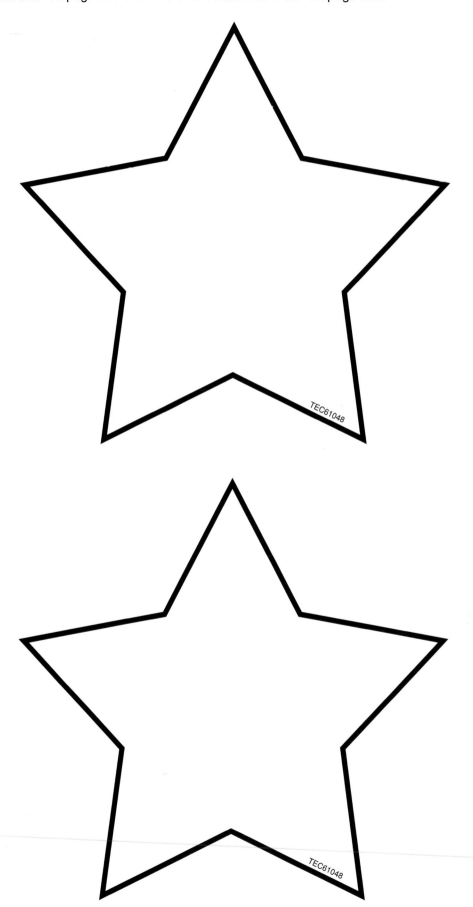

Where's Wormy?

For each student in a small group, program a copy of the lotto board (page 303) with different consonants, making each board unique. Cut out a copy of the picture cards on page 302 and place them in a container. Also, cut green pipe cleaners into one-inch pieces to resemble worms. Give each student nine worms to use as game markers.

To begin, the first player takes a card, names the picture, and announces the corresponding initial consonant. After confirming his response, each player who has the letter covers it with a marker. Players take turns drawing cards until a player removes the worm card and automatically wins or until a player covers three spaces in a row (horizontally, vertically, or diagonally) and announces, "Wormy!"

an apple fan

Apples Aplenty

Review the sound of short a with an "a-peel-ing" activity! Enlist students' help in compiling a list of words that contain the short a sound as in the word *apple*. Then have each child incorporate an apple cutout into a picture that depicts one of the listed short a words. To complete the project, help each child add a caption to her picture.

Collecting Leaves

Use this crisp idea to review a variety of skills! Program a class supply of leaf cutouts for a desired skill such as odd and even numbers, addition facts, high-frequency words, spelling words, shapes, or time. Place the leaves in a large paper grocery bag. Gather students in a circle and inform them of the chosen skill. Empty the bag into the center of the circle. Invite each child to quickly pick up a leaf and return to the circle. Next, have each child, in turn, share his leaf and demonstrate the desired skill. Then collect the leaves and play another round!

Five is odd!

5 14 22

Who's That Ghost?

Turn this creative idea into a mystery bulletin board. Give each student a 6" x 9" piece of white construction paper and ask him to draw a picture of himself from head to toe. (Encourage each child to use the full length of the paper.) Have each student cut out his self-portrait and glue it to a 9" x 12" sheet of colored construction paper. Next, have each student trim another 6" x 9" piece of white construction paper into a ghost shape and attach it at the top of the cutout with a dot of glue. At the bottom of the paper, direct each student to write three clues about himself. Mount the papers on a bulletin board with the title "Who's That Ghost?" Have students guess whom each ghost represents by reading the clues. By lifting the ghost shape, the answer will be revealed.

This ghost likes pizza, plays football, and has brown hair.

Which Book?

Celebrate Children's Book Week—annually the week before Thanksgiving—with this intriguing idea! Display several books on the board ledge. Secretly choose the book you plan to read to youngsters. Then give clues about the book, such as "The book is nonfiction" or "The book's title has four words." Continue giving clues until the correct guess is made. Then invite youngsters to settle in as you read the story aloud.

Ablaze With Math!

Recognize Fire Prevention Week in October with this red-hot idea! Draw on the board a large fire shape. Write several addition or subtraction problems on the fire. Fill a squirt bottle with water or board cleaner and place it near the board. Invite a volunteer to solve a problem. After her classmates verify her answer, have her help to extinguish the fire by squirting the problem and erasing it. Continue in the same manner for each remaining problem. Then congratulate your junior firefighters for a job well done!

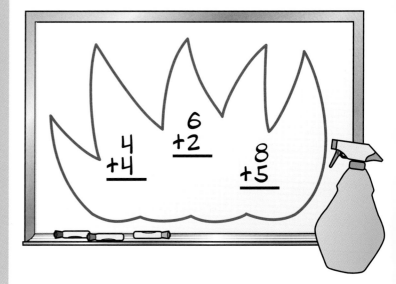

An Orderly Patch

Youngsters poke around the patch to put pumpkins in order! Program a supply of pumpkin cutouts with different numerals. In an open area of the classroom, spread the pumpkins on the floor to represent a pumpkin patch. Invite five students to each choose a pumpkin from the patch; then direct them to line up in order from least to greatest. After their classmates confirm the order, have students return their pumpkins to the patch. Continue in the same manner until each child has had a turn.

We're Thankful!

Include students' families in this Thanksgiving booklet-making project! Give each child a seven-inch paper circle for each member of his immediate family plus one extra. To make the booklet cover, invite each child to sponge-paint a circle to resemble turkey feathers. Then direct him to cut out a personalized copy of the turkey pattern on page 303. When the paint is dry, have him glue the turkey to the feathers.

To make the booklet, ask each child to write the name of a different family member on each circle and then staple the pages behind the cover. Encourage each youngster to take his booklet home and ask each family member to write a message telling what he is thankful for. When the messages have been entered, instruct him to bring his booklet to school to share with classmates.

Gobblin' Up Vowels

Youngsters identify vowel sounds while decorating a fine-feathered turkey! Have each child trace her hand on a sheet of construction paper and then cut it out. Direct her to label each finger (feather) with a different vowel and add details to resemble a turkey. Once all the turkeys are made, announce a word that contains a desired vowel sound. After students identify the vowel sound, have them color the corresponding feather on their turkeys. Continue in the same manner for each remaining vowel.

Thanksgiving-Feast Favorites

Right after the Thanksgiving holiday, have students brainstorm a list of foods that were featured at their holiday dinners. Illustrate and label several of the food items along the bottom of a grid; then have each child graph one or two of his favorite foods on the list. Students will like finding out what foods were enjoyed most at the Thanksgiving feasts.

		William					Cathy
		Jenny		Linda			Cordelia
Ralph		Alexander		Willow		Giles	Andy
Giles		Angel		Ralph	Jenny	William	Alexander
Cathy	Willow	Gina	Gina	Cordelia	Angel	Andy	Linda
turkey	gravy	stuffing	corn	sweet potatoes	dinner rolls	cranberry sauce	pumpkin pie

Picture Cards

Use with "Where's Wormy?" on page 299.

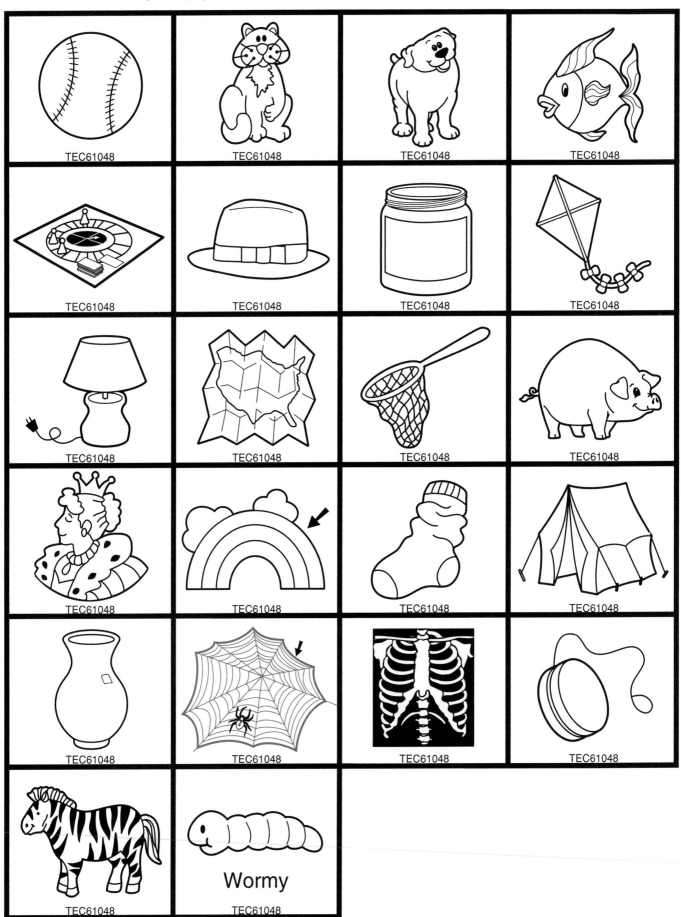

©The Mailbox® • Superbook® • TEC61048

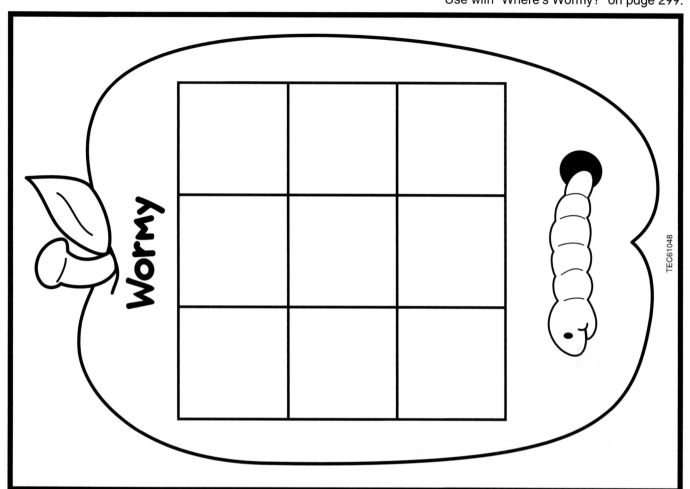

TEC61048

Turkey Pattern
Use with "We're Thankful!" on page 301.

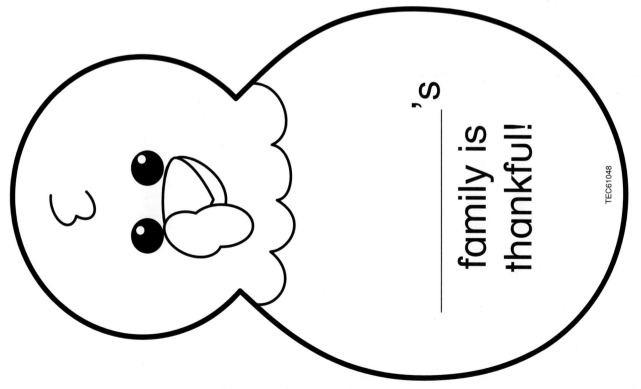

TEC61048

Picture-Perfect Grandparent

Draw.
Complete each sentence.

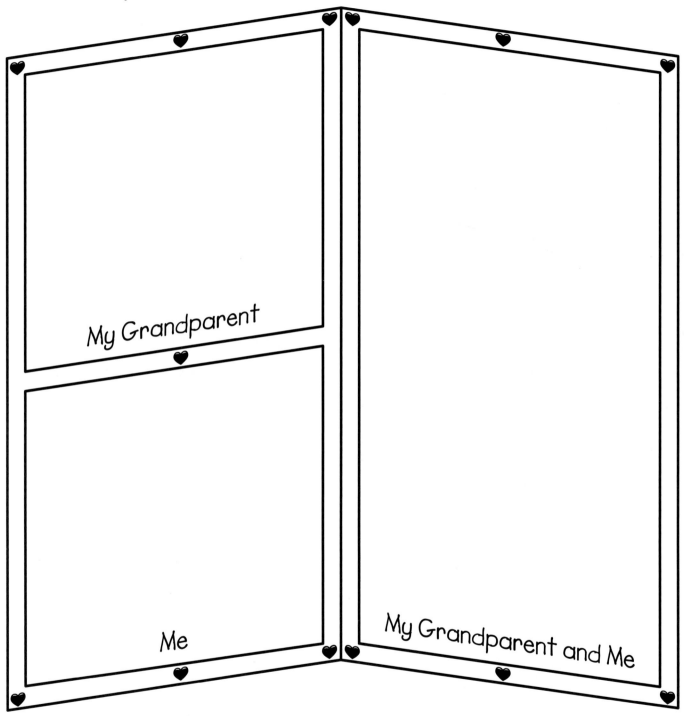

My grandparent is _____.

We love to _____

_____.

WINTER

Twelve Days— Revised

Turn your students into songwriters by having them rewrite lyrics for "The Twelve Days Of Christmas." Divide students into 12 groups and assign each group a verse from the song. Instruct each group to create a new verse for the song. Then use chart paper to record your students' new verses. Practice the revised song after it's complete. If desired type and print a copy of the lyrics for each child to take home. Expand on the idea by relating art projects to the 12 items students chose. This song also provides a fun way to review ordinal numbers.

Twelve Days of Christmas

First day—box of candy
Second day—basketballs
Third day—video games

Winter Words

The result of this booklet-making project is a cool writing reference! Write a student-generated list of winter-themed words on the board. Give each child a snowpal cutout (pattern on page 308) and several three-inch construction paper squares. Direct her to draw buttons down the center of one square and write and illustrate a different winter word on each remaining square. After she stacks the squares with the buttons square on top, help her staple the stack to the center of her snowpal. To complete the project, have each student personalize her snowpal and add desired details.

I baked 5 star cookies and 4 tree cookies. How many cookies did I bake in all?

Cookie Capers

Youngsters cook up story problems with this sweet idea! On a large sheet of construction paper, draw a simple cookie jar, leaving ample space for writing at the bottom of the paper. Make a copy of the prepared paper for each child. Arrange shallow trays of brown paint along with holiday-shaped cookie cutters for easy student access. A child makes several cookie-cutter prints in two different styles on her cookie jar. Then she writes a corresponding story problem below the jar. When the paint is dry, youngsters color the cookies and then trade papers with each other to solve the cookie capers!

Hanukkah Gifts

Good for One Sticker!

...od ...r 15 Minutes of Free-Reading Time

Giving coins is a traditional part of the Hanukkah holiday. Make some coin coupons to give to your students in honor of this special Jewish celebration. Cut several yellow construction paper circles per student and write a variety of redeemable items on the coins. Gather a class supply of resealable plastic bags; then place a few coins inside each one. Distribute a bag to each student and allow her to redeem the coin coupons as desired.

Good for Your Choice of Lunch Partner

Helping Hands for Kwanzaa

Kwanzaa is a holiday not only for giving handmade gifts but also for celebrating many virtues. Students can explore both aspects of this African-American holiday by making helping-hand coupon booklets to give to their families. Help each child make a booklet by placing four hand-shaped sheets of white paper between hand-shaped construction paper covers as shown. Have the child decorate the cover in traditional Kwanzaa colors of red, green, and black. On each page of a student's book, have her write a chore that can be done to help the family or a family member. Have students present the books to their families on the third day of Kwanzaa, *ujima,* when collective work and responsibility are observed.

Start the Year on the Right Foot!

To make a New Year's Day card, have each child trace his foot onto colorful construction paper and cut it out. Next, have each child fold a 9" x 12" sheet of white construction paper in half to create a card; then have him glue the foot shape to the card's front. Instruct each student to write "I'm starting the year on the right foot..." on the front of the card. Have each student complete the inside of his card by writing and illustrating what he plans to do in the new year. Encourage each child to present his card to his family on New Year's Day.

Peace Train

Enlist students' help in completing this thoughtful display while remembering Dr. Martin Luther King Jr. Mount on a wall a cutout of a train engine (pattern on page 66) and the title "Get on the Peace Train." Provide each student with a colorful train car (pattern on page 66) and have her write a peaceful thought. Post each train car behind the engine to complete the display. If desired, have each child complete a copy of page 310 to learn more about Martin Luther King Jr.

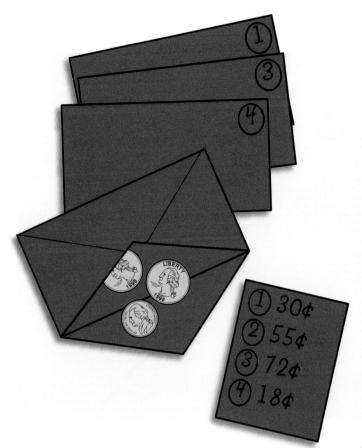

Chinese New Year Money Fun

To celebrate the New Year, Chinese children look forward to receiving gifts of money in red envelopes. Invest in this tradition by creating a money-practice game to enhance your classroom celebration of the Chinese New Year. Number a class supply of red envelopes; then place a combination of plastic coins in each envelope. Establish an answer key listing the number of each envelope and the coin value enclosed in each one. Distribute an envelope to each child, have him determine the coins' value, and then have him check the answer key before trading with another student. If desired, place the envelopes and answer key in a center for students to explore.

Valentine Kisses

Encourage your students to give some love to a family member on Valentine's Day with this sweet project. Cut a six-inch candy-kiss shape from tagboard for each student. Then have each student write a message of love on a 1" x 12" strip of white paper. Then have the student glue the message strip to the top of the shape. To complete the project, have her cover the tagboard shape with foil. Send each student home with her message of love, and encourage her to give it to a family member to show how much she cares.

Love Is...

This student-made book is full of love! Give each student an 11-inch paper strip and have her write "Love is" and then complete the sentence. Then have her illustrate her sentence on a sheet of white paper. To create the book, have each child mount her sentence and picture on a 12" x 18" sheet of pink or red construction paper. Bind the completed pages between construction paper covers. Your students will enjoy reading the class collection of love definitions on Valentine's Day.

Check out the skill-building reproducibles on pages 309 and 310.

Love is ice cream.

Snowpal Pattern

Use with "Winter Words" on page 305.

Time for Winter!

Write each time.

____ : ____   ____ : ____   ____ : ____   ____ : ____

____ : ____   ____ : ____   ____ : ____   ____ : ____

____ : ____   ____ : ____

____ : ____

Martin Luther King Jr.

 Cut.

 Glue each strip to a sheet of paper.

Draw matching pictures.

Put in order. Staple.

Martin Luther King Jr.

Martin Luther King Jr. studied hard in school.

1

©The Mailbox® • *Superbook*® • TEC61048

Martin became a preacher.

2

Dr. King dreamed that all people would be treated the same.

3

He gave speeches.

4

We celebrate his birthday to remember how he helped people.

5

Note to the teacher: Give each child five 5½" x 8½" sheets of paper. Then have her follow the directions above to make a booklet.

SPRING

I will practice my spelling words every night.

Julian

Goals Are Growing!

Help youngsters discover the sweet smell of success! Guide each child in setting an academic goal such as reading every night, learning math facts, writing neatly, or always completing homework. Give each youngster a construction paper flower cutout (patterns on page 314) and a flowerpot cutout. Direct him to personalize the flower and write his goal on the flowerpot. Then have him connect the cutouts with a green pipe cleaner. Display the completed projects with the title "Growing Toward Our Goals!" Periodically refer students to the display and encourage them to discuss the progress of their goals.

Seeing Green

Here's a fun activity to help your students see green on St. Patrick's Day. Have your class brainstorm a list of items that are green. List the responses on the board. Have each student choose one item from the list to depict. Provide students with a variety of green papers such as wallpaper, construction paper, tissue paper, or wrapping paper. Next, have each student use the different papers to create his green item and then glue it to a large sheet of white construction paper. Ask each child to write a caption about his picture. Display the completed pictures with the title "Seeing Green."

Flowerpot Families

To prepare for this center, label each of three plastic flowerpots (or plastic cups) with a different word family. Add a small amount of play dough inside each flowerpot. Also, program several flower cutouts (patterns on page 314) with words from the three word families. Glue each flower to a craft stick (stem). Place the flowers and pots at a center. A visiting youngster chooses a flower and reads the word. Then she finds the matching pot and pushes the flower stem into the play dough. She continues in this manner until all the flowers have been sorted.

Bunny Tales

Hop right into spring by having your students write rabbit stories. Cut booklet covers and writing paper into ovals and staple each booklet to secure the pages. Have students decorate their covers to resemble bunnies. Ask your students to compose rabbit-related stories on the booklet pages. Provide title suggestions, such as "How the Bunny Got Its Tail" or "The Bunny That Saved Easter!" After the stories have been written, have each student title her booklet "Bunny Tales"; then give each child a cotton ball to glue to the back cover of her booklet. Give each student an opportunity to read a story to her classmates before displaying the project.

Mother, May I?

Mothers are sure to flip for these student-made cards, which are full of good intentions! For each student, fold a 9" x 12" sheet of construction paper in half lengthwise. Have her write "Mother, may I…" at the top and draw a special picture for her mother below. Then help each student cut the top layer of the paper from the edge to the fold to make five equal-size flaps. To complete the project, ask her to write under each flap a different task that she could do to help her mother. Encourage each child to take her card home and invite her mother to open a different flap every day until all of the tasks are completed.

> 41   < 41

65

65 is greater than 41.

Eggs and Baskets

Give a game of comparing numbers an "egg-citing" twist! Program a class supply of plastic eggs or egg cutouts with different numerals up to 99; then place the eggs in a basket. Choose a number that you did not program on an egg. Write the number on opposite ends of the board and add a different inequality sign (< or >) to each. Have each student remove an egg from the basket and line up at the corresponding side of the board. In turn, ask each youngster to insert her number into the math sentence. After each child has had a turn, collect the eggs, reprogram the board with a different number, and play again.

Mom's Special Card

Creating a Mother's Day card will be a snap for your students with this creative method. Provide several *M* and *O* templates as well as a supply of colorful wallpaper samples or gift wrap. Have each child trace and cut out two *M*s and an *O* from different designs. Provide each student with a 9" x 12" sheet of construction paper and have him fold it in half to form a card as shown. Then have each student glue his letters on the card's front to spell "MOM." Each child can then personalize the inside of his card with a special message.

Welcome-Back Bulletin Board

At the year's end, have your current students help you create a bulletin board to welcome new students the following year. Ask each child to decorate a face shape to resemble herself. Then distribute segments of sentence strips and ask each child to write words that describe her year in your class. Post the comments and personalized pictures on a display; then cover the entire board with newsprint or other material for protection during the summer. As you prepare your class for the start of school, unveil the board for an attractive first-day display.

First-Class Dad

Even though Father's Day often occurs after school is out for the summer, youngsters can still prepare ahead of time for that special day! Invite each student to write and draw on a sheet of paper a special message to her father. Then instruct her to glue it to a slightly larger sheet of construction paper. Help her roll the message into a scroll and tape it closed. Next, have her glue a personalized copy of the label on page 314 to the scroll and tie a length of string around it. Encourage each youngster to present her message to her father and to remind him to wait until Father's Day to open it!

First-Grade Memories

During the final month of school, ask students to discuss their most memorable experiences in first grade. On a sheet of drawing paper, ask each child to write and illustrate a description of an event or activity that he thought was special. Display the memories around the room. On the final day of school, send each child home with his favorite first-grade memory. If desired, have each child complete a copy of page 316 to record more first-grade memories.

Check out the skill-building reproducibles on pages 315 and 316.

Flower Patterns
Use with "Goals Are Growing!" and "Flowerpot Families" on page 311.

TEC61048

TEC61048

Father's Day Labels
Use with "First-Class Dad" on page 313.

To _____

Love, _____

FIRST-CLASS

Do not open until Father's Day!

TEC61048

To _____

Love, _____

FIRST-CLASS

Do not open until Father's Day!

TEC61048

Earth's Friends

 Cut. Glue to show things that are good for the earth.

Save cans.   Recycle paper.   Plant a tree.   Litter.   Clean up!   Don't pollute.

Note to the teacher: Use this page to commemorate Earth Day in April.

First-Grade Follow-Up

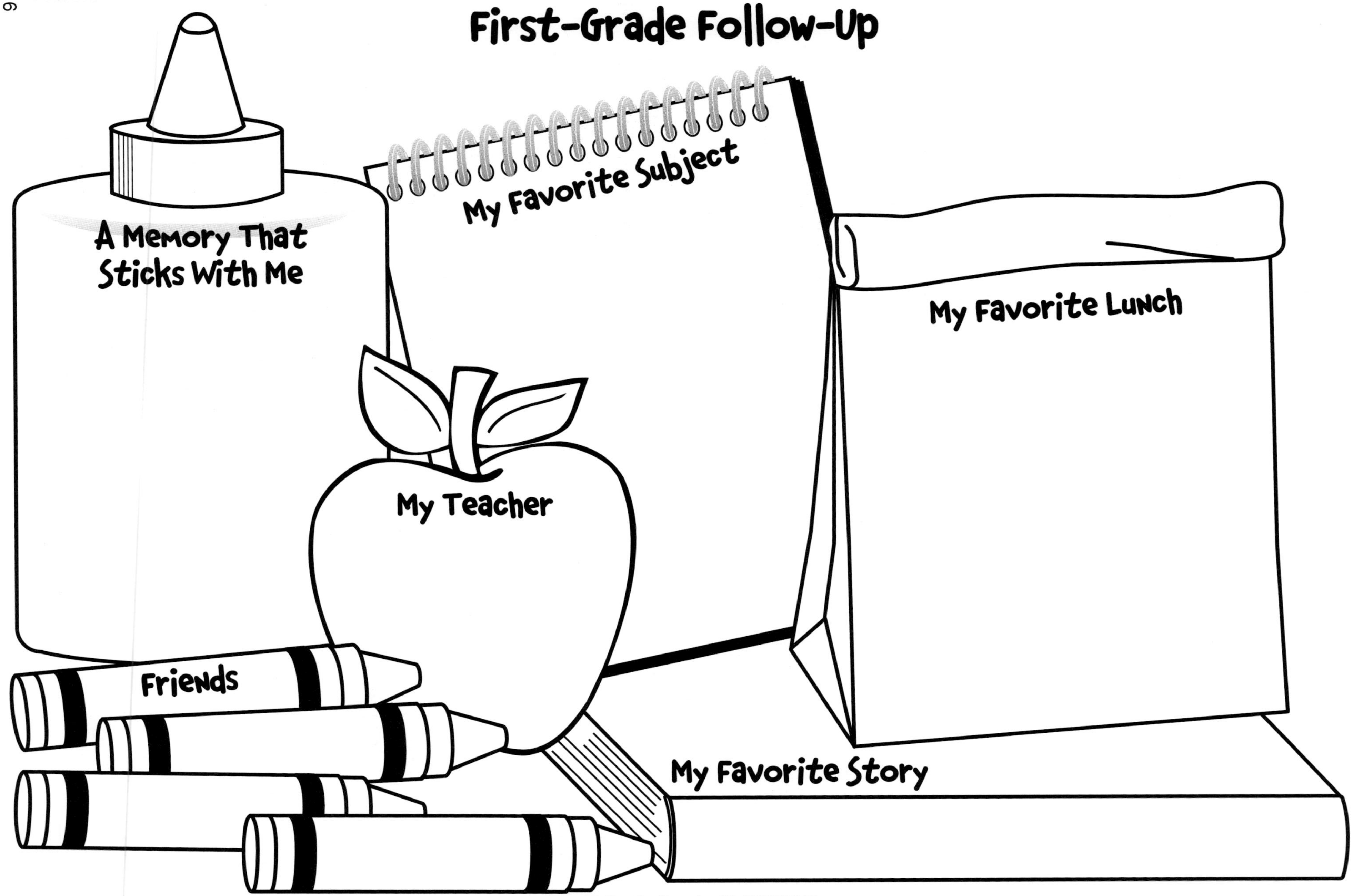

My Favorite Lunch

My Favorite Subject

My Favorite Story

My Teacher

A Memory That Sticks With Me

Friends

Index